Humanism and the Culture
of Renaissance Europe

In this updated edition of his classic account, Charles Nauert charts the
rise of humanism as the distinctive culture of the social, political, and
intellectual elites in Renaissance Europe. He traces humanism's emergence in the unique social and cultural conditions of fourteenth-century
Italy and its gradual diffusion throughout the rest of Europe from the
late fifteenth century onwards. He shows how, despite its elitist origins,
humanism became a major force in the popular culture and fine arts of
the fifteenth and sixteenth centuries, and the powerful impact it had on
the Protestant and Catholic Reformations. He uses art and biographical
sketches of key figures to illuminate the narrative and concludes with an
account of the limitations and eventual transformations of humanism at
the end of the Renaissance. This comprehensive account of the development and significance of humanistic culture will be essential reading for
all students of Renaissance Europe.

CHARLES G. NAUERT is Professor Emeritus of History at the
University of Missouri, Columbia. His major publications include
several essays on pre-Reformation academic and religious controversies
and *The Age of Renaissance and Reformation* (1977).

NEW APPROACHES TO EUROPEAN HISTORY

Series editors

WILLIAM BEIK *Emory University*

T. C. W. BLANNING *Sidney Sussex College, Cambridge*

New Approaches to European History is an important textbook series, which provides concise but authoritative surveys of major themes and problems in European history since the Renaissance. Written at a level and length accessible to advanced school students and undergraduates, each book in the series addresses topics or themes that students of European history encounter daily: the series embraces both some of the more 'traditional' subjects of study, and those cultural and social issues to which increasing numbers of school and college courses are devoted. A particular effort is made to consider the wider international implications of the subject under scrutiny.

To aid the student reader scholarly apparatus and annotation is light, but each work has full supplementary bibliographies and notes for further reading: where appropriate chronologies, maps, diagrams and other illustrative material are also provided.

For a list of titles published in the series, please see end of book.

Humanism and the Culture of Renaissance Europe

Second edition

CHARLES G. NAUERT

University of Missouri, Columbia

CAMBRIDGE
UNIVERSITY PRESS

CAMBRIDGE UNIVERSITY PRESS
Cambridge, New York, Melbourne, Madrid, Cape Town, Singapore, São Paulo,
Delhi, Tokyo, Mexico City

Cambridge University Press
The Edinburgh Building, Cambridge CB2 8RU, UK

Published in the United States of America by Cambridge University Press, New York

www.cambridge.org
Information on this title www.cambridge.org/9780521547819

First published 1995
Reprinted five times
Second edition 2006
5th printing 2011

Printed in the United Kingdom at the University Press, Cambridge

A catalogue record for this publication is available from the British Library

ISBN 978-0-521-83909-9 Hardback
ISBN 978-0-521-54781-9 Paperback

Contents

Illustrations

Preface

This book aims to present a comprehensive account of the development and significance of the humanistic culture of Europe (north as well as south) in the age of the Renaissance. It is based on the researches of more than a generation of scholars active since about the end of the Second World War. At that time, critical attacks on the traditional picture of Renaissance civilization established by Jakob Burckhardt had produced so much doubt about the meaning, and even the existence, of a Renaissance that many historians abandoned use of the term itself, a situation brilliantly demonstrated in Wallace K. Ferguson's *The Renaissance in Historical Thought* (1948). In the aftermath of that historiographical demolition, I myself wrote a dissertation which systematically avoided use of the dread term 'Renaissance', and not a single member of my examining committee challenged or even mentioned the omission. Yet leaving 'the Renaissance' and 'humanism' out of the history of the Renaissance age was not a viable position, as I found when I undertook to revise my dissertation into a book that addressed the intellectual problems of the sixteenth century, and found in an even more pressing way when I faced the task of explaining the Renaissance to a class of college freshmen in a lecture of fifty minutes. Whether historians like the concepts 'Renaissance' and 'humanism' or not, the centuries to which those terms are conventionally applied really did exist and must be faced, since they contributed in important ways to the subsequent development of Western society and civilization.

In my teaching and in preparing this book, I have had the guidance of a host of scholars who have gone back to the sources and have created the materials out of which one can derive a credible account of the rise of humanistic culture and its historical significance. In my own thinking about the age, the crucial influences have been a handful of stimulating articles by Theodor E. Mommsen, whom I never met, and the publications and personal encouragement of Hans Baron, Paul Oskar Kristeller, and my own mentor, William J. Bouwsma. To go beyond this short list would be invidious, for I have learned from a whole generation of colleagues. Most of their names appear in the Bibliography, and I can only hope that I had the good sense to make constructive use of what their publications offer.

I owe special thanks to my colleagues in the Department of History at the University of Missouri-Columbia, especially for enabling me to have a year free from teaching to work on this book. I dedicate this book with love and thanks to my wife Jean and our sons Paul and Jon.

Preface to the Second Edition

A decade after the appearance of the first edition, the opportunity to prepare a revised second edition has permitted me to introduce a number of changes in the text. Some of these are relatively minor revisions made in the interests of clarity and readability. Obviously, the new Bibliographical essay includes a number of important publications that appeared since my earlier work. Three changes, however, are more substantial. First, new publications on Italian education have caused me to rethink the treatment on that subject, now located in Chapter 2. Unfortunately, the story of the 'educational revolution' of the Italian Renaissance has become more complicated, though the revised account still maintains that a significant transformation in the nature of Italian grammar-school education took place during the fifteenth century. Second, new publications on what I have called Italian pre-humanism and on the role of 'civic humanism' (if any) in the development of Renaissance Italy have led to some rethinking of my earlier treatment, though I remain unconvinced that the basic idea of a historically decisive connection between political and intellectual history in Quattrocento Florence should be abandoned. As a result of these two areas of revision, the original Chapter 1 has been divided, with the new Chapter 2 beginning with the emergence of humanism as the dominant culture of the elite classes not only in Florence but throughout Italy. That emergence of humanism and the mechanisms (such as education) by which it took place are the main theme of the new Chapter 2.

A third change is a new section (also in Chapter 2) on the role of women in the history of Renaissance humanism. This is partly a response to an objection voiced by a learned reviewer of the first edition, but it also reflects my own reaction to teaching in a generation when women's history emerged as a major historical specialty. In general, the most successful products of the turn towards the history of women have been in social history; cultural and intellectual history of women has been less productive, more anecdotal. Though I have been able to present some examples of women who aspired to become learned humanists and a larger group who became successful writers of vernacular books, women were still pushed to the margins of intellectual life. Mastery of Latin (and preferably, also Greek) was the essential key for entry into the world of humanistic learning, and it functioned to screen almost all females except a few daughters of high-ranking and wealthy families out of the pool of potential scholars. Hence female humanists were very few, and even those few were marginalized. For female writers in the vernacular languages, conditions were a little better. The spread of literacy in the vernacular, the growing number of translations of classical literary works into modern languages, and above all, the rise of the printing industry enabled a number of intelligent and persistent women to gain recognition as writers. Their number was small, but at least it represents a beginning in the entry of women into active participation in the world of literature.

I want to repeat my earlier thanks to my family and to my colleagues at the University of Missouri-Columbia, and also to thank the editors of the Cambridge University Press for their interest and helpfulness.

Introduction

The last thing readers want from the authors of history books is arcane historiographical debates among contending schools of interpretation. Yet in the case of Renaissance humanism, any serious reader needs some knowledge of where we have been since 1860, when the Swiss historian Jakob Burckhardt put forward what long remained the dominant concepts of the key terms, 'Renaissance' and 'humanism', in his masterpiece of cultural history, *The Civilization of the Renaissance in Italy.* Although few specialists today would give unqualified endorsement to his description of the age, it was profoundly appealing to his contemporaries, and it still has much to offer.

Burckhardt's book quickly captured the imagination of educated readers because it was a subtle and learned synthesis of opinions about the Renaissance that had been accumulating for centuries and had grown powerful during the Age of the Enlightenment (Ferguson 1948). Burckhardt seemed to confirm a story that had already become prevalent but had never before been given such a powerful and coherent presentation. This story, or historical myth, was the product of the secular intellectuals of the eighteenth and nineteenth centuries who were searching for the origins of their own beliefs and values. According to this story, after the collapse of ancient civilization in the fifth century AD, a thousand years of darkness and barbarism ensued, with the Christian church acting simultaneously to preserve some few shreds of ancient civilization and to suppress any intellectual or religious revivals that might weaken the stranglehold that the higher clergy and the warrior aristocracy held over the minds as well as the bodies of ordinary people. Eventually, however, a revival of commerce and urban life (the reasons for which were rarely explained) laid the foundations for a rediscovery of ancient literature and simultaneously for a secular, even anti-religious, set of values. These values, which constituted a new and distinctly modern philosophy of life, glorified the individual and the attractions of earthly life; and they were strongly reinforced by the rediscovered pagan literature of Antiquity. The new secular, individualistic values were inherently incompatible with

Christian belief. This worldly philosophy of life came to be called 'humanism', and it reflected a comprehensive rebirth (i.e., a renaissance) of high civilization that drew its main ideas and inspiration from ancient times. Those who had been brought up in this humanistic philosophy overthrew the social and economic restraints of feudal, pre-capitalist Europe, broke the power of the clergy, and discarded ethical restraints on politics. They laid the foundations for the modern absolute, secular state and even for the remarkable growth of natural science at the end of the Renaissance. In short, they ended the Middle Ages and ushered in the modern world. This is a rather straightforward story. It is especially attractive to secular-minded intellectuals who still often call themselves 'humanists'. It dominated prevailing views of Renaissance humanism from the publication of Burckhardt's book until well into the twentieth century. It has only one major flaw: both in its general thrust and in virtually every detail, it is untrue.

The preceding account of Renaissance humanism contains just enough half-truths to make it plausible. Rather oddly, the author who created it, Jakob Burckhardt, was no uncritical admirer of the materialistic, power-hungry bourgeois culture of his time. His masterpiece is far more subtle than the preceding simplified account would indicate. Virtually every work on the Renaissance for two generations accepted its conclusions without serious question. But the twentieth century witnessed a growing reaction against 'Burckhardtian' orthodoxy, partly because fresh research challenged specific points but also because the bloody and violent history of the twentieth century made it hard to accept the liberal, optimistic faith in progress that Burckhardt's book seemed to imply.

The attack on Burckhardt's Renaissance

Of particular importance in the twentieth-century reaction against Burckhardt was the growth of scholarship on medieval history, which made the conventional view of a dark and barbarous Middle Ages increasingly hard for well-informed historians to swallow. The stark contrast between a culturally 'dark' Middle Ages and an enlightened, 'modern' Renaissance melted away as medievalists discovered squarely in the Middle Ages all the essential traits supposedly typical of the later period, and also discovered within the Renaissance many traditional elements that seemed to prove that the Middle Ages lived on into the Renaissance. Medievalists found renaissances (that is, periods of classical revival) in 'their' period also – in Carolingian France, Anglo-Saxon England, Ottonian Germany – though not, perhaps significantly, in any century of Italy's Middle Ages. One of these medieval revivals, the 'twelfth-century

Renaissance', has established itself firmly in the historical vocabulary. The great American medievalist Charles Homer Haskins made that concept canonical with his *The Renaissance of the Twelfth Century* (1927). Haskins argued that the term 'renaissance', in the sense of emergence of high culture, including significant enthusiasm for classical Latin literature, was an obvious characteristic of the twelfth century and that this cultural renewal is the direct ancestor of all subsequent European civilization. Others went further and claimed that *the* Renaissance, the real one, the one that marked the fundamental transition of Europe from a backward to an advanced civilization, occurred not in Italy in the later fourteenth century but in France in the twelfth century. For a time in the late 1940s and the 1950s, the very idea of a Renaissance came under attack.

Yet the concept and term 'Renaissance' have survived, though still contested. The main reason is that whatever terms historians might apply, the historical realities that Burckhardt described cannot be dismissed with quibbles about the proper terms to use. A flood of new studies vastly enriched historians' understanding of the period. By the 1950s, these studies had produced new ways of thinking about Renaissance culture, new ways of defining such fundamental terms as 'humanism' and 'Renaissance'. Books by Myron P. Gilmore (1952) and Denys Hay (1961; 2nd edn 1977) are important early steps in synthesizing this new research.

Many of those who joined in the attack on Burckhardt spent their energy denying the appropriateness of his terms rather than in discussing the major traits of the period. No serious scholar now believes that before the Italian Renaissance, Europe lay sunken in darkness, barbarism, and superstition for a thousand years. It is true that Petrarch and other humanists claimed to have restored civilization after a millennium of cultural darkness. This claim may contain profound truths concerning the Renaissance period. But concerning the Middle Ages, it is patently false, so false that no one whose opinion counts now holds it.

Thus the beginning of wisdom for anyone who wants to understand the culture of Renaissance humanism is to realize that the high civilization of the Renaissance developed out of the high civilization of the Middle Ages and always retained marks of that origin. The medievalists are at least partly right: the Renaissance is not the beginning of the cultural dynamism of Western society, but rather a highly significant reorientation of an advanced civilization already two or three centuries old. As Haskins demonstrated beyond dispute, many of the major authors of ancient Rome were not only known but well known in the schools of the High Middle Ages. From the thirteenth century, the curriculum of all universities was based on the works of Aristotle, one of Antiquity's greatest philosophers. Humanism was not, as many people have assumed, a worldly rival philosophy that displaced a pious scholastic philosophy during the Renaissance. For one thing, humanism was not a philosophy at all (an issue that will be treated later). In the professional study of philosophy and natural science, scholasticism (and Aristotle) retained a mastery unshaken and almost unchallenged right through the Renaissance centuries, all the way down to the collapse of Aristotelian science in the time of Galileo and Descartes. The humanistic culture did not produce a new philosophy to replace this scholasticism, which continued not only to exist but also to develop along lines that were intellectually sound and philosophically fruitful.

Yet Burckhardt was right in detecting the emergence of a new culture and also in identifying at least one of its major sources. Part One of his book links the new humanistic culture of Italy to a unique set of social, political, and economic conditions. At first glance, this new culture might seem to be the simple reflex of the emergence of capitalism, commerce, and cities in northern Italy from the late eleventh century. But there are difficulties with the cruder forms of this purely materialistic explanation, the most obvious one being chronology. Urban growth and commercial expansion can be traced as early as the eleventh century. Why did the new culture not attract a large following until almost the end of the fourteenth century? Since many historians of the period are now convinced that the 1340s witnessed the onset of the new capitalist economy's first great depression, it even seems that the new culture did not develop until the capitalist economy was in a prolonged decline. In any case, there is no simple connection between the birth of capitalism and the new humanist culture.

Italy's unique social character

Yet it is true that Italy during the twelfth and thirteenth centuries had become the most highly developed, the wealthiest, the most urbanized region of Europe. North of the Alps, the scholastic philosophy, Gothic art, and vernacular literature of these centuries seem to be clearly associated with the clergy and the feudal aristocracy that dominated the Middle Ages. Italy was not totally free of this older aristocratic and clerical culture. But Gothic art and architecture never gained full dominance in Italy, and the scholasticism that developed in Paris first penetrated Italian universities during the lifetime of the earliest humanists and never became a prominent element in Italian civilization (at least not until the conservative Catholic religious reforms of the late sixteenth century).

The dynamic part of Italy, the north, was dominated not by clerics and feudal nobles but by wealthy urban merchants; and during the twelfth and thirteenth centuries, the cities of northern Italy in alliance with the popes broke the military and political power of the German kings, who called themselves Roman emperors and attempted to control northern Italy. Instead of developing a strong, centralizing monarchy based on feudalism as France and England did, Italy became a jumble of urban republics that exercised *de facto* independence, a point developed at some length by Burckhardt. Although the people of these urban communes were sincerely Catholic and were periodically swept by waves of religious revivalism, the position of the clergy in Italian city life was marginal. The cities were ruled by wealthy merchants and modest tradesmen and artisans, though from the thirteenth century, more and more of them came under the control of military despots who offered protection from internal class conflict and outside invasion.

In such a society, based on individual property and private contract, the most important educated groups were those who dealt with commercial and industrial activities. These were the lawyers and the notaries, those who drew up and interpreted the rules and written agreements that made trade on a large scale possible. As Italian capitalist society developed, there was an acute need for men skilled in drafting, recording, and authenticating contracts and letters. These were the notaries, specialists who did not need the long and costly education provided by law schools but who did receive a training in Latin grammar and a style of rhetoric called *ars dictaminis*. Such training in letter-writing and drafting legal documents was often given by apprenticeship, but at major centres of legal study such as Padua and Bologna, there were professional teachers who not only taught the conventional legal forms of various kinds of business documents and the correct type of handwriting for documents of public record but also provided some instruction in Roman law. At first, the duties of notaries required little more education than the ability to read and write. But as the scale and complexity of Italian business transactions grew and as a growing proportion of Italy's urban male population became literate, professional notaries had to differentiate themselves from the general literate population by acquiring more sophisticated skills, such as a good mastery of Latin, the language of the law courts, and the ability to embellish documents and letters with quotations from classical and Christian authors. In addition, the need for lawyers and notaries to study, ponder, and apply Roman law predisposed them to develop an interest not only in the law but also in the language, literature, institutions, and customs of Antiquity. Although humanists of the Renaissance generally pointed to Petrarch and Boccaccio as the pioneers of the cultural renewal that they claimed to be leading, they sometimes alluded to precursors who lived in the closing decades of the thirteenth century. Not by mere coincidence, these precursors (sometimes now labelled pre-humanists) were all either lawyers or notaries.

Paduan 'pre-humanism'

Padua, a university town especially noted for the study of law and medicine, held the earliest known cluster of enthusiasts for the language and literature of ancient Rome. The central figure was a judge, Lovato dei Lovati (*c.* 1240–1309). His few surviving poems show that he had a thorough knowledge of ancient Latin poetry. Lovato energetically defended ancient poetry against those who preferred modern vernacular verse. He was active in the discovery and reburial of the supposed remains of the Trojan Antenor, the mythical founder of Padua. He was also an admirer of the Roman dramatist Seneca. His study of Seneca's texts gave him a clear understanding of the metrical structure of ancient Latin poetry, producing the earliest Renaissance treatise on metrics. While his poetic work shows a strongly classicized Latin diction, his prose works are written in the prevailing medieval Latin of the legal profession.

Although Lovato was a talented writer and a striking personality who showed many characteristics of humanism, he remained relatively little known outside Padua. His younger contemporary Albertino Mussato (1261–1325), who was a notary by profession, became widely known throughout Italy; and perhaps for that reason, many more of his writings survive. Though he sometimes still interprets classical myths and poets in the allegorical medieval way, his underlying approach to poetry and history is innovative. His prose style was influenced by the Roman historian Sallust; and his own historical works were influenced by Sallust, Caesar, and especially Livy, ancient Rome's most famous historian. His poems were also modelled on ancient poets. His admiration for Seneca's tragedies reflects the influence of Lovato, whom he regarded as his master. Mussato used Seneca's tragedies as a model for the first secular drama written since Antiquity, the *Ecerinis*. Significantly for future developments in Italian humanism, the play was political propaganda encouraging Paduan citizens to resist the attempts of the tyrant of Verona to incorporate Padua into his principality.

One of the most puzzling characteristics of the Italian cultural situation is that Florence, the city associated with the later flowering of humanistic culture, played a modest and largely derivative role in this pre-humanist movement. A few individuals had personal connections to classicizing Paduan lawyers and notaries, but in general Florence at the end of the thirteenth century was not a highly learned place. It was not a university town, and, with the exception of the convents of the mendicant orders, there seem to have been few libraries of classical texts. Yet the city was growing and prospering immensely in the late thirteenth century, and it contained a large population of lawyers and notaries, the group most active in the early classical culture of Padua. Conventional scholarship associates the first great Florentine literary and intellectual figure, Dante Alighieri (1265–1321), with medieval rather than Renaissance culture. The most important Florentine precursor of Dante was a notary, Brunetto Latini, who was broadly learned, but in a manner that links him to the encyclopaedic tradition of the Middle Ages. Indeed, Latini spent several years of exile in France and wrote his major book in French. The prospering merchant class of Florence was developing an intellectual life dominated by its own needs and interests, not those dominant among university professors and clergymen. Yet it was not cut off from medieval scholasticism. Dante claims to have attended 'the schools of the religious and the disputations of the philosophers' during the 1290s, probably meaning that he attended lectures on theology at the Dominican and Franciscan friaries. The libraries of these two flourishing convents were the only places where Dante could have gained access to the broad range of books, both ancient and medieval, reflected in his poetic and prose works.

Yet while the unusual erudition of Latini and Dante seems to reflect predominantly medieval culture, the fact that both were laymen and both were chiefly concerned with practical moral and political questions rather than abstract, speculative ones (such as logic, metaphysics, and theology) demonstrates that the new social reality of late medieval Italy was producing new cultural initiatives. What these Florentine intellectuals lacked was a clear conception of a far-reaching cultural renewal to be brought about by assimilation and reinterpretation of classical literature and by conscious repudiation of the values of medieval civilization. These new directions were the discovery of yet another Florentine, Francesco Petrarca (or Petrarch). It may be significant that Petrarch was a Florentine who never resided in Florence, the son of a political exile who became a functionary at the papal court in Avignon. Thus Petrarch grew up not in Italy but in southern France. And surely it fits the emergent pattern of the early classical revival that though he never practised law, he received a university education in Roman law. With him, a new cultural ideal, the ideal of humanism, emerged in Italy. That emergence is the subject of the following chapter.

1　The birth of humanist culture

Both the classical enthusiasms of Paduan lawyers and notaries and the literary works of Florentines like Brunetto Latini and Dante show that about 1300 the prosperous educated laymen in the Italian cities were groping their way towards a new culture distinct from both the chivalric culture of the medieval nobility and the scholastic culture of the clergy. This was a natural response to the conditions of their life. Since the nineteenth century, historians have labelled this new culture 'humanism', though that abstract term was coined by a German scholar in 1808 and appears nowhere in the writings of the Renaissance itself. The term that did exist then was 'humanistic studies' (*studia humanitatis*), used to designate a cluster of academic subjects much favoured by humanists. By the first half of the fifteenth century, the term 'humanist' (in Latin, *humanista*) had come into use, originally as student slang used to designate masters who taught those particular academic subjects: grammar, rhetoric, poetry, history, and moral philosophy. 'Humanism', the bundle of subjects taught by 'humanists' in the Latin grammar schools and university faculties of liberal arts, made no claim to embrace the totality of human learning, nor even all of the traditional seven 'liberal arts' (embracing the *trivium*, or grammar, rhetoric, and dialectic, and the *quadrivium*, or arithmetic, geometry, astronomy, and music) that in theory were studied by all who received the bachelor and master of arts degrees from a university. The *studia humanitatis* did not include the subjects taught in the three higher faculties of medieval universities: law, medicine, and theology.

To our own era, which has cast aside most of its classical heritage, it may seem odd that an educational and literary movement that embraced only grammar, rhetoric, poetry, history, and moral philosophy could have become quite literally epoch-making. Since the eighteenth century, efforts have been made to equate humanism with something broader and more obviously significant, the rise of a new philosophy that was generally defined as a glorification of human nature and an exaltation of this-worldly goals in place of the otherworldly values that supposedly dominated life in the Middle Ages. But this way of thinking about humanism ran up against irrefutable evidence that leading humanists (beginning with Petrarch himself) were still deeply moved by otherworldly religious values.

In the Renaissance itself, humanism was never defined as a philosophy or taught as an academic subject. All serious study of philosophy throughout the Renaissance was founded on one or another of the rival forms of medieval Aristotelianism – scholasticism. Although humanist scholarship eventually diffused knowledge about other ancient philosophical traditions besides the Peripatetic or Aristotelian, only Aristotelian philosophy was taught in the schools. This scholastic philosophy remained dominant until the rise of the new physical science in the seventeenth century demolished the credibility of Aristotelian natural philosophy. Outside the academy, Platonism or Stoicism or some other ancient system may have been a philosophical rival to scholasticism for certain individuals. But humanism never was, because it was not any kind of philosophy at all. Among twentieth-century scholars, Paul Oskar Kristeller led the opposition to all attempts to define humanism as a philosophical rival to scholasticism. Aside from his awareness of the actual origins and contemporary meaning of the term *studia humanitatis,* one of his principal motives seems to have been historiographical. The kind of windy, undocumented blather about 'humanist philosophy' that dominated discussions of the Renaissance in the nineteenth century cannot stand up against any serious study either of medieval civilization or of the writings of the leading humanists themselves. It is true that from the time of Petrarch, humanists frequently attacked scholasticism; but this was largely an outgrowth of educational and curricular disputes, not of philosophy strictly speaking. Humanists objected to the narrow, trade-school approach that dominated scholastic education. They also denounced the scholastics' reluctance to incorporate some fairly limited curricular changes that the humanists demanded. Sometimes they attacked scholasticism (as Petrarch did) because it seemed too materialistic and rationalistic, too subversive of religious faith. They did not present their age with a comprehensive new philosophy, because they had none to offer. There is no identifiable set of philosophical doctrines that all humanists held and that could possibly be used to define them as a distinct philosophical school. Most of their writings had nothing to do with philosophy. Kristeller concludes, 'the Italian humanists on the whole were neither good nor bad philosophers, but no philosophers at all'.

On its own terms, this position is unassailable. But it leaves modern students with the problem of explaining why humanism seemed so important, both to contemporaries and to later historians. Perhaps to the graduate of nineteenth-century classical schools, the humanis attain a purer, more classical Latin style and a broader kn ancient Latin and Greek literature may have seemed epoch-making; but to the present generation, which has virtually renounced study of Greek and Latin, why should such achievements seem important? It is a fair question, made all the fairer because a significant part of the ancient Latin literature that survives today was known, read, studied, and even loved throughout the Middle Ages.

The question of how thoroughly lost the 'lost' classical books really were is worth pondering. In the case of Greek texts, which in general were far less known than Latin books in the Middle Ages, the works of Aristotle were of interest to the medieval Arabs; and in the late twelfth and early thirteenth centuries, when the intellectual life of Christian Europe reached a level where Aristotle seemed relevant to its concerns, nearly all of his works were made available in Latin translation within the lifetime of one generation.

Also worth pondering is the historical fact, widely known but seldom reflected upon, that from the conquest of Constantinople by the Fourth Crusade in 1204 down to 1261, that city and many other centres of medieval Greek culture were ruled by puppet princes installed by Venice and other Italian cities. A steady stream of Italian merchants and administrators went east and lived for many years in the Byzantine capital. Western churchmen flocked to the east to persuade or compel the Greeks to accept religious union with Rome. Yet none of this thirteenth-century contact seems to have aroused much interest in ancient Greek language and literature. In the case of both Latin and Greek, perhaps what is the important and overlooked point is not the availability of ancient books (which were always potentially present) but the change in outlook that made acquisition of those books and mastery of a difficult language worth the trouble.

A change of mentality

Western Europeans *could* have recovered Greek language and literature in the thirteenth century as easily as in the fifteenth, but they did not seize the opportunity. The scarce Latin manuscripts that humanists of the early fifteenth century took pride in 'rediscovering' were all available during the high-medieval period, but they were not 'discovered' – that is, few readers knew of their existence. In the case of both classical Latin and Greek, something had changed between the early thirteenth century and the early fifteenth century. This change was a change of mentality, of values, that made the tedious mastery of the classical languages and diffusion of classical texts seem worth the effort.

Historians of culture have often assumed that the Renaissance recovery of ancient languages and literatures was somehow easy because Italy as the homeland of ancient Roman civilization had never quite lost touch with that civilization. But this gratuitous assumption is never proved, for the simple reason that it cannot be. Not only the 'twelfth-century Renaissance' but all of the earlier medieval classical revivals (Carolingian, Alfredian, Ottonian) were centred north of the Alps. In the Renaissance period, some important discoveries of little-known manuscripts were made in Italian libraries, but the most significant ones came out of libraries north of the Alps, where medieval civilization had flourished while Italy remained culturally backward. Poggio Bracciolini (1380–1459), the most spectacularly successful humanist discoverer of lost manuscripts, made his greatest finds at the monasteries of Cluny in Burgundy and St Gallen in Switzerland.

Petrarch, the first major figure of humanism, received his early education and his inspiration to revive ancient Latin language and literature while growing up near Avignon, an area that was culturally French, not Italian. The papal curia during its 'Babylonian Captivity' at Avignon (1305–77) was a lively centre of interest in the classics during Petrarch's youth. Petrarch himself had French as well as Italian friends who shared his devotion to Roman literature. In fact, both France and England had a number of enthusiastic students of classical Latin literature during the early fourteenth century, though these men approached ancient texts within the medieval tradition and did not show the distinctive characteristics of Petrarch's scholarship. At least some of the 'brightness' claimed for the Renaissance by Italian humanists and some of the 'darkness' they attributed to the Middle Ages may be the result of their contrasting their own achievements not with the most advanced culture of the Middle Ages, the French, but with that of their own Italy.

Thus the mystery of humanism's broader significance remains unsolved. If the Middle Ages already possessed a substantial portion of surviving classical literature and could have possessed most of the rest if they had taken the trouble, simple 'rediscovery of the classics', even the Greek classics, cannot be the decisive element in Renaissance humanism. If humanism, the *studia humanitatis,* embraced only a small cluster of academic subjects, does it have any lasting significance except for those who have an antiquarian interest in the development of literary and linguistic studies? Why did the humanists – and a great number of their contemporaries, including the rich and powerful men who paid the bills – think that the growth of humanistic studies represented a fundamental turning-point in the history of the world? If humanism was not a philosophy, was it anything more than the pastime of a band of literary dilettantes? That is precisely the charge levelled against it by some historians of science (Thorndike), who seem to have blamed the humanists for the failure of seventeenth-century scientific advances to flow immediately from the promising advancements made by fourteenth-century scholastic scientists at Paris and Oxford.

The answers to these questions must follow several directions, and must avoid the trap that captured many of Burckhardt's early disciples, that of defining and justifying humanism as a new philosophy that led directly to the modern world. Kristeller is clearly right on this issue: it was not a philosophy. But as some of his critics have pointed out, Kristeller defines both philosophy and humanism very narrowly. He was a careful scholar and insisted that history, even intellectual history, must rest on documents. Yet if the humanists' programme is not exactly a philosophy, it does have some philosophical implications. An attempt to define these may help to explain why humanism not only claimed to be but actually was an important force in human history.

Meaning of *studia humanitatis*

One approach focuses on the term *studia humanitatis,* a Latin phrase with classical origins. It appears in the work of Cicero, the Roman author most admired by Renaissance humanists. In *Pro Archaia,* a defence of the social utility of poetry, Cicero spoke of 'the humanities and letters' (*studia humanitatis ac litterarum*). While his own meaning for this phrase is not entirely clear, his use of *humanitas* in other places suggests that the humanities were those subjects that boys must study in order to develop their full potential as human beings. Thus he seems to have used the term to include all of the liberal arts – that is, the subjects (traditionally seven in number) appropriate to the education of a free man. Here he meant a Roman male citizen who had the right and also the duty to share in the governance of the Roman republic, and who did not have to earn his living through physical labour at one of the mechanical or servile arts. The general education given to such a young man under the republic and early empire was focused largely on attaining skill in Latin oratory (hence on grammar and rhetoric) and on an appreciation of his privileged heritage and obligations as a participant in government (hence also on the history of Rome and on moral philosophy). As this Ciceronian ideal was passed down through later classical books such as the widely read *Noctes Atticae* of Aulus Gellius, the phrase *studia humanitatis* implied a programme of education for the ruling elite of the republic, somewhat akin to the Greek term *paideia* or the modern German term *Bildung,* a word that is properly translated not only as education but also as culture. Thus the *studia humanitatis* implied a broad general education, but they also implied a strong emphasis on the oratorical skills and the social values most needed by a ruling elite, precisely the subjects embraced by the humanists' programme of study: grammar, rhetoric, poetry (a special application of rhetoric), history (which dealt largely with politics and with the consequences of moral decisions), and moral philosophy (which included the issue of political obligation).

As a comprehensive educational programme, however, the *studia humanitatis* had certain philosophical implications. One implication in the area of moral philosophy was an obligation of the person educated, the free Roman citizen, to participate in the life of the community, and hence in politics. The conditions that had encouraged the growth of this educational ideal were replicated to some degree in Italy from the twelfth century onward. As the German emperors lost effective control of Italy, many cities in the north and central parts of the peninsula had become self-governing republics. Although these city-republics were often unstable because of class rivalries and old political enmities, all of them passed through a stage of republican political life. Even if they came under the rule of an authoritarian ruler (as most eventually did), they still retained some republican institutions and practices. In a rough way, therefore, their political structure and practices came to resemble the condition of ancient Greece and ancient Italy. Literate people quickly saw this similarity and turned to the history of Rome for inspiration and guidance.

Any republic formulates and applies public laws and policies through a process of discussion and debate. Thus the Roman educational system, which had no appeal for the aristocratic and clerical rulers of the Middle Ages, provided exactly the kind of training in oratorical skills and fostered exactly the sense of obligation to public service needed for those who governed the Italian communes. At first, this attraction to humanistic studies was felt mostly by judges, lawyers, and notaries. In time, however, as the chaotic political conditions of the thirteenth century gave way to established republics or despotisms in the fourteenth and fifteenth centuries, the social groups who dominated political life found in a humanistic education precisely the kind of education needed to prepare their sons to govern. The humanist programme of education was conceived by an intellectual who was also a great poet, Petrarch. But its eventual success in becoming the educational *paideia* of the Italian elite classes resulted not from its being artistically appealing but from its being practical.

Humanism and the Florentines

The outstanding example is the republic of Florence. By the late fourteenth century, after almost a century of political, social, and economic upheaval, the wealthy merchant families had gained effective control of the political system, while still preserving some share in government for members of the twenty-one legally recognized professional, commercial, and artisanal guilds. At precisely this same period, not only educational theory but also the actual practice of upper-class families strongly favoured a humanistic education, rather than merely a commercial apprenticeship, for the sons who were destined to grow up to be rulers of the republic. Thus whether it be called a 'philosophy' or not, humanism certainly did provide a common educational formation for the families that ruled Florence in the fifteenth century. While many historians partially or wholly reject Hans Baron's famous thesis (see pp. 30–34 below) about Florentine 'civic humanism', it is hard to escape the impression that there was a symbiosis between republican politics and humanistic education. Students of fourteenth-century Florentine political debates have found that while about 1350 historical references to Roman experience were rare, the practice of citing examples from ancient times grew during the later fourteenth century. A young Florentine who lacked oratorical skills and mastery of classical history would be at a disadvantage if he wished to participate actively in political life.

Redefining 'practical' learning

Another broadly philosophical attitude that grew up naturally in a society that defined participation in the making of political decisions as a primary obligation of citizens was a tendency to doubt the validity and utility of abstract generalizations and to challenge the emphasis on logic, metaphysics, and natural science that had dominated medieval education. Political decisions may be influenced by scientifically demonstrated facts, but politics is not a science based on absolute certainties. It is an art that involves making choices among alternative proposals, each of which offers (or claims to offer) certain advantages. No matter what the proponents of any proposal may claim, no political decision is made with the absolute certainty that inheres in a conclusion of geometry or formal logic. Politicians offer (and make) only choices based on calculations of probability. Whereas the scholastic education of the Middle Ages, which exalted logic above all the other liberal arts, seemed suited to the needs of men seeking the absolute certainty required in theology and natural science, it did not seem very attractive to young men who saw their future in making the debatable, merely probable determinations required in government or the law courts. The humanistic arts of grammar (that is, clear and correct writing and speaking) and rhetoric (that is, persuasive argument and the making of practical decisions on the basis of probability) seemed far more useful for young men of the politically dominant class.

Humanistic education claimed to provide rhetorical skills that would help such young men participate effectively in political life. It also claimed to provide an emphasis on moral training and moral obligation that seemed directly relevant to a ruling elite. This emphasis was notoriously lacking in traditional university education, which concentrated on logical analysis, Aristotelian science, and professional training in law, medicine, or theology. Universities trained experts and specialists. But the life of wealthy urban Italians seemed to require instead a broad general education with special attention to learning to speak effectively and to developing a sense of social responsibility. Ancient Roman society had faced similar conditions and had developed a style of education, oratorical or rhetorical in nature, for the preparation of its young aristocratic men. The ethical works and oratorical treatises of Cicero reflected (and indeed imparted) precisely such a rhetorical education. By the late fifteenth century, these works had become standard textbooks for study of humanistic subjects.

What is hard for modern people to grasp but seemed obvious to Italians of the Renaissance is that education in humanistic subjects appeared practical while education in logic and natural science, the dominant subjects in the medieval liberal-arts curriculum, seemed to breed idle debate about purely speculative issues that were useless for real life. What was useful was not primarily knowledge of facts about nature (even if the facts were true) but the making of wise moral choices. This moral goal and the related need for skill in persuading others through aptly shaped speech and writing already found clear expression in Petrarch. Rhetorical skill and character development became and remained the advantages claimed for humanistic education, even though recent scholarship suggests that actual classroom practice gave far more attention to questions of Latin style than to close analysis of the moral issues raised by the treatises and orations of Cicero and other classical moralists whose books were studied in the schools (Black, pp. 29, 32–33, 315–16, 323–24).

Although this conception of education does not constitute a 'philosophy', it implies some important opinions about human nature. First, though not in any formal sense sceptical, it suggests that intellectual mastery of absolute truth, the metaphysical certitude exalted by medieval Aristotelian philosophy, was probably beyond human ability and certainly was not necessary for everyday living. It implies that the ultimate goal is not knowledge of truth, as the tradition of Thomas Aquinas taught. Instead, those humanists who addressed such matters usually declared that the purpose of human life is to make sound moral decisions in the course of daily living. Such decisions involve making choices based on probability, not certainty. Thus humanistic thought from its very origins, not only in Petrarch but even in Cicero, who was a self-proclaimed follower of Academic scepticism, defined the goals of intellectual life in modest terms. This rejection of scholastic intellectualism is evident in the works of Petrarch's most important Florentine disciple, Coluccio Salutati (1331–1406). He taught that the goal of life is not to know God, who is beyond our limited understanding, but to love God, something that depends on faith rather than reason. In real life, people are guided more by emotion than by reason, and the true business of life is to make sound ethical judgements. Thus a degree of intellectual relativism is built into the humanists' mentality. Any debatable issue involves matters that can be determined only at the level of probability. If absolute certainty could be obtained, then debate, discussion, and persuasion would be preposterous. There is no debating the truth of the Pythagorean theorem; but questions like whether to choose this alliance or that, to make war or peace, to marry or remain single, to invest in a certain business or not, can be decided only by choosing between alternatives that seem more or less probable. Practical moral judgements involving everyday experience, not the Pythagorean theorem, constitute the real business of life. Humanistic education, offering special attention to the making of probable decisions and moral choices, seemed far more practical, far better suited to the human condition, than training in speculative and scientific questions.

Thus humanism surely implied – indeed, openly proclaimed – opinions about human nature, about the scope and limits of human reason, even about the ultimate goal of human life, that were philosophical in nature. The success of humanism in defining the goals and methods of education rested on its suitability for the political and social needs of the time. Poetry was indeed more practical than physics; and the fact that this sounds strange to the modern ear may not rest entirely on our possessing a better understanding of physics. It may also reflect the spiritual, ethical, and social poverty of the modern world.

Classicism: medieval and Renaissance

The preceding pages suggest that although Renaissance humanists undeniably knew more classical literature than medieval scholars did, the real cultural change had little to do with how much was known. Medieval civilization also depended heavily on its inheritance from Antiquity, a condition well symbolized by the almost exclusive use of Latin for all serious thought, and also by the dominant position held in the universities by Aristotle. The Renaissance difference rested partly on the different social milieu. Medieval civilization was the creation of feudal and clerical elites. But already by the twelfth and thirteenth centuries, Italy had become an entirely different kind of society.

Although individual Italians played major roles in the cultural life of the High Middle Ages (Thomas Aquinas, for example), Italy played a marginal role in the creation of medieval civilization. Italian universities were dominated not by scholastic philosophy and theology but by their law and medical faculties, which met the needs of an urban, commercial society ruled by laymen. In vernacular literature, poetry in medieval Italy was written in French, not Italian. In classical studies, which were essential in a society that used Latin for public worship and for all advanced education and scholarship, Italy remained a laggard until the closing decades of the thirteenth century.

The new culture of humanism was an enduring solution to the need of this distinctive society for a type of culture and education suited to its character. Ancient educational and literary practices, products of a society of self-governing cities, provided both inspiration and specific details for the new Italian culture that began to stir in the late thirteenth century and developed rapidly in the late fourteenth century. Inevitably, a society of cities, engaged in commerce and practising at least *de facto* political self-rule by local citizens, viewed and evaluated ancient literature differently from a society whose intellectuals were mostly priests and whose life was controlled by feudal nobles and high-ranking clergymen. Thus part of the difference marked by the rise of humanistic culture is purely sociological.

Changing intellectual habits

Renaissance classicism also differed from medieval classicism in fundamental intellectual habits. From late Antiquity through the Middle Ages, classical (and also Christian) texts were conceived as 'authorities' – that is, as bundles of factual statements about specific individual things or issues. Each specific statement might be determined to be true or false, but in either case it was regarded as what one authority had said on its subject. In effect, each known work of an authoritative writer was dissolved into a bundle of individual statements; and each statement tended to be quoted and understood without the slightest attention to the context in which it had originally stood, still less with any attention to the historical circumstances or the original intention of the author. As the cathedral schools of northern France were eclipsed by the professionally oriented universities, this disaggregation of classical literary texts into bundles of unrelated statements became even more marked. The individual statements were known in Latin as *sententiae* (opinions), and university scholars collected anthologies of such *sententiae*, completely divorced from their original context and hence often also divorced from their original meaning. Such collections included the famous *Sic et Non* (*Yes and No*) of Peter Abelard and the book that became the standard manual for study of theology, the *Book of Sentences* (or *Book of Opinions*) of the twelfth-century theologian Peter Lombard. Such books were organized according to debatable issues (*quaestiones*), with the excerpts favouring and opposing a specific conclusion arranged under a statement of the question. Logical analysis would then be used to determine which contending opinion was correct and to explain or refute the contrary set of opinions. A philosophical or theological work covering a broad range of issues was a *summa*, such as the famous *Summa theologiae* of St Thomas Aquinas. This was the scholastic method of intellectual discourse. Its great virtue was that it probed each issue in an orderly and rational way, collecting the various possible opinions and making a determination of the opinion deemed correct. The great intellectual vice of this method was that it simplified and distorted the opinions of its authorities by reducing each author's opinion to a single statement, totally divorced from the original context.

This was precisely the weakness to which humanist critics began objecting in the fourteenth century. From Petrarch onward, humanists insisted on reading each opinion in its literary context, abandoning the anthologies and subsequent interpretations and going back to the original source in search of the author's real meaning. To put it another way, classical (and early Christian) authors re-emerged as real human beings, living at a particular moment in history and addressing their remarks to specific issues that might have no connection at all with the issues for which medieval anthologists used the author's words. To a student working from a scholastic anthology, ancient authors were essentially bundles of disaggregated opinions, not real, individual human beings whose writings reflected their own situation and addressed specific current issues rather than general and universal ones. Petrarch and his successors found this whole method – the very foundation of medieval learning – intellectually flawed and even dishonest. Behind their complaints about textual and stylistic inadequacies of scholastic texts is this much deeper objection.

Thus the humanists thought the traditional medieval approach to classical texts to be invalid in principle. Scholastic thinkers applied these excerpted opinions to their own questions, not those of the original authors. In practice this meant that they wrote interpretations or commentaries reshaping the ancient material so that it served their own purpose. Hence humanists rejected all the commentaries that had accumulated about the words of an ancient author like Cicero or Aristotle, and demanded a return to the full original text. The only valid interpretation of a passage in an ancient book was one that took into account the whole work and also, more broadly yet, the historical milieu in which the author wrote. To read merely in order to pluck out information on narrowly defined issues was to miss the point – indeed, it was to distort the point.

Petrarch's conception of history

Medieval civilization had a very weak understanding of the uniqueness of historical events. Renaissance humanists sensed this defect and objected to it. Humanist thought was historically conditioned, and the rise of a new sense of history was the crucial innovation associated with the Renaissance, underlying the 'rediscovery' and reinterpretation of classical texts, the emphasis on 'practical' rather than 'speculative' knowledge, the keen sense of the limitations of human reason, and in general the whole revulsion from medieval tradition that became the most striking trait of Renaissance thinkers. Indeed, although modern scholarship has for some time recognized that a distinctive attitude towards history was a major characteristic of the Renaissance, the full significance of this change has not been sufficiently emphasized. The distinctive Renaissance way of reading classical literature was a direct outgrowth of a new way of think-ing about history, a way that is embedded in the term *Renaissance* itself. Petrarch invented this new way, and his invention explains why, even in his own lifetime, he was regarded as the crucial innovator, responsible for the emergence of a new era in civilization.

In simple terms, Petrarch's invention was the concept of historical dis-continuity. As he looked at conditions in his own troubled century, he concluded that the modern age was worthless. Indeed, he defined the whole period of history since the decline of Rome as a 'dark age'. When Petrarch defined this post-classical or 'modern' age, the age we now call medieval, as a dark age, he meant an age of barbarism, ignorance, low culture. This polemical and obviously inadequate description of the med-ieval millennium is untrue and unjust concerning the Middle Ages, but it is still a true historical fact concerning the Renaissance, for his fellow humanists fully shared his opinion. They also shared his conviction that their own classical scholarship was bringing that darkness to an end, and that high civilization, which had flourished in ancient Greece and Rome, was being reborn in their own time and through their own efforts. In short, they claimed that after the centuries of 'darkness', they were bring-ing about a cultural rebirth: a Renaissance. Since the new age of high culture that they hoped to inaugurate would constitute a third distinct epoch of human history, in effect Petrarch and his disciples had divided history into three parts: first Antiquity, third the new age of high culture that was just beginning, and second, in between the others, a Middle Age, an age that the humanists (unfairly, perhaps, but fervently) regarded as an age of darkness and barbarism. The humanist intellectuals of the Renaissance were the first to define, and even to name, the preceding centuries as a distinct historical period, a Middle Age lying between the high culture of Antiquity and the incipient high culture of reborn Antiquity.

Secular human history for Petrarch, therefore, does not consist of an undifferentiated flow of time and events as it had for even so gifted a medieval thinker as Dante. Instead, it consists of discrete cultures, each of which has distinctive characteristics. Any literary work or other record of a particular age must be viewed in relation to the culture, and even the particular circumstances, from which it arose. This does not mean that past experience is irrelevant to present times, but it does mean that past experience can neither be used nor comprehended until it is seen in historical context. This historical-mindedness, this sensitivity to what texts, historical records, and even single words had meant originally, is the basis for the radically new way in which Renaissance humanists interpreted classical authors, even authors well known to the Middle Ages, such as Aristotle or Cicero or St Augustine. Renaissance thought was in a sense just as tightly bound by authority as medieval scholasticism had been, but it viewed its authorities differently because their statements were no longer viewed as absolute declarations of eternal truth but as statements made by specific individuals under specific circumstances. Both scholastic thought and humanistic thought criticized their authorities, but the scholastics did so through logical analysis of individual statements, while humanists did so by trying to comprehend the unique circumstances in which an author had written. To the humanist, truth seemed particular, conditioned, and subject to many limitations.

Humanism was not a comprehensive system of philosophy as scholastic Aristotelianism had been and continued to be, but it was a distinct method of intellectual procedure. Since scholasticism also was essentially an intellectual method rather than a single set of doctrines or conclusions, a subtle clash of intellectual methods underlies the many overt and accidental causes for the conflicts between humanists and scholastics that marked the intellectual history of the Renaissance.

The humanists' new historical consciousness strongly affected their own self-perception. Although Petrarch was never brazen enough to say this openly, the full implication of his claim that his renewal of classical studies would usher in a new age of high civilization was clear enough. It meant that his own work was literally epoch-making. He was in effect declaring something like this: 'In addition to the ancient age of light, of high civilization, and the modern [we would say medieval] age of darkness and barbarism, there is a third age, a new age of light, and it begins with me!' This sense of standing at a turning-point in human history, and of reviving lost civilization, explains what often seems an exaggerated sense of self-importance, an outlook that Jakob Burckhardt labelled 'individualism' and demonstrated largely with reference to the humanists' thirst for fame. Burckhardt himself saw clearly that mere interest in classical language and literature could not be taken as the defining trait of Renaissance civilization since the whole of medieval civilization lived in the shadow of Antiquity. The Renaissance 'rediscovery' of the classics was not so much a real rediscovery as a habit of viewing the classics in a new historical perspective.

Renaissance humanism, conceived as 'a new philosophy of life' or a glorification of human nature in secular terms, melts away into vagueness as soon as the critical historian tries to define the terms of that philosophy or that glorification. Except in the vaguest sense, there is no definable set of common beliefs held by all or nearly all of those who are acknowledged to be humanists. Likewise the central attribute of Burckhardt's interpretation, a new spirit of individualism, proves to be so nebulous that it threatens to become a universal human tendency that finds expression in all historical periods. Burckhardt made the mistake of putting a secondary characteristic, a heightened sense of individualism, in place of the truly primary characteristic, the new historical consciousness that emerged in the thought of Petrarch. This sense of being engaged in the restoration of true civilization after many centuries of barbarian darkness finds its first clear statement in the works of Petrarch, and some such claim is common to virtually all of those writers (Salutati, Valla, Ficino, Erasmus) whom historians identify as the crucial figures in the history of humanism. The claim is of course wholly unfair to the cultural achievements of the Middle Ages, but it was repeatedly made. It was the defining characteristic of Renaissance humanism, and anyone who wants to understand humanism must take it into account.

Petrarch's classicism

The preceding discussion of the meaning of humanism points repeatedly to the poet Petrarch (Francesco Petrarca, 1304–74) as the real founder of the new culture. Petrarch himself knew and praised the writings of Lovato and Mussato, but he also believed that he alone had been the first to form a clear idea of the necessity and the possibility of bringing back to life the inner spirit of ancient Roman civilization. He joined his intense love of ancient Latin literature to a sweeping repudiation of medieval culture. He transformed classicism into a weapon in his struggle to regenerate the world and to create a distinctive new culture built on the solid foundation of a lost but retrievable Antiquity. His alienation from current tradition and his dream of cultural regeneration stand out clearly in his Latin works.

Petrarch's contribution to the revival of classical scholarship is important because it is rooted in his historical consciousness of a separation between ancient and modern (what we would call medieval) civilization. His Paduan predecessors had acquired new factual knowledge, such as Lovato's discovery of the principles underlying the metrical structure of Seneca's tragedies. But Petrarch's achievements were much greater, displaying a sensitivity to both ancient language and ancient culture that surpasses his predecessors. Several of his own manuscripts survive in modern libraries, and his marginal notes demonstrate remarkable ability to trace references and allusions made by ancient authors. More easily understood, but probably not so truly revealing of his talent, was his success in finding lost works of ancient literature. Cicero, his favourite author, had been widely known throughout the Middle Ages, but some of his major works had fallen out of use. In 1333 at Liège Petrarch found one of Cicero's most famous orations, *Pro Archaia*, especially important because it upholds the social utility of poetry. Even more significant was a discovery made in 1345 at Verona, where he found three collections of Cicero's personal letters. This discovery allowed Petrarch to comprehend the personality of Cicero, whom he had venerated previously as an eloquent orator and a great moral philosopher but had never before glimpsed as a real man driven by human ambitions and fears.

Petrarch is historically important not only for his efforts to rediscover lost works but also for his efforts to resolve some of the inner conflicts that Christian classicists had always faced. One such conflict was that between the urge to flee worldly involvement in order to contemplate God and the urge to seek wealth and fame in worldly life. The monastic tradition in medieval Christianity had exalted the contemplative over the active life, and Petrarch did write a book extolling the monastic life. In general, however, his praise for monasticism emphasized personal withdrawal for study rather than specifically monastic activities. Although Petrarch sought out and charmed many powerful and wealthy patrons to advance his career, he personally was inclined to the life of the isolated scholar. He never practised law, the profession for which he had studied. He never conducted a business. He never participated as an active citizen in the life of Florence or any other political community. Hence his own experience explains why despite his admiration for ancient Rome, he showed little real understanding of the Roman ideal of citizenship, and also why he was shocked when the newly discovered letters of Cicero revealed that the author whom he had admired as a philosopher burned with desire to abandon philosophical studies and to plunge back into the turbulent politics of the dying Roman republic. Nevertheless, Petrarch did perceive enough of the Roman character to praise the ideal of public service expressed in Cicero's famous dream-fantasy, the *Somnium Scipionis*. Despite Petrarch's own dependence on the patronage of the papal curia, he bluntly denounced the worldliness and corruption of the hierarchy and agitated for a return of the popes to Rome and for a serious (if vaguely conceived) reform of the church. He idolized the grandeur of ancient Rome and urged a restoration of Roman power.

Petrarch felt divided within his own soul, torn not only between the active life and the contemplative, but also by the tension between his longing to lead a moral regeneration of Christendom, on the one hand, and his worldly desires for love and fame, on the other hand. In several of his works he reveals his own anguish in a subjective way not typical of medieval authors. In his *Secretum*, an imaginary dialogue between himself and St Augustine, he lays bare his doubts – not doubts about the truth of Christianity but doubts about his own worthiness as a Christian. Despite the imaginary Augustine's warnings of the dangers of worldly ambition, Petrarch cannot repudiate the ancient pagan authors whom he loves, such as Cicero, for they have been the source not only of his eloquent mastery of Latin language but also of his moral insights.

Union of eloquence and virtue

The hermeneutic principle underlying Petrarch's approach to classical texts is his conviction that genuine eloquence and genuine moral wisdom are united in the great Roman authors like Cicero and Vergil. In one of his late works, defending Christian faith against Aristotelian rationalists, he upholds Cicero's superiority over Aristotle as a moral philosopher precisely in terms of Cicero's ability to join moral wisdom with eloquence, thus appealing to the emotional as well as the intellectual nature of human beings, the will as well as the intellect. Aristotle is too narrowly intellectual to stir people to moral action. Petrarch attributed Rome's greatness to the moral grandeur, the 'virtue' or patriotism, of Romans like Cato and Cicero, men who devoted their lives to public service and who always (he claimed) put the welfare of society before personal advantage. He believed that the melancholy condition of Italy in his own time could be remedied only if Italians recaptured the moral qualities, especially devotion to the welfare of the community, that had been the true secret of Roman greatness. The union of moral virtue and eloquent persuasive power was the distinctive excellence of the Rome that he loved. Roman greatness could be restored if young Italians were properly educated in wisdom and eloquence.

Inevitably Petrarch's thought led him to the idea of revolutionizing education. His objection to medieval scholastic learning was that it was too narrowly intellectual to inspire a band of heroes who could lead Italy back to ancient greatness. Scholastic learning seemed to be focused on two main goals: the sophistical analysis of concepts and the study of abstruse scientific questions, both goals that were irrelevant to the need for moral guidance and inspiration. Petrarch himself never became a teacher, but several of his admirers and disciples did. Humanism inevitably implied criticism of the intellectualism and scientism of the scholastics (and of Aristotle, their philosophical model), and it also implied efforts to end the dominance of logic and natural science in education and to replace them with the ethical and rhetorical emphasis that had dominated Roman education.

2   Humanism becomes dominant

Petrarch raised most of the issues of humanistic culture and set many of the directions in which it moved during the two centuries following his lifetime. He also became a famous literary personality in his own time. Nevertheless, he was a deracinated intellectual with no fixed abode and no real sense of belonging to a community. His exquisite lyric poetry and his classical learning did indeed point towards a new direction for Italian culture, but in the short run his constituency was mainly the wealthy, leisured clergymen and the secular princes whose patronage assured his material existence. What saved Petrarch's work from becoming merely a literature of the court was the adoption of his ideals by the prosperous lay intellectuals of the Italian cities, particularly Florence, which in the late fourteenth century and throughout the fifteenth century was by far the most important centre of humanistic culture. Modern scholars have probed the history of this great city, trying to understand why it outstripped all the other cities where humanism was also developing. Perhaps there is no definitive answer to the mystery of Florentine cultural leadership. Florence was by no means the only city with the wealth and the literate population needed to support the new culture. One special advantage of Florence may have been a lack. Unlike Padua, Bologna, Pisa, and several rival cities, Florence did not have a university at all until 1349. Even after that date, the local university never played a dominant role in cultural life. Hence local intellectuals were relatively free from the traditionalism and professionalism of university life. Petrarch's distaste for scholasticism was shared by many of the wealthy and literate laymen who were groping their way towards a new culture that seemed compatible with their own experience of the world.

Despite objections that have been expressed to the idea, there is no denying that the new humanistic culture had a certain affinity for republican political ideals and practices (Baron 1966). As one after another of the cities of northern Italy came under the control of a despot during the thirteenth and fourteenth centuries, Florence became more and more unusual in preserving its republican constitution. Florence was never a democracy in the modern sense, but until the republic was abolished by force in 1532, it was always ruled by boards and commissions of its own citizens. Thus the city was governed by a process of discussion, debate, and accommodation that distinguishes all true republics from the authoritarian and private decision-making procedures of despotism. The privileged, wealthy, and educated oligarchy that dominated the republic was self-consciously republican and looked back to the ancient Roman republic as its model. Petrarch's exaltation of Rome was therefore potentially attractive to the Florentine ruling elite. Petrarch was only nominally a Florentine, but his literary works attracted favourable attention from a number of citizens. In 1350, Petrarch himself passed through Florence (his first visit to his 'native' city) on a pilgrimage to Rome. He met several local literary figures, most notably Giovanni Boccaccio (1313–75). This encounter turned Boccaccio himself from a career of writing vernacular prose tales in the medieval tradition, such as his famous *Decameron,* to a career dominated by classical studies. Boccaccio's greatest service to Renaissance humanism was that he recognized the originality and greatness of Petrarch and became the central figure in a group of avowed disciples at Florence. Through his efforts, Petrarch's ideas first gained a foothold in the city.

Salutati and Florentine cultural hegemony

After Boccaccio's death in 1375, leadership of the Florentine humanists devolved upon two younger men. The first was Luigi Marsili (1342–94), a native Florentine and an Augustinian friar who had studied theology at Paris and was Petrarch's chosen successor in his struggle against the irreligious tendencies of Italian scholasticism. His convent became the meeting-place for a humanistic literary circle. The other successor to leadership was even more important. Coluccio Salutati, chancellor of the republic from 1375 until his death in 1406, was the decisive figure not only in making humanism fashionable but also in establishing the cultural hegemony of Florence throughout Italy. By Petrarch's death in 1374, there were little bands of admirers in many Italian cities, and Florence had no obvious advantage. By Salutati's death, however, Florence was beyond question the centre of the new culture, and humanism was becoming the cultural standard for members of the local ruling class. Part of this change was the result of his scholarly work on classical texts. He was the first to make frequent citation of Cicero's *Familiar Letters,* one Ciceronian treasure that had escaped Petrarch's notice. He also accumulated what was for the time a huge manuscript library of more than 800 volumes, thus providing local humanists with a resource for study that had been lacking. Furthermore, as a professional notary in charge of the diplomatic correspondence of the republic, he developed personal contacts with educated people all over Italy, so that he became the central figure of his generation for the exchange of both information and inspiration derived from classical study. His official documents, which were intended to function as propaganda for the city and which contemporaries found strikingly effective, conformed to traditional diplomatic etiquette but still contained enough classicism to impress a generation that admired the works of Petrarch. Within a few years of taking office in 1375, his letters had made him by far the best-known humanist of his time. Under his influence, humanism became a collective undertaking that attracted classical enthusiasts all over Italy, thus establishing itself as the cultural norm of the educated classes.

Salutati also advanced the standards of humanistic textual and linguistic scholarship. He was active in the work of textual emendation. He was aware, as few predecessors had been, that Latin style had changed even in ancient times. For example, he showed that in late Antiquity the second-person pronoun for direct address, *tu* (thou), had been replaced by the more formal plural form, *vos,* a change that carried over into many modern European languages (*vous* in French, *voi* or *Loro* in Italian, *Sie* in German, *you* in English) and except where diplomatic protocol prevented, he returned to use of the classical *tu.* Unlike Petrarch, he did not hesitate to cite scholastic authors and even to employ their unclassical technical terms when it seemed appropriate; but Salutati shared Petrarch's reservations about the secularism and materialism of contemporary scholastic philosophy.

One of Salutati's greatest contributions to the scholarly side of humanism was his role in reviving the Greek classical heritage. No careful reader of the leading Roman authors could fail to observe the profound impact of Greek learning on Latin literature. Petrarch made some attempt to learn Greek, but with little success. Salutati realized that knowledge of the Greek sources was essential to a deeper understanding of Roman authors. In 1396 he persuaded the Florentine government to offer a handsome salary to Manuel Chrysoloras, the leading Byzantine classical scholar, if he would come and teach in the local university. He then recruited the first group of pupils among his humanist friends. Chrysoloras' teaching between 1396 and 1400 created a critical mass of humanists who could teach the next generation and who also began the study and translation of Greek literature. When Chrysoloras subsequently lectured elsewhere in Italy and at Paris, his teaching aroused no comparable enthusiasm. Only at Florence, where Salutati had carefully fostered the heritage of Petrarch and Boccaccio, were Europeans ready to undertake the assimilation of Greek civilization.

Like Petrarch, Salutati faced the question of whether to prefer the active or the contemplative life, but he was less equivocal than Petrarch had been, largely because his own experience as a public official made him better able to understand the ideal of public service and duty that had inspired Romans like Cicero but had shocked Petrarch when it took the form of ambition for political office. Though as an orthodox Christian he accepted the excellence of the monastic vocation, in general he believed that the natural goals of life lie on earth and are bound up with active participation in the moral and political life of the community. The life of the Christian is full of constant trials and struggle, not of retreat from action, though of course its final goal is the peace and quiet of heaven. His rejection of the Thomistic emphasis on intellectualism and on contemplation as the goal of life in favour of the Franciscan emphasis on human will and the love of God reflected his defence of the active life of the Florentine layman.

Salutati attracted a following of talented younger men. The calibre of these admirers of Salutati, many of whom came from outside Florentine territory, documents the emergence of Florence as the leading centre of humanistic studies. Despite his own personal piety, Salutati, unlike Petrarch, never really hesitated in adopting the ideal of active life for himself. As a married layman with a family to support and also as a professional notary constantly involved in property transactions and government business, he plunged into a life of political engagement. Indeed, his success as the republic's principal civil servant, which made him a central figure in Italian diplomacy, rested on his skill at applying the humanistic art of rhetoric (persuasive speech and writing) to the task of making the hard moral (that is, political) choices required by the politics of the day. His humanistic learning was not just an ornament. It was essential to his success. His keen understanding of issues and his ability to apply his knowledge of both ancient and recent history to the analysis of current problems made him a source of political strength, especially as the republic struggled for survival against the aggressive duke of Milan, Giangaleazzo Visconti, at the turn of the century. During the most intense part of the struggle in 1401–2, Salutati's diplomatic correspondence served as effective propaganda for the Florentine cause, which he redefined as the defence of political liberty against a tyrant. To his own generation, Salutati's achievements demonstrated that a life of humanistic study was intensely practical.

Critics of humanistic studies

By the end of the fourteenth century, study of humanistic subjects was becoming fashionable among the educated elites of Italian cities, not only at

Florence and other republics but also at the courts of despots like the duke of Milan, who employed a former pupil of Salutati to be his chancellor and to produce anti-republican, anti-Florentine propaganda. But this craze for classical studies did not pass unopposed. Some of the objection was religious. All Christian students of pagan literature, even in ancient times, had to face the question whether their studies would undermine their own faith and morals. Salutati insisted that both the eloquence and the moral reflections available in pagan authors had great value for Christians. Despite his personal piety, however, in 1405 he came under attack by a conservative but very learned Dominican friar, Giovanni Dominici. Dominici's *The Night-Owl* was a direct attack on the humanists' use of ancient pagan authors in teaching young students. He denounced the humanists as pagans and charged that they neglected and despised Christian books. He contemptuously rejected all of the standard justifications for use of the classics in education, insisting that Christianity and pagan literature were flatly incompatible. Salutati himself shared some of these reservations. He wrote a moderate, cautious reply but never published it.

Conservative friars were by no means the only critics of the humanist programme. Although more and more Florentine fathers were choosing a humanistic education for their sons, there were old-fashioned businessmen who thought study of Latin grammar and poetry useless for practical men. In addition, many tradition-minded Florentines were shocked by the provocative and irreverent behaviour of some humanists. A Florentine patrician named Cino Rinuccini wrote an *Invective Against Certain Calumniators of Dante, Petrarch, and Boccaccio*. Here he charges that arrogant young humanists, carried away by excessive reverence for the classics, showed contempt for the three great Florentine authors of the fourteenth century. He also charges that their enthusiastic study of Varro, the ancient authority on Roman religion, reflected sympathy for ancient paganism. Perhaps just as serious was his charge of bad citizenship. He accuses these unnamed humanists of despising matrimony and the duty of providing children for the future, of preferring to lead disorderly and dissolute lives, and of deliberately avoiding the burdens of public office which they, as members of prominent families, were expected to bear. They repudiated both family and civic duty and preferred to spend their lives in leisured and unproductive study of pagan authors.

This attack could not have been aimed at Salutati. Despite his lifelong involvement in classical studies, he was a devoted public servant, a married man, father of a family, and deeply devout. He was also a warm admirer of the three great Florentine authors of the preceding century. But the accusations do suggest that some Florentines perceived humanism as a threat to tradition. Rinuccini probably had in mind several of

Salutati's young followers, such as the wealthy patrician Roberto de'Rossi, who never married, avoided public office, and devoted his life to his books and studies, and Niccolò de'Niccoli (1363–1437), perhaps the most obvious case. Later in the century, the humanist Giannozzo Manetti wrote of Niccoli: 'At no time whatever did he give himself over to striving after public offices, . . . or to marriage in order to have children, but he preferred to live a happy life with his books, without much property or honours, unmarried, free of worries about transitory things, in leisure, peace, and tranquillity.' If such individualistic and antisocial views had become typical of humanism, it would found little favour in Florentine society.

Civic life and humanistic learning in Florence

But there were forces within humanism working against such an individualistic and irresponsible alienation from society. The most admired Latin author, Cicero, had plunged into the turmoil of politics and explicitly taught that a truly virtuous man puts service to the community at the top of his list of values. The union of rhetorical eloquence with moral and political concerns that typified Cicero's ideas on education was directly linked to political action. Salutati demonstrated in his own career as chancellor that the humanistic union of eloquence with morality was socially useful. The great majority of those who became humanists had a vested interest in the welfare of their city and could hardly miss the point that humanistic studies seemed the ideal preparation for an active career in public service. Modern research has largely undermined Burckhardt's impression that the typical humanist was an impoverished intellectual without much stake in society. Certainly at Florence, the leading humanists were either born into the wealthy ruling elite or else were talented immigrants (like Salutati) whose services to the city government or to wealthy citizens earned them considerable prestige and prosperity. In the early fifteenth century most Florentine humanists had much to defend in the existing social order.

Some historians, notably the German-born American scholar Hans Baron, have suggested that an acute military and political threat to the republic of Florence had a revolutionary impact on both the political ideology and the cultural life of the city. Between 1385 and his unexpected death in 1402, the duke of Milan, Giangaleazzo Visconti, pursued an expansionist foreign policy that endangered the power and independence of Florence. Most historians, with the advantage of hindsight, think that the danger to Florentine independence was not so great as contemporaries believed. But many citizens seem to have felt that their city was in grave danger. Baron argued that this sense of crisis produced a decisive shift in both the political outlook and the humanistic culture of the city. Faced with the loss of independence, the ruling elite rallied to the defence of their republican constitution and interpreted the political crisis as a struggle between their own 'republican liberty' and the 'tyranny' of the Milanese duke. Inspired by the example and the propaganda tracts of their chancellor Salutati, Florentines embraced an ideal of republican government that had its roots in the political thought of Cicero. Thus at Florence, Baron concluded, humanism underwent an historic transformation from an individualistic and apolitical literary movement into a political ideal that took the Roman republic as its model and taught that citizens should regard an active life and service to the republic as the highest secular goals of life. Baron labelled this ideology 'civic humanism'.

Some of Salutati's political tracts argued that republicanism in the style of ancient Rome was the best form of political life, though in other writings he upheld the traditional medieval opinion that monarchy is the best form of government because it mirrors the governance of the universe by God. He made much of his discovery that Florence, which had been thought to be a foundation by Julius Caesar, had actually been planted as a colony by the republican general Sulla, so that its origins were linked to the republic, not the empire. According to Baron, an important cultural result of this association of the city's independence with republican ideology was that the ruling classes patronized humanists and came to prefer classical education for their sons. Humanistic education glorified ancient Rome. It also cultivated precisely those oratorical skills that seemed useful for citizens of a republic that determined policy by debate and discussion.

Baron viewed Salutati, who demonstrably did much to promote humanistic learning in Florence and throughout Italy, as the initiator of the transformation. Although in his theoretical tracts he accepted the medieval preference for Rome's universal monarchy, the actual world in which he lived was not ancient Rome but a chaotic mix of small and middle-sized states that were *de facto* independent. Many of these states, notably the papacy and the duchy of Milan, pursued policies that endangered the interests of Florence. In justifying his city's cause, he found in the stirring example of republican Rome not only a source for his political propaganda but also an inspiration for his diplomatic efforts in defence of Florentine independence. Baron concluded that the historical achievement of Salutati was his association of the humanist movement with the rediscovery of Rome's republican heritage.

Bruni's republican ideology

The most important consequence of the republican element in Salutati's thought, according to Baron, was that the ablest of his young disciples,

Leonardo Bruni of Arezzo (1370–1444), was converted from scholarly aloofness to an active defence of republican political values. Beginning with two dialogues written at the peak of the Milanese crisis in 1401–2 and culminating in a remarkable *History of the Florentine People* (1415–29), Bruni defended republicanism as the best form of government and cited the example of ancient Rome as proof. His writings presented a radical reinterpretation of history, both ancient and modern. Historians in the Middle Ages virtually without exception accepted the claim of the medieval Holy Roman Empire that the empire of Augustus marked the culmination of ancient history and was providentially created to prepare the world for the incarnation of Christ, and that the medieval German emperors were lawful successors of the ancient Roman Empire. Bruni swept aside this imperial myth by presenting a totally different history. Ancient civilization both at Athens and at Rome was the product of the free discourse and unfettered thought of citizens who ruled themselves under republican constitutions. The growth of authoritarian power under the Roman emperors destroyed political liberty, the republican constitution, and ultimately ancient civilization itself. Imperial tyranny crushed freedom, and freedom is essential to a flourishing civilization. Thus the ancient world had died, creating a permanent break in history.

Bruni further claimed that the emergence of republican self-government in the cities of Tuscany during the twelfth century was the ultimate cause of the revival of learning. Even more clearly than Petrarch, he defined a radical break in historical continuity at the end of the Roman world; thus he reinforced the Renaissance concept of a rebirth of civilization. Bruni's republican ideology repudiated traditional preference for the contemplative life (either monastic or scholarly) over the active life of a citizen. In his laudatory biography of Dante, he praised the poet as the ideal man: father of a family, active citizen, poet, and philosopher. Far from being incompatible with literary greatness, Dante's active secular life was a condition of his greatness. Perhaps with apolitical, purely literary classicists like Niccolò Niccoli in mind, Bruni added: 'And here let me say a word in reproof of the many ignorant folk who suppose that no one is a student except such as hide themselves away in solitude and leisure; whereas I, for my part, never came across one of these muffled recluses from human conversation who knew three letters.'

Baron's concept of 'civic humanism' was challenged from the beginning and continues to evoke scepticism from many scholars. Although his interpretation had widespread support in the 1950s and 1960s (especially in North America), it has lost ground in recent decades (Celenza, pp. 36–38). Baron's emphasis on the specific 'crisis' of 1401–2 as the turning-point in the transformation of humanism from a literary movement to a dominant one has proved the least successful of his conclusions. His broader claim that there was a link between humanistic learning and republican politics, however, has had a more durable influence. According to him, 'civic humanism' provided the wealthy elite that dominated Florentine society with a useful political ideology based not only on a perceived affinity between republican Rome and republican Florence but also on the conviction that active participation in the social, political, and economic life of the city was a moral obligation of the elite groups who had always dominated political life. An influential criticism of Baron suggests that his concept of 'civic' humanism is rooted not in his fifteenth-century sources but 'in the political and intellectual history of the Weimar Republic which Baron as a young German liberal had fervently supported before the German Nazis forced him into exile' (Godman, p. 293). The ideals that Baron discovered in his 'civic humanists' were coloured by his own convictions about the essence of a civilized modern society (Connell in Hankins 2000, p. 16). Baron, however, traced these ideals back to Greek and Roman Antiquity as reflected in the political thought of Aristotle (whose *Politics* Bruni translated into Latin), Cicero, and the major Roman historians. He contended that the humanists, especially Bruni, recaptured the political spirit of the Roman republic for the modern world.

A related debate among historians concerns the question whether Bruni himself had any true commitment to republican ideology. After trying unsuccessfully to become Salutati's successor as chancellor, they observe, this alleged republican left Florence and became a secretary in the papal curia, a hotbed of authoritarian political principles. Yet after the pope whom he served left office, Bruni (who was not a Florentine by birth) chose to settle in Florence (1415) and acquired citizenship there. From that time, he spent much of his literary effort working on his history of the city, and after being appointed chancellor in 1427 he devoted much effort to opposing a new wave of military threats from the dukes of Milan.

A number of critics of 'civic humanism' dismiss the influence of republican political ideology on Florentine culture by pointing to the undemocratic reality of the city's political system. Behind a façade of republican forms, real power was concentrated in the hands of a small group of wealthy families. Yet this objection is not valid. Republicanism is not identical to democracy, and in the modern sense of the term, neither ancient Rome nor medieval and Renaissance Florence was ever a democracy or ever aspired to be. Renaissance Florence, like ancient Rome, was ruled by an aristocracy of wealthy families. The actual extent to which the less wealthy citizens shared power varied from time to time and ever since the founding of the republican constitution in 1293 had been a recurring issue in local politics. Even under the informal principate of the Medici family (1434–94), the city remained formally a republic; and the ease with which the citizens drove out Piero de'Medici in 1494 after he lost popular favour shows that Medicean hegemony had rested on tacit consent by the citizens. Florentines still revered their republican constitution. After the expulsion of the Medici in 1494, those who dominated local politics laboured to devise ways of preserving but reforming their republican polity. Their goal was to maintain the long-established dominance of the wealthy classes while preserving at least the appearance of popular participation and preventing any one person or faction from gaining excessive power. Florentines still regarded themselves as citizens, not subjects. 'Civic humanism' did not threaten the traditional domination of the city by wealthy patrician families. Indeed, the attraction of humanistic education to the dominant classes was their belief that such education was the most practical way to prepare their sons for the role they would be expected to play as leaders in the next generation.

In Florence, the last great exponent of civic humanism was Niccolò Machiavelli. Readers of his most famous work, *The Prince*, should remember that he repeatedly expressed his opinion that if conditions made it feasible, a republican government was preferable to all other forms, even though he also made it clear (in *The Prince* and in his other major political work, *The Discourses*) that the success of a republican constitution depended on historical circumstances and that some societies (including, he came to fear, his own beloved city) were morally unfit to rule themselves. His own political career (1498–1512) during the struggle to reform the republican constitution shows that his sympathies were for a moderately aristocratic republic that provided all propertied citizens some voice in political life.

The writings and personal examples of Salutati and Bruni helped to transform humanistic culture from being little more than the hobby of a few eccentric literary figures inspired by Petrarch into the shared culture of the elite classes of Renaissance Italy. This central contention of Hans Baron has not been effectively overturned. As a major force in the life of the Quattrocento, humanism depended ultimately on the conclusion by hard-headed businessmen, oligarchs, and princes that humanistic studies were useful to those who ruled. Study of Cicero and the Roman historians kept alive an undercurrent of interest in republican government, and some students of early modern political thought have pointed to the Florentine political tradition of Bruni and Machiavelli as well as to their ancient sources, Aristotle and Cicero, as a significant influence on the birth of English republicanism during the civil wars of the 1640s and even on the republicanism and political liberalism associated with the American and French revolutions of the late eighteenth century (Pocock).

Perhaps, as one recent study suggests, the real struggle over the direction of Italian culture in the fifteenth century was not so much between republican and monarchical tendencies but between humanistic studies conceived as a useful preparation for an active life devoted to politics, business, and family and those same studies conceived as preparation for a life devoted to philosophical contemplation and textual scholarship (Godman). Humanism was pulled in two quite different directions: towards preparation of youths for active careers in public life (a 'practical' ideal), and towards pure scholarship, either the contemplative Neoplatonism of Marsilio Ficino and his disciples or the philological, textual scholarship exemplified by Angelo Poliziano.

Humanism at the despotic courts

Although Florentine republicanism waned under Medicean dominance in the later fifteenth century and was finally suppressed (along with the republic itself) in 1532 by Medici dukes backed by Spanish and papal armies, the idea that men educated as humanists were especially suited to political life was not destroyed, for it was not necessarily limited to its original venue, the republic of Florence. Even in Salutati's time, the political skills possessed by men trained in humanistic studies had led to the employment of humanists to glorify princes and produce propaganda for them. For example, Salutati's most important tract of republican theory was an answer to an anti-Florentine pamphlet by Antonio Loschi, a former member of his own literary circle who had become chancellor of Milan. If Florence could be presented as the offspring of republican Rome and the home of political liberty, the Milanese duke could be hailed as a great ruler who, like Augustus, would impose unity and peace on all of Italy. The ideal of civic humanism upheld by Bruni could easily be adapted to justify service to a generous and beneficent prince. Humanists possessed the skills needed to serve as chancellors, ambassadors, and political propagandists in the now-stylish humanistic fashion.

Florentine styles in humanism seem to have spread most rapidly at the smaller courts: the Carrara rulers at Padua, the Este at Ferrara, the Gonzaga at Mantua, all of whom employed humanists for public office and patronized the new culture. The larger Italian courts, such as Naples, Milan, and the papal curia, were rather slower to catch the Florentine style, though all of them harboured humanists from an early date. The papacy in particular found humanists, with their elegant Latin style and their verbal facility, desirable for secretarial positions. Bruni himself spent several years in papal service. Rather surprisingly, Italy's second great republic, Venice, was slow to respond to humanism. One reason for

Venetian aloofness may have been the city's remarkable political stability, which depended on careful preservation of tradition. Another was her policy of abstention from Italian wars and alliances until the early decades of the fifteenth century. In the fifteenth century, however, Venice began seeking mainland provinces and mainland alliances, and thus her leaders gradually were drawn towards the new culture. Even so, not until the city faced direct armed conflict with the papacy in 1509 did the Venetian ruling class embrace something akin to the republican political ideology of Florentine humanism.

By the middle decades of the fifteenth century, humanistic culture had become the norm for the privileged classes of northern Italy; and even in less socially advanced regions like the kingdom of Naples or Rome, humanists strongly influenced the society of the court. The rhetorical and linguistic skills of men educated as humanists could be useful to princes as well as to republics, and for much the same purposes: as secretaries, as public administrators, and as propagandists, also as educators of the children of rulers and their closest advisers. The ability to speak and write a Latin closely modelled on the language of ancient Rome, possession of a fund of ready knowledge about ancient history and literature, and even a little knowledge of Greek became normal expectations of an educated man in Italy. These distinctively Renaissance cultural attainments were joined to the ideal of service to society (often expressed as service to a prince) that constituted a non-republican version of 'civic humanism', though often joined with more traditional courtly skills in horsemanship, military arts, ability to write vernacular verse and also to sing, play a musical instrument, and conduct a lively conversation. Although not published until 1528, *The Book of the Courtier* by Count Baldassare Castiglione reflects the elegant Renaissance court of the duchy of Urbino in the late fifteenth century. It illustrates, as well as any single book can, how humanism became a major element in the culture of Renaissance Italy's 'beautiful people'.

The search for ancient texts

Castiglione gives little sense of one important aspect of Quattrocento humanism, the continuation and virtual completion of earlier humanists' search for lost masterpieces of ancient literature. The manuscript discoveries of Petrarch and Salutati have been discussed above, and the effort continued into the new century. The eccentric Niccolò Niccoli through his correspondence directed an endless search for new literary treasures, and with considerable success. One of his correspondents located in Germany works of the Roman historian Tacitus that were totally unknown in Italy. Poggio Bracciolini had even greater luck while in Germany for the Council of Constance. His finds in northern libraries included several unknown or imperfectly known orations of Cicero, and texts of Silius Italicus, Lucretius, Manilius, Ammianus Marcellinus, Asconius, Valerius Flaccus, Statius, and Petronius – a whole library of classical works. His most striking discovery, however, occurred at St Gallen in Switzerland, where he found the complete text of the *Institutes of Oratory* of Quintilian, a work known previously only from fragmentary manuscripts. Quintilian was second only to Cicero as an authority on classical rhetoric, the foundation of both Roman and humanistic education. The *Institutes* were not just a technical manual on speech-making but set forth a whole programme of education for a citizen qualified for high office by his combination of oratorical skills and moral integrity.

The work of Chrysoloras in planting the study of Greek among Florentine humanists meant that recovery of Greek literature, pagan as well as patristic, became a part of the humanist programme of cultural restoration. When Chrysoloras returned to Constantinople in 1403, one of his Italian pupils, Guarino Guarini of Verona, accompanied him and spent five years perfecting his mastery of the language and literature of ancient Greece. On his return to Italy in 1408, Guarino brought back fifty manuscripts of Greek books not available in Italy. The Sicilian humanist Aurispa collected no fewer than 238 Greek manuscripts, including the previously unknown dramatic works of Aeschylus and Sophocles. In 1427 the humanist Francesco Filelfo returned from seven years as secretary to the Venetian legation in Constantinople, carrying a trove of forty ancient authors. Translating these texts was especially important because although many students in humanistic schools studied some Greek, relatively few could read it with ease. Thus full recovery of the Greek cultural heritage depended on the making of Latin translations. Leonardo Bruni was an active translator, and he also set forth new ideas about standards for literary translations. His teacher Chrysoloras had been critical of the word-for-word method employed by medieval translators, and Bruni's *On Translation* developed this point and defended a less literal method that sought to express ideas in ways natural to the new language.

By the 1430s, the best Italian Hellenists were linguistically prepared to cope with the flood of Greek philosophical ideas and disputes brought west by the Byzantine scholars who attended the Council of Ferrara–Florence (1438–9). The way was prepared for the wave of enthusiasm for Platonism that swept through Florentine intellectual life in the second half of the century. The practice of employing humanists for positions in the papal curia had also made Rome an important centre of humanistic learning despite the varying personal interests and intellectual mediocrity of several popes of this period. The election of Pope Nicholas V (1446–55) was especially important. He not only collected a large library that marks the foundation of the Vatican Library but also brought together a team of scholars to prepare Latin versions of the whole body of Greek learning, both Christian and pagan. The plan could not be fully carried out during his relatively brief pontificate, but it expresses the determination of fifteenth-century humanists to assimilate the full range of Greek literature.

For the modern world, the humanists' frenzied search for ancient texts may be hard to appreciate. But the modern critical editions that make ancient literature, history, and philosophy readily available to modern readers depend on the classical scholarship of the Renaissance. Western civilization would be immensely poorer without the writings of Plato, Aeschylus, Sophocles, Aristophanes, Herodotus, Thucydides, and Polybius among the Greeks, and Livy, Tacitus, Lucretius, and Quintilian among the Latins. Yet all of these authors were either unknown or little known until the manuscript discoveries of the fifteenth century. By the end of the Renaissance period, the modern corpus of both Greek and Latin classics was virtually complete, and the Greek portion available in Latin translation. The new art of printing from the 1450s diffused these discoveries more widely and helped to ensure their survival.

Valla and critical method

If modern historians have difficulty in sharing the excitement that Renaissance humanists felt about the hunt for lost works of classical literature, they should be somewhat more impressed by the humanists' invention of the distinctively modern art of historical criticism. Medieval writers sometimes showed awareness that errors had crept into their classical, patristic, and even biblical texts. In general, however, they were remarkably naive about the accuracy and authenticity of the texts they used. The Middle Ages were a forger's paradise, and both literary texts and legal documents were frequently manufactured to order if they seemed necessary but did not exist. In addition, many texts that were genuinely ancient were attributed to the wrong author. Even Aristotle, the most intensely studied secular author, acquired an annex of pseudo-Aristotelian works, many of which ought to have been (but were not) easily rejected simply on the basis of their incompatibility with opinions expressed in his many genuine works. Among Latin authors, both the letters of the younger Pliny and the *Natural History* of the elder Pliny were known throughout the Middle Ages but were thought to be the work of a single author. The rather simple feat of distinguishing uncle from nephew (the nephew in one letter even describes the dramatic death of his uncle during the eruption of Mount Vesuvius) was not achieved until one of the early humanists pointed out the obvious.

Humanists from Petrarch onward became aware that many classical texts contained omissions, interpolations, and textual errors as a result of simple scribal mistakes that had accumulated through centuries of re-copying. Thus humanists sought not only to find lost works but also to detect and remedy textual errors, either through comparison of multiple manuscripts or through conjecture based on their sense of the author's style or the general context. Yet even at its best, the early humanistic work of criticizing and emending ancient texts was haphazard.

A decisive step towards sounder critical methods was the work of Lorenzo Valla (1407–57), a Roman humanist whose most enduring connections were with the papal curia. He studied at Mantua in the famous school of Vittorino da Feltre, taught rhetoric for a time at the University of Pavia, met the chief Florentine humanists of the 1420s, and spent many years in the service of the king of Naples before finally returning to Rome as a secretary in the papal chancery. Most recent scholars agree that in terms of sheer intellectual power and originality, Valla was the ablest of all the Renaissance humanists. He had a keen intellect and a driving ambition to excel at scholarship. He was one of the few humanists of his generation who had a marked interest in philosophical issues, and in every field that he touched, he tended to take unconventional, even extreme, positions.

But most relevant here is that as a humanist rhetorician and grammarian, Valla hit upon the second of the two truly new ideas in Renaissance thought (the first being Petrarch's discovery of historical discontinuity). This idea, which no ancient or medieval thinker had seen clearly, was that human language, like everything else outside of the material world, is a cultural artifact, so that language undergoes historical development and changes with the passage of time. In terms of his own main field of interest, grammar, this meant that the attempt of all previous humanists to write better Latin lacked a secure foundation because they failed to take linguistic development into account. The effort to write an eclectic 'classical' style, which was typical of earlier humanists, really produced no style at all because modern authors uncritically chose grammatical usage and vocabulary from ancient authors who may have lived six or seven centuries apart. Valla insisted that anyone who wants to write good Latin must define some one period, preferably the late republic and the early empire, and use only the words and grammatical practices found in authors of that period. Here he was tacitly accusing virtually all of his predecessors and contemporaries of stylistic incompetence. To make matters worse, he not only dared to suggest that the revered Cicero was not a sure guide on matters of style and that the recently rediscovered rhetorician Quintilian was superior, but he also was sharp enough to detect stylistic flaws in the writings of respected contemporaries, and rude enough to make his opinions publicly known.

Valla's principle of linguistic change was the foundation of modern linguistics. It found its most popular expression in his *Elegances of the Latin Language* (*c.* 1440). This is a guide to classical style, usage, and grammar, based inductively on close study of the leading authors of the Latin Golden Age. One of the longest and most valuable parts presents a careful, comparative study of the precise meanings of individual Latin words, a sort of fifteenth-century precursor to Fowler's *Modern English Usage,* all the more valuable in an age when, professionally speaking, humanists lived and died professionally by their ability to write superior Latin. When printing came to Italy a decade after his death, the *Elegances* was printed early and often. It became the best guide to a good Latin style; and by 1536, the death of Erasmus, who admired it greatly, fifty-nine editions of this long and costly book had been printed.

The fruitfulness of Valla's critical mentality is well represented by his *Emendationes Livianae,* which demonstrated obvious factual errors in Livy's history and showed that even the greatest historians must be subjected to critical analysis. What this work on Livy demonstrates is that Valla's brilliant insight into philological criticism was part of a broader historical criticism leading to drastic re-evaluation of historical documents. This led him to make attacks on the conventional legal scholarship of his day and to challenge the credibility of many popularly accepted documents, such as the supposed correspondence between the Apostle Paul and the Roman philosopher Seneca.

The most famous exercise of his critical method was a tract he wrote on behalf of his employer King Alfonso of Naples when the king was at war with the pope. His *Declamation on the Forged Donation of Constantine* (*c.* 1440) attacked the authenticity of a document that medieval popes used to justify their claim to possess political (rather than only religious) authority over all of Western Europe. The Donation purports to be a grant of political authority by the first Christian emperor, Constantine, to Pope Sylvester I. It is a blatant forgery made in the eighth century (four centuries after Constantine). But it had been included in the collections of canon law and had been cited by papal apologists during their conflicts with the medieval German emperors. A few critics had cautiously wondered about its authenticity. But Valla did not merely wonder. He subjected the document to intensive critical examination, applying principles of both historical and linguistic criticism, two ways of thinking little prac-

tised in the Middle Ages. First Valla advanced purely theoretical objections. Such a grant would never have been made by a competent emperor
like Constantine, and even if it had been offered, a saintly pope like
Sylvester would have refused it, for he had no worldly ambition. This rhetorical thrust at the political ambitions of the current pope could have
been made by any medieval defender of royal power. Valla's second line of
argument was more innovative, involving a basic principle of historical
criticism. This was the demand for independent corroboration. If
Constantine really did transfer control over the Western provinces, where
are the other evidences of Sylvester's rule? Where are the laws, charters,
and other documents issued in his name, and the lists of officials he
appointed? Where are the coins struck bearing his image? Which contemporary or later chroniclers recorded the events of Sylvester's reign?
Turning to the text itself, he subjected it to close verbal analysis. For
example, 'Constantine' speaks of his new capital of 'Constantinople', but
that name was never used in his time. Again, the 'emperor' speaks of the
optimates as if they were Roman nobles, but any student of Roman history
should know that they were an aristocratic political faction during the
civil wars of the late republic. Most telling of all, however, is Valla's devastating application of philological science: the language used in the document is not the Latin used in genuine documents of the fourth-century
imperial chancery but shows characteristics of a much later phase in the
degeneration of classical Latin. For example, why did the author use
the medieval word *banna* for *flag*, when any Roman would have written
the correct word, *vexillum*? Leaving aside the question why Constantine, a
layman, would presume to grant a bishop authority to ordain priests, why
does the document use the medieval term *clericare* for *ordain*? Valla also
pointed out grossly unclassical grammatical forms. In short, the document must be a forgery. Both historically and linguistically, it contains
gross anachronisms. The Middle Ages had absolutely no sensitivity to
anachronism, as art historians and literary historians have repeatedly
noted, because it was quite innocent of the concept of historical discontinuity and periodization that Petrarch had invented.

Valla's critical attack was devastating, though in fact the papacy did not
quit citing the Donation in defence of its political claims for several centuries. In 1519, the German humanist Ulrich von Hutten brought out the
first printed edition of Valla's treatise as Evangelical propaganda against
the popes, intended to show that their claims to authority were founded
on deliberate lies. But Valla did not conceive his tract as an attack on the
papacy at all, only as an attack on the *political* claims that the current pope
was making against the king of Naples.

While his development of the concept of linguistic change and the invention of philological and historical criticism were his greatest achievements, Valla was also one of the best Hellenists of his generation. He produced Latin translations of Homer's *Iliad,* Herodotus, and Thucydides. His most historically significant application of Greek, however, was his *Annotations on the New Testament.* He had observed serious stylistic defects in the currently used Latin Bible, the Vulgate, and sought to remedy these defects by referring to the Greek original. He insisted that serious New Testament scholarship must refer to the Greek text, and that difficult passages in the Vulgate could be clarified by consulting the Greek. What he eventually produced was a set of notes on specific passages where unclear phrases or apparent errors could be remedied by looking at the Greek. This pioneering effort attracted little attention until 1504, when the greatest of the northern humanists, Erasmus, found a manuscript of Valla's *Annotations* in a monastery near Louvain. He published it the following year, an important step in the development of his own biblical scholarship.

The most fruitful part of Valla's work, his creation of a scholarly method of philological and historical criticism, was little understood by his contemporaries. The sceptical, critical approach to documents that he conceived was too disruptive of tradition, too contrary to mental habits inherited from the Middle Ages, to be widely accepted. Of his philological achievements, only his *Elegances,* a practical guide for humanists who wished to develop a good Latin style, was widely circulated before the sixteenth century.

By the time of Valla's death in 1457, humanistic studies were the height of fashion in Italian courts and cities. The large number of humanists contending for choice appointments such as positions in the chanceries of the papacy and the various cities and courts led to bitter feuds among the humanists, who built their reputations in part by pulling down the reputations of their rivals. Valla himself had played this game skilfully, but his immense originality, so admired by modern historians of humanism, was not so evident to his contemporaries.

The ablest of those who did continue Valla's line of scholarship was Angelo Poliziano (1454–94). He is the earliest Renaissance scholar whose emendations to classical texts still appear in the notes of modern editions. Poliziano published only one major work, the *Miscellanies* (1489), a set of brief critical essays on a varied list of textual issues. This was a pathbreaking book in a number of ways. First and perhaps most important was his new way of using manuscripts. Humanists had always searched for unknown manuscripts, but their use of manuscript sources in editing and annotating the classics was unsystematic and uncritical. When they determined which of several discordant wordings to follow, their procedure was arbitrary and haphazard. In practice, they relied on their own personal sense of good Latin style when they made their textual choices. They were really guessing. Poliziano repudiated conjectures, focusing attention instead on the manuscripts themselves. His guiding principle was that the oldest available manuscript was the most likely to be close to the original wording. Even its errors would be closer to the correct wording than the accumulated guesses and scribal errors of many generations of copyists. He demonstrated a practical way of examining a group of manuscripts and establishing their relationships. Poliziano also realized the need to consult collateral sources, especially inscriptions and laws, and to seek out Greek parallels since many Latin authors had closely followed Greek models. His knowledge not only of Greek language but also of its literature was so thorough that he was able to uncover the correct wording and meaning of many passages in Latin authors that had puzzled all predecessors. With this comparative method, he established another basic procedure of modern classical scholarship.

Great as his achievements were, however, there were also limitations. Poliziano represents brilliantly that aspect of Renaissance humanism that developed into professional classical philology. But he wrote for a tiny elite of scholars, mainly the intellectuals clustered about the household of his patron Lorenzo de'Medici. Like the Florentine Neoplatonist philosophers, who were his friends and associates, he had no interest at all in the republican political ideology of older humanists like Salutati and Bruni. He showed no interest in promoting active participation in government or in glorifying family life or drawing historical parallels between ancient Rome and modern Florence. His interest in Antiquity was remote from everyday life. He made humanism truly scientific, but he also made it (or his kind of it) irrelevant to civic life. The careers of Poliziano and his friend Ermolao Barbaro of Venice, the other outstanding humanist scholar of his generation, mark the peak of Italian humanism. Both men died in 1494. After them, there were still talented humanists in Italy, and in the new century the papal curia at Rome asserted its cultural leadership in humanism as well as in art and music. But the truly creative figures of sixteenth-century humanism were northerners like Erasmus, Budé, Scaliger, and Casaubon; and it was in their work that the scholarly creativity and intellectual challenge to tradition found in the work of Valla and Poliziano lived on.

Education in late medieval Italy

Petrarch's dream of a cultural and moral regeneration of Christian society, based on the union of eloquence and philosophy, had important implications for education. Furthermore, he repeatedly expressed his contempt for the barbarous (that is, post-classical) Latin that was currently used, and for the preoccupation of the universities with subjects like logic and natural science that he considered speculative and useless for the real business of human life. His attacks on traditional education seem directed mostly at the universities.

In Italy, however, the pressure to teach a more classical style of Latin and to give greater attention to study of classical literature was directed not primarily at the universities (as would be true a century later north of the Alps) but at what today would be called the secondary level. Italian universities were essentially federations of professional faculties (mainly law and medicine, with modest provision for theological study). Unlike northern universities, which admitted boys at the age of thirteen or fourteen who still had to complete their study of the liberal arts before they were qualified to enter a professional faculty, they enrolled youths of about eighteen years who had already completed most of their preparatory study and were ready to begin professional study of law or medicine (Grendler 2002, pp. 3–5; cf. Grendler 2004, pp. 3–12). The Latin grammar schools of Italy, which taught boys who had already learned to read but had studied Latin grammar at only a very elementary level, became the target of humanist disciples of Petrarch who wanted to introduce a more classical style of writing and pre-university education.

Petrarch himself had not put forward a detailed programme of educational reform. Between the twelfth and fourteenth centuries, Italy had created a large number of Latin grammar schools, some founded and controlled by city councils but for the most part privately owned by an experienced master who taught boys a usable, practical, but unclassical kind of Latin. Their purpose was to prepare boys for university education in one of the three secular professions: lawyers, physicians, and notaries. Parallel to the grammar schools was an alternative network of *abbaco* (abacus) schools, which taught in the vernacular and provided instruction in commercial arithmetic, geometry, and accounting to boys who planned commercial careers and did not intend to study at a university. Nearly all of these schools, those teaching Latin grammar as well as those teaching *abbaco*, were under the control of laymen, either the governing councils of cities that maintained communal schools, or private schoolmasters. Whatever the institutional form, schools had to cater to parents who paid the cost of schooling and expected the schools to conform to their own aspirations for their sons. Church-controlled schools were not numerous or important by the later medieval centuries (Grendler 1989, pp. 6–7, 10–16). Communal schools became quite common in smaller Italian cities since the leading citizens wanted their sons to receive a useful preparation for secular careers either in the university-based learned professions or in commercial life (for which the *abbaco* schools had been created). In larger cities, which had more diverse educational resources, communal schools were not so important. Advanced Latin grammar was taught to the sons of wealthy families by private tutors and to less affluent boys by self-employed schoolmasters.

By the fourteenth century, this array of schools provided an opportunity for sons of moderately prosperous families to study either *abbaco* or Latin grammar. Some boys spent time in both types of school. The widespread availability of schools made literacy in the vernacular fairly common among urban males. The grammar schools expected boys to come with a very elementary beginning in Latin grammar acquired in elementary schools. The real goal of elementary teaching was to impart vernacular literacy; serious study of Latin began in the grammar schools (Black, p. 41). At this secondary level, the traditional grammar book, the *Ars minor* of the late Roman grammarian Donatus, was deemed too superficial to take students very far. The other principal ancient manual of grammar, the *Institutiones grammaticae* of Priscian, however, was too detailed and too poorly organized to meet the needs of students, though some teachers drew material from it. In the twelfth century, there were several attempts to adapt Priscian to the needs of Italian students, and a text sometimes called the *Donado* but more commonly the *Ianua* (=*Doorway*) came into use, organized in a catechetical (question-and-answer) form. Study of manuscript grammars suggests that medieval and early Renaissance grammarians taught students to write simple Latin with a straightforward style that imitated contemporary Italian rather than classical Latin. Thus boys learned a Latin that followed the word order of the Italian vernacular; in other words, they learned what today would be called medieval Latin. Contemporary France, with its intellectual life centred in the new university at Paris, had considerable influence on Italian schools, reflected in the widespread adoption of the *Doctrinale*, a versified grammar-book composed in 1199 by the French master Alexander of Villedieu. This book, with its doggerel Latin verses and unclassical vocabulary and style, later became an object of ridicule for humanists, who blamed it for the 'barbarous' style of contemporary academic Latin. Nevertheless, the *Doctrinale* had many virtues. It was thorough and well organized, and even its despised doggerel verses were useful because they helped students to memorize the rules of the language. Use of the *Doctrinale* and similar versified grammars, most of them French in origin, became common in Italy during the thirteenth century. Even grammars written mostly in prose often included verse passages as mnemonic aids.

By the second half of the fifteenth century, new humanistic grammars that aimed to teach a classical style of Latin came into use in Italian schools. Yet even these works by critics of the *Doctrinale* followed its definition of the topics to be covered and its order of presentation. Many of them, though not the most famous one, Niccolò Perotti's *Rudimenta grammatices* (1468; first printed in 1473), included excerpts from the *Doctrinale* or other versified grammars as mnemonic aids (Black, pp. 124–36). Alexander's doggerel verses no longer were the primary textbook used in good Italian grammar schools of the later fifteenth century, but teachers referred to the *Doctrinale* because of its thoroughness and its helpful verses. Modern scholars have generally assumed that use of the *Doctrinale* had become rare (though not totally absent) in Italy before 1500 (Grendler 1989, pp. 139, 168, 182); but recent studies have shown that it circulated widely in manuscript in fifteenth-century Italy. It was brought into print early and reprinted often (at least forty-six Italian editions by the end of 1500), and continued to be reprinted in Italy throughout most of the sixteenth century. The last Italian edition appeared in 1588 (Black, pp. 153–57). Use of the *Doctrinale* seems to have died out in German schools and faculties of arts from about 1520, but not in Italy. Use of this 'barbarous' medieval Latin grammar persisted longer in the homeland of Renaissance humanism than in any other country.

The Classics in late medieval schools

One series of changes that did occur in late medieval Italian schools, however, was in the list of texts read by students of grammar. The rise of universities in both northern Europe and Italy seems to have brought to an end the relatively widespread study of ancient Latin authors (mainly poets) that had developed during the twelfth century. Grammar schools in the thirteenth century adopted contemporary reading materials designed to hurry the pupils along and impart just enough mastery of Latin so that the students could do the work expected in the professional faculties of universities. There was little time for ancient poetry. Indeed, not only did the proto-humanistic programme of the great French cathedral schools of the twelfth century go into eclipse, but there was a corresponding change in Italian grammar schools that amounted to 'nothing less than a collapse of the study of the ancient Roman classics' (Black, p. 75). The author of the *Doctrinale*, Alexander of Villedieu, was openly scornful of the literary curriculum that had prevailed in the cathedral schools. A prominent teacher at Bologna boasted that he never imitated Cicero or taught his rhetorical works.

The favoured replacements for Cicero's rhetorical writings and the ancient Latin poets were short, simple books that promoted Christian moral values. Some were late classical works such as the *Consolation of Philosophy* by Boethius or a Latin abridgment of Homer's *Iliad* that stems from the first century AD. Others were recent products, written in the same post-classical style used in the *Doctrinale*. Examples are three Latin word-lists: *Papias* (an anonymous work of the eleventh century), *Derivationes* (written about 1200 by Hugutio of Pisa), and the *Catholicon* (a Latin glossary and grammar written about 1286 by a Genoese Dominican friar). Also widely used were collections of moral maxims in metrical form, like the anonymous and widely used *Physiologus* (probably written in the eleventh or twelfth century) and *Facetus* (really a manual of good manners, written in the thirteenth century by John of Garland). Grammar schools also taught certain works from late Antiquity, such as the *Disticha Catonis*, a collection of moral maxims that had been used in imperial Rome and remained in use into the sixteenth century, and Aesop's *Fables*, a collection of prose tales translated from Greek into Latin (Grendler 1989, pp. 113–14; Black, pp. 198–200). The common characteristic of most of these schoolbooks that replaced classical poetry in the late medieval classroom is that they were not primarily (or not at all) literary works in any sense, but utilitarian manuals written to help students master simple Latin grammar promptly and then get on to the serious business of professional study in a university.

The rise of the so-called Paduan pre-humanists in the later thirteenth century and the work of the first major figure of Renaissance humanism, Petrarch, were early reactions against this thirteenth-century rejection of classicism. Petrarchan influence may help to explain a limited return to study of classical authors in fourteenth-century Italian schools. As in the earlier Middle Ages, the authors read in school were poets, especially Horace, Ovid, and Lucan. The short moral treatises of Cicero (for example, *De senectute* and *De amicitia*), which had been widely read in good twelfth-century schools but dropped from use in the thirteenth century, did not benefit from the early stages of this classical revival. Instead, schoolmasters taught the tragedies of Seneca and poems by Statius and Claudian. They also brought back a late classical text widely used in the early Middle Ages, Boethius's *Consolation*.

Use of classical authors as textbooks in Italian grammar schools continued to grow in the fifteenth century, and so did humanists' complaints about the continued study of post-classical books that departed from the stylistic, lexical, and grammatical standards of Antiquity. For most of the century, however, this movement back to classicism was by no means radical. Most of the traditional Latin curriculum of the later Middle Ages continued in use, including the old *Ianua* for the most elementary level of grammar, and some minor Latin authors (*Disticha Catonis*, Aesop, and especially Boethius) and Christian Latin poets like Prudentius. Though much criticized by humanists, versified medieval grammar-books, including the *Doctrinale*, remained in use.

The two most famous new humanistic grammars, *Regulae grammaticales* (*c.* 1418) of Guarino da Verona and the *Rudimenta* of Niccolò Perotti, mark a clear shift towards cultivation of a more nearly classical style, and Guarino's manual was deliberately written to be shorter than the medieval grammars. Both authors avoided the scholastic terminology found in the medieval grammars. In practice, Guarino still relied on the *Doctrinale* to supplement his brief textbook, and he included some mnemonic verses borrowed from older grammars. Perotti, who wrote a half-century later, eschewed mnemonic verses entirely; but his adoption of the question-and-answer format found in the ancient *Ars minor* of Donatus and the medieval *Ianua* may have been intended to provide an alternative form of mnemonic aid.

An educational revolution?

Some historians of Italian education regard these new humanistic grammars as evidence of a drastic educational revolution, marked by a decisive shift from medieval to humanistic Latin even though some medieval elements survived (Grendler 1989, pp. 167–69, 172–74). Others place more emphasis on continuity with medieval education, describing a combination of innovative approaches with important survivals of medieval practices (Black, pp. 124–35, 153–57). Despite its unclassical elements, the *Doctrinale* offered practical solutions to the task of teaching a style of Latin that may not have been classical but was usable for the ordinary business of the time. Medieval grammarians faced and largely solved the problem of teaching the language to students who, unlike ancient Roman schoolboys, were not native speakers of Latin; and their Renaissance successors borrowed from them because they faced exactly the same problem.

In Renaissance Italy as in the three preceding centuries, schoolmasters began by teaching their pupils what was known as 'natural order' but would now be called simply 'medieval Latin'. This was a plain, unadorned style that followed the word order of the Italian vernacular: subject first, verb next, object at the end. In the early stages of study, there were no pretensions of stylistic elegance and no conscious rhetorical element. Basic grammatical correctness (verb forms, case endings, and the like) was the overriding concern. In ancient times, study of rhetoric had followed grammar; and several of the medieval grammars included some elements of rhetoric at the end of the course, usually based on the pseudo-Ciceronian (but genuinely classical) treatise *Rhetorica ad Herennium*. As was the case with grammar, late medieval Italian schools began by following French models of rhetoric, notably the *Poetria nova* by Geoffrey of Vinsauf (written about 1208–13). Despite its versified form and its title, *Poetria nova* was used not to teach prosody (the techniques of versification) but to teach Latin prose composition. Geoffrey's book concentrated on matters of style, distinguishing between the 'natural style' and various types of what the author called 'artificial style', that is, styles intended to create a desired rhetorical effect. The type of artificial style most commonly taught was that used in letters and documents composed by the notaries who drafted letters and public documents for both individuals and institutions.

This way of writing Latin was known as *dictamen* or *ars dictaminis*. Notaries learned it either through apprenticeship or by attending classes affiliated with a university faculty of law. It was still the type of rhetoric taught to advanced grammar-school students in the fourteenth and early fifteenth centuries. Even humanists used it when they composed the kind of documents for which this elaborate, formal (and unclassical) style seemed appropriate. For example, Salutati, the first of the great humanistic chancellors of Florence, who had been educated as a notary and engaged in private notarial practice, composed documents in *dictamen* style for his clients. When he secured the influential job of chancellor of the republic of Florence (1374), he continued to write his public documents in the notarial style even though he had become an admirer of Petrarch and in his personal correspondence and scholarly writings adopted a style modelled as closely as possible on the rhetorical practices of classical prose authors, especially Cicero.

The growing devotion of humanists to classical style gradually produced a change in the rhetorical instruction that came at the end of grammar-school education. Perotti's *Rudimenta*, written in 1468, denounced several practices common in *dictamen* style, including some recommended by Geoffrey of Vinsauf. Perotti rejected these practices as 'barbarous'. He cited passages from Cicero's letters (one of the major rediscoveries of humanistic textual scholarship) as examples of preferable style. This new direction in stylistic education was developed at length in the *Isagogicus libellus* (also called *Elegantiolae*) of the Sienese humanist Agostino Dati (1420–78), which was first published in 1470, reprinted more than a hundred times by the end of the incunable period in 1500, and repeatedly reissued in the sixteenth century. Though Dati followed Geoffrey's aim of teaching stylistic elegance, the preferred style was no longer *dictamen*, which now seemed hopelessly 'barbaric', but the practices of Roman classical authors, especially Cicero, who was increasingly accepted as the best (for some, the only) model for Latin prose. Like Geoffrey and other teachers of *dictamen*, Dati assumed that users of his book would already have acquired the ability to write grammatically correct Latin in the natural or plain style – in other words, conventional medieval Latin. Also like Geoffrey, Dati intended to upgrade this plain style to a more elegant kind of written Latin; but his goal was not *dictamen* but a humanistic or classicized style attained by reading Cicero's works and by careful imitation of his usage. This shift in the rhetorical goal and stylistic model of Latin composition represents one of the two major elements in the transformation of instruction in Latin from medieval to Renaissance standards, a change that matured in the second half of the fifteenth century.

The other major element was a further increase in the study of classical Latin literature. Accompanying this change were frequent attacks on the traditional textbooks such as the *Doctrinale* (although, as shown above, the *Doctrinale* long survived as a handy mnemonic aid). The usual lexical reference works such as the *Catholicon* and short moral tracts like *Physiologus* also remained in use. The revived study of classical authors by fourteenth-century teachers initially restored classroom use of ancient poets like Horace and Ovid who had been commonly studied before the anticlassical turn of the thirteenth century. Italian masters of grammar also introduced some classical texts that had been neglected during the earlier Middle Ages, such as the tragedies of Seneca, the historical work of Valerius Maximus, and the *Achilleis* of Statius – in general, more poetry than prose. Late classical and early Christian authors (Boethius, Aesop, Prudentius, Prosper of Aquitaine) received increased attention in class. The made-to-order reading materials associated with the anticlassical phase got less attention but did not disappear overnight. The principal absentees in this revival of classical authors were, oddly, the two greatest Roman writers. The poems of Vergil were not frequently studied, and Rome's greatest prose author, Cicero, did not immediately regain the classroom presence that his short moral tracts had held before 1200.

In the fifteenth century, though medieval grammatical, lexical, and moral books by no means disappeared from the classroom, some major Roman poets were restored to use: Horace and Ovid, the satirists Persius and Juvenal, and the plays of Terence. An important innovation was the rise of the greatest Latin poet, Vergil, not only the *Aeneid* but also the *Eclogues* and *Georgics*. For the first time since Antiquity, Vergil became the most widely studied Roman poet, a status that he has retained ever since. The historian Sallust gained entry to many schools. Most striking of all, however, was the rise of Cicero. His moral treatises (*De amicitia*, *De senectute*, *De officiis*), which had dropped out of school use in the thirteenth century, came back into favour; and surviving manuscripts show by their plentiful marginal notations that these works were studied closely. There is some evidence of classroom use of his orations, but in general the Ciceronian texts restored to use were the ones that had been widely studied before 1200.

The late fifteenth century experienced a significant further change in preferences for classroom usage. A number of major humanists (Lorenzo Valla in particular) criticized the Latin style of Boethius as a fount of undesirable linguistic practices; and after mid-fifteenth century, his *Consolation of Philosophy*, which had been a favourite of fourteenth-century teachers, seems to have dropped out of use rapidly, at a time when in northern Europe, printers were still producing many editions for use in schools. The late fifteenth century also experienced a decline in the formal study of the lesser Latin authors, both ancient and medieval, who had traditionally been read at school (Black, pp. 270–71). By 1500, the authority of Cicero ruled over matters of Latin style, to such an extent that some of the ablest humanist authors, notably Poliziano in fifteenth-century Florence and Erasmus in sixteenth-century northern Europe, protested against a narrow, intolerant Ciceronianism that rejected all words, forms, and usages not found in Cicero even if they appeared in other ancient authors. In theory, the eclectic Latin style defended (and written) by great neo-Latin authors like Poliziano and Erasmus may seem to have been a wiser preference. Yet the authority of Cicero as not only the best but almost the only guide to superior Latin prose style prevailed. Writing good eclectic Latin like Erasmus required a remarkable linguistic sensitivity and an incomparable mastery of ancient Latin and Greek literature. A handful of great scholars could achieve such a style, but ordinary schoolmasters could not define it clearly and teach it systematically to schoolboys. Ciceronian style may have been restrictive and may have contributed to the decline of Latin as a living language in post-Renaissance times. But Ciceronian style was teachable, and well before the end of the sixteenth century, it had established a mastery that still rules the modern Latin classroom.

As they agitated for the adoption of a more classical Latin and for the abandonment of the medieval handbooks, humanists justified their preference for classical authors by claiming that the best Latin authors (except for some sexually titillating or philosophically materialist passages, mainly in the poets) were valuable for the moral indoctrination as well as the stylistic development of their pupils. Especially during and after the late fifteenth century, the most successful humanist schoolmasters presented themselves as teachers of a literature that shaped moral character as well as Latin style. Like much in the humanist educational programme, the claim to teach morality as well as Latin grammar was not entirely an innovation. Ever since late Roman times, grammar-school education involved study of texts that dealt with moral issues, beginning at a very simple level with the *Disticha Catonis*. The short treatises of Cicero that were widely used in twelfth-century schools, had been dropped from use in the thirteenth century, and then restored to use in the fifteenth century dealt with moral questions; and the medieval textbooks that replaced most classical texts (including Cicero) in the thirteenth century included many titles that dealt with moral issues.

Yet the humanists' claim of a link between humanistic education and indoctrination in moral philosophy has been challenged. Even though some books on moral topics were taught, study of commentaries that were used in teaching suggests that moral issues were mentioned only cursorily and that classwork concentrated on the tedious process of memorizing the meaning and etymologies of words and on questions of style. Teachers gave little attention to the general ideas of Cicero or any other author studied. What really counted was mastering the mechanics of the language and developing a proper 'classical' style. Interest in the ideas contained in the texts was superficial. Ordinarily, the teacher provided no more than a smattering of general information about the author. Command of grammatically correct Latin and development of an eloquent style modelled on Cicero, not formation of character, were the true goals of Italian grammar schools. Humanist careers depended on superior Latin style, not on superior moral character (Grafton and Jardine, pp. 20–22). A recent study based on analysis of the commentaries and notes that reflect day-to-day activity in the classrooms of fifteenth-century Italian schoolmasters concludes that these glosses and commentaries concentrate on philological questions, not moral ones (Black, pp. 27–29, 275–88). Renaissance Italian schoolboys were indeed exposed to books that discussed moral issues, but the focus of their study was on the grammar and Ciceronian style of these books, not on their moral doctrines. The beneficial moral effects of the readings were taken for granted and were often lauded by educational theorists, but they received little attention in class. The moral benefit was simply assumed; hence teachers did not feel obliged to go deeply into moral questions.

A significant difference of opinion has arisen concerning the extent and timing of the changes that humanism brought into Italian secondary education. Robert Black, on the basis of his analysis of a great number of manuscripts that were used in the schoolroom, contends that the truly revolutionary change in Italian schools occurred early, in the twelfth and thirteenth centuries, when the emergence of universities imposed new demands on grammar schools (both Italian and northern). The study of

Latin grammar then was divided into two quite distinct levels: a very elementary introduction of young boys to Latin grammar, employing only
Latin readings but in practice intended mainly to confer vernacular literacy; and a more advanced secondary or grammar-school level that prepared a limited number of boys for university study and other careers that
required effective command of Latin. Although Black concedes that there
was also an important change favouring Ciceronian style in the later
fifteenth century, he finds the medieval period the most innovative phase
in Italian education. Even the most famous humanistic grammarians of
the fifteenth century, Guarino da Verona (1418) and Niccolò Perotti
(1468), followed the broad structure and definition of topics covered by
the remarkably innovative medieval grammar-books they affected to
despise. Black concedes that the humanists did change the teaching of
Latin grammar (and also of rhetoric), but he contends that the changes
developed more slowly than the humanists wished and were less innovative than they claimed. He does not deny that by about 1500, humanists
had decisively transformed the type of Latin being taught from medieval
and scholastic to classical and rhetorical. They also restored the study of
the major Roman authors, especially Vergil and Cicero.

By contrast, Paul Grendler (1989, pp. 140–41), studying mainly the
educational treatises of humanist educators and the structure of schools,
regards the educational changes of the fifteenth century as a genuine educational revolution. He describes this revolution as a transformation of
Italian grammar schools from centres for the teaching of traditional Latin
style (either scholastic or notarial) into centres for the establishment of
the new humanistic culture that had been inspired by early humanists like
Petrarch and brought to maturity by the humanist schoolmasters of
the fifteenth century. This new direction in education made humanism
the approved culture of the social classes that shaped the life of Italy in the
fourteenth and fifteenth centuries; and it also, when transplanted into the
rest of Europe, reshaped all European education into a classical mould
that remained dominant until at least the late nineteenth century.
Grendler does not deny that a highly developed network of schools (communal and private) had developed in Italy before the new humanist
culture became influential, nor does he deny that many medieval elements persisted in Renaissance schools. Likewise, Black does not deny
that significant changes took place in the goals and content of secondary
education during the fifteenth century, though he suggests that those
changes had not gone very far until sometime after 1450. The two historians disagree on which set of changes was the more significant.

Research by other scholars may cast light on this discussion. There is
plenty of evidence that as early as the late fourteenth century, ambitious

fathers belonging to the elite classes that ruled the cities of northern and central Italy were seeking humanistic education for their sons. This pressure for a new direction in schooling was founded on the conviction that an education based on study of the Latin classics would be more useful to patrician youths than study of the textbooks that had come to dominate the school curriculum during the thirteenth century. In Italy the pre-professional education of boys took place mainly in the grammar schools, which were either controlled by civic authorities or, if they were owned by a self-employed schoolmaster, had to cater to the wishes of the parents who paid the teacher's fee. Changes in the curriculum to accommodate the parents' desire for a more classical education were introduced gradually and without much conflict, since schoolmasters were governed by the market for their services. Italian grammar schools were institutionally simple, consisting merely of an established schoolmaster and whatever assistants he chose to employ at his own expense. A headmaster could not afford to be too far ahead of fashion, but neither could he afford to give the impression that he offered an old-fashioned curriculum.

The education of boys in the arts of grammar and rhetoric was very different in northern Europe, for most of it took place in the liberal-arts faculties of universities, which boys entered as young teenagers. Unlike grammar schools (and also unlike Italian universities, most of which were closely controlled by the local municipality), northern universities were autonomous institutions. Their faculties were much more independent and were in a position to resist some of the pressures exerted by humanists for the introduction of new goals, practices, and courses of instruction. Hence the transformation of grammatical and rhetorical study north of the Alps, especially in Germany, where most governments were weak and universities were nearly self-governing, faced greater institutional resistance and at times led to sharp and noisy (though for the most part, purely local) conflicts when humanists began pushing hard for educational reform in the years just after 1500.

Women and the new learning

Renaissance society continued the misogynistic tradition of the Middle Ages, assigning a subordinate role to women, who both by custom and by law were assumed to be always subject to control by some man – a father, a husband, or (for some widows) their own adult sons. Unlike men, who were identified by occupation and social and political rank, women were identified by their relationship to a male authority-figure, as somebody's daughter, wife, mother, or widow. Until the Reformation, the church offered an alternative to marriage: a celibate state as a member of a

monastic community. But female convents, just like prospective hus-
bands, expected a woman to provide a dowry, so that the monastic option
was generally available only to women of the propertied classes. A nun
vowed to obey her monastic superiors; and ultimately even the highest-
ranking authority of a female monastery was subject to the male clergy.

These social limitations meant that in general a woman was expected to
have little or no formal education. Child-rearing, housekeeping, and
religious devotion were regarded as the only necessary and permissible
activities for women, though by the thirteenth and fourteenth centuries, a
significant minority of aristocratic and urban middle-class women
received some education, usually limited to vernacular reading and
perhaps elementary arithmetic. Except for a handful of highly privileged
women, this education did not progress much beyond bare literacy. Girls
from urban centres and aristocratic households might attend schools,
usually segregated by sex and often taught by female teachers who themselves had only a rudimentary education. Reading was a useful attain-
ment for a young woman of the middle and upper ranks, and so these
schools taught pupils to read the vernacular – with emphasis on books of
devotion, lives of the saints, and (in the better Italian schools) vernacular
works by respectable authors like Dante and Petrarch. Even so, the most
important subjects were the traditional female skills of spinning and
needlework. Of course religion, defined in terms of simple devotion but
not complex theology, was omnipresent, since respectable women were
expected to be devout and – until marriage – virginal. Some elementary
schools in Italy included girls as well as boys, but once a few years of elementary schooling were finished, formal education ended for the girls.
Only boys would go on to more advanced schools where they would begin
the study of Latin grammar or else (in the Italian *abbaco* schools) the
study of commercial arithmetic and book-keeping in preparation for mercantile careers. Girls, who had only the two options of monastic life or
marriage and motherhood, had no need for the skills developed in
grammar schools. The dominance of Latin as the language of higher education and all serious intellectual discourse meant that with rare exceptions, language skills as well as social pressures barred women from
participation in intellectual life.

These educational practices excluded nearly all women, even ones
from privileged families, from direct access to humanistic culture, for
which effective command of Latin was essential. By the sixteenth century,
as the new technology of printing stimulated production of vernacular
translations of Greek and Latin classical authors, intelligent and intellectually curious women might gain familiarity with bits and pieces of the
classical heritage and the works of some modern humanists by reading

translations. Since even the most privileged women, once they married, were occupied with domestic management and child-rearing and in their younger years with frequent pregnancies, even those who were able to read had limited opportunity to pursue anything that might be called study. Only in their youth before marriage, or else after their children were grown and their spouses dead, could the handful of exceptionally privileged women who learned Latin pursue an intellectual life as humanists or (more commonly) as authors of vernacular books. Nearly all of the few women who became humanists or vernacular authors abandoned their attempts at intellectual life when they married. The rare exceptions were those who were widowed early in life and were independently wealthy, or somehow (usually because they had access to family wealth) managed to remain single without subjecting themselves to the surrender of autonomy associated with monastic life.

After centuries of neglect, the study of educated women of the late Middle Ages and the Renaissance has flourished in recent decades. One unavoidable conclusion is that female humanists were few. Furthermore, even those few women who did acquire the linguistic skills and literary knowledge associated with humanism found themselves forbidden by social custom and traditional clerical and academic misogyny to associate freely with the leading figures (all male) of classical scholarship. Unlike male humanists, learned women found no professional employment in which they could apply their learning. Women were excluded from all universities and so could not qualify for careers in law or medicine. They were (with the exception of the few whom hereditary succession transformed into sovereign rulers, such as Elizabeth I of England) excluded from any formal share in political life and so could not become governmental secretaries or clerks as ambitious and successful male humanists could. A handful of the few who became skilled in Latin were able to find employment teaching the most elementary level of Latin grammar. No matter how learned or socially well connected she might be, a woman could never become a teacher in the Latin grammar schools where classical study in Renaissance Italy was centred. No woman was eligible to become a member of any university faculty.

The exclusion of talented women from the humanist community could be humiliating. A classic case is the experience of two daughters of a noble family of Verona whose widowed mother employed a male tutor who had been educated at Ferrara in the famous court school founded by Guarino da Verona. Both sisters gained fame in their home town for their erudition, and both received encouraging letters from humanists living nearby. When the elder daughter, Ginevra Nogarola, married at age twenty, however, like nearly all married female humanists she permanently abandoned her studies. Her younger sister, Isotta Nogarola (1418–99), was more persistent. She continued her studies throughout a long life. But she never married, and at age twenty-three, she abruptly withdrew from society and thereafter lived as a pious recluse, pledging herself to virginity and changing the focus of her studies and her writing from classical to religious studies. With the guidance of a friendly Venetian nobleman, she pursued a programme of private philosophical study modelled on university education. This eccentric turn was acceptable in her society, but only because she lived a reclusive and devout life.

Isotta's adoption of this reclusive life was a natural reaction to her youthful attempts to participate, if only by correspondence, in the contemporary scholarly world. At age eighteen, she tried to correspond with prominent political figures, ecclesiastics, and humanists who lived beyond the limited region where she and her sister were known. Some of the addressees did not reply at all. Some of those who did reply praised her extravagantly, but others made light of her learning and let her know that no woman could be regarded as a fellow-scholar. One anonymous letter (with no apparent evidence except her intellectual interests) accused her of sexual promiscuity and even incest. Most humiliating of all was the response of the famous Guarino Guarini, a native of her own city and the teacher of her own tutor. To her initial letter, he sent no reply at all. When she wrote again to protest his silence, Guarino's reply chided her for her abject appeal for recognition and warned her that if she continued to act like a woman, she would never gain recognition by the world of scholars. Even Isotta herself assumed that women are inherently inferior to men. In one of her works written on the question whether Adam or Eve bore the greater burden of guilt for original sin, she maintained that Eve's guilt was less because female nature was inherently inferior. Eve could not be the greater sinner, for as a woman she had been made imperfect; Adam, as a man, had been made perfect, and therefore his sin was more culpable.

Another example of how learned women were belittled even while being praised is the experience of Cassandra Fedele (1465–1558). The daughter of a prosperous family that for generations had provided civil servants to the republic of Venice, Fedele was educated by her father, who employed a humanistic monk to teach her Latin and Greek and who freed her from having to master the domestic skills that usually dominated the education of Venetian girls. Her father seems to have wanted to enhance his own reputation by presenting his bright daughter as a prodigy. His effort was successful. While still an adolescent, Cassandra was allowed to present public lectures at the University of Padua (though not, of course, as a member of any faculty), to the people of Venice, and even in the presence of the city's chief executive, the doge. In 1487, at age twenty-two, she published a little book containing four of her Latin letters and one oration. She corresponded with noted scholars, including the prominent Florentine humanist Angelo Poliziano and the Florentine chancellor Bartolomeo Scala and his daughter Alessandra, another rare female humanist of the time. She even received an invitation from Queen Isabella of Spain to join the royal court. Regarding her as a local treasure, the Venetian Senate forbade her to leave the city. The surviving works of Fedele, however, though they demonstrate her competence in Latin and her familiarity with the classics, also reveal that her literary and intellectual attainments were unoriginal and limited. What made her a celebrity was her precocity and her ability to deal with matters ordinarily deemed to be beyond the intellectual ability of any woman. She was an oddity, not a truly important scholar. As she lived into her twenties and thirties, she came to seem less remarkable. In 1498, at age thirty-three, still beautiful but no longer a prodigy in any sense, she married a physician. Normally, as in the case of Ginevra Nogarola, marriage would have ended her scholarly career forever. But she bore no children, and her husband's death in 1520 left her free to resume her studies but also poverty-stricken because of her husband's poor financial management. Her youthful celebrity was long past, and her petitions to the Venetian government and to the pope for financial assistance brought no help. Her own kinfolk provided grudging and limited support. When she was aged eighty-two, after years of neglect, her petition for assistance caught the sympathy of Pope Paul III, who persuaded the Venetian Senate to make her prioress of a local orphanage. She lived out the remaining eleven years of her life in that modest role, though she had one final experience reminiscent of her youthful fame. In 1556 the republic chose her – now remarkable for her great age – to deliver a Latin oration welcoming the visiting queen of Poland to the city.

Modern scholars have identified a small number of other learned women who gained some contemporary reputation. None of them, however, made major contributions to classical scholarship. Almost without exception, they were the privileged daughters either of wealthy and influential families or of prosperous and highly educated middle-class fathers who indulged a beloved girl by letting her receive a serious education. Learning Latin, of course, was the decisive step. Most contemporaries regarded learned women as oddities, even as potentially dangerous anomalies whose activities and ambitions threatened the divinely ordained order of nature.

Highly intelligent women who did not claim to be learned humanists but who read widely, at least in the vernacular, had greater success as authors of vernacular books, an activity that still might arouse the hostility of social conservatives but at least did not pose a challenge to the male monopoly on serious scholarship. A number of women became well-regarded vernacular poets and writers of prose fiction. Most of these, too, came from privileged families that provided them with a substantial education. Not all of them were aristocrats. The French author Louise Labé (*c.* 1520–66) was the daughter of a Lyonese tradesman (but a prosperous one). She received an unusually thorough classical education, and her verse elegies show familiarity with the works of Catullus and Ovid. She published not only love sonnets but also a mythical dialogue on the blindness of love that reflects familiarity with the genre of Italian Renaissance *facetiae.* Her poems show ironic awareness of the dominance of masculine values in literary treatments of love, and the introduction she wrote for her *Œuvres* (1555) was something of a feminist manifesto. Most of these successful female authors, however, came from much higher up in the social scale. A famous example is the pious and reform-minded poet Vittoria Colonna (*c.* 1492–1547), who achieved considerable personal influence. Like most female intellectuals, Colonna, born into a powerful family of the Roman aristocracy, had no children and became a wealthy widow at an early age. Thus she was free to pursue religious meditation and write vernacular poetry that was published (without her consent) during her lifetime and reprinted frequently. An even higher-ranking figure was Marguerite of Angoulême (1492–1549), who was the sister of King Francis I of France and by her second marriage became queen of the small border kingdom of Navarre. But although she was an active patron of French (male) humanists and religious reformers and a vernacular author of considerable ability, she was not sufficiently versed in ancient languages to become a humanist rather than a patron of humanists. Her writings included vernacular poems, prose tales, and tracts of religious meditation. More closely linked to French humanism was Marie de Gournay (1565–1645), who became a protégée of Michel de Montaigne and later an editor of his works and a promoter of his literary reputation. Gournay, the daughter of a noble but impoverished family, became learned in Latin language and literature and was so devoted to study that she successfully resisted family pressure to provide for her own security by marrying. Her literary prominence resulted from her discovery of Montaigne's *Essays* in 1588 and her success in making the elderly author her own literary patron. Although she genuinely revered Montaigne's learning and literary achievement, she also knew and to some degree resented that her own prominence was dependent on his endorsement and his willingness to make her a sort of adoptive daughter and informal literary executor. Like recognition as a genuine humanist, true literary prominence remained a predominantly masculine preserve.

3   Humanism and Italian society

By the closing decades of the Quattrocento (the fifteenth century), humanism dominated the culture of the ruling groups in all important Italian cities, from Rome north to the Alps. Although Florence deservedly has received the most attention and provides the best evidence of a link between the new culture and an ethic of political action and public service, humanism fitted almost as neatly into the need of the many princely courts for a distinctive lay culture and for a cadre of classically educated administrators and advisers to the ruler. Even the papal curia at Rome found the linguistic and scholarly skills of humanists useful in the chancery, the department that drafted papal letters and many other official documents. Although the sympathy of Pope Nicholas V for humanism, expressed in his library and his programme of sponsoring translations from the Greek, quickened this process, humanists played an important role in curial administration even under Paul II (1471–84), who began his pontificate by dismissing many curial humanists and even arrested several of them in 1468 on trumped-up charges of impiety that probably masked his fear of political conspiracies. By 1500, Rome was on its way to outstripping Florence as the most brilliant centre of humanistic culture, just as it was also taking leadership in the patronage of art.

Printing and the new culture

The rise of curial and courtly humanism and the growing dominance of humanist schoolmasters in the Latin grammar schools of the peninsula did much to establish humanism as the major force in Italian culture. Another source of humanism's growing dominance was the new art of printing. Printing developed during the 1450s in a Germany that was still virtually untouched by the new culture, but Italy was the first foreign country reached by the new art. By 1465 two German printers, Conrad Sweynheym and Arnold Pannartz, had set up shop at Subiaco near Rome, and in 1467 they moved on to Rome. Their first products reflected the Renaissance: a Latin grammar, a work of Cicero, and a book by the

Latin patristic author Lactantius. The real future of printing in Italy, however, lay not in clerical Rome but in Venice, the bustling international trade centre, which by the end of the century was beginning to dominate the Italian book market. The first Venetian printer opened his shop in 1469. Even in humanistic Italy, classical and humanistic books were by no means the only, or even the largest, part of the market. Little, cheap devotional tracts in Italian, such as meditations and lives of the saints, were probably a bigger item. Printing did not immediately change the contents of book production, though it vastly increased the quantity. With a turn of the press, books, formerly rare and costly hand-produced objects, became plentiful and much cheaper.

By 1500, many classical texts had been printed in Italy, nearly all of them (even Greek authors) in Latin. Copying by hand inevitably introduced unintentional errors into every single copy made; and humanists since Petrarch and Salutati had been aware that all manuscripts of their beloved classics had gradually been corrupted. When humanists were bound to the old manuscript technology, as soon as an editor had made his corrections, the process of textual corruption started all over again with the making of new copies. From the late 1460s, the printing of classical works caused an important change in the textual reality. Even if the text used for printer's copy was far from perfect, printing produced a standardized frame of reference, the hundreds of identical copies having exactly the same words on exactly the same lines and pages. Thus printing stabilized the text of a classical work (or any book); and all future emendations by editors could be made with reference to the standard printed text. The advent of printing made textual improvements by humanist editors permanent and cumulative in a way impossible for manuscript books. One reason why the fifteenth-century classical revival became a more permanent and more central part of Western culture than any medieval classical revival is that the gains made by fifteenth-century textual scholars were firmly anchored and widely diffused in the text of thousands of printed books.

But printing did far more than stabilize scholarly editions of the classics. It also diffused them, and with them, the interests and ideas that they reflected. Before printing, most books existed in only a few copies. Now, even the earliest printers turned out at least two or three hundred copies of every book they set up in type. The cost of books fell, and Rome in 1472 may have experienced history's first glut and price-crash in the book market. The medieval classroom depended on the *lectura*, the word-for-word dictation of the textbook, simply because few students could afford a copy. Now each student could be expected to have a copy of the book, and many of the old forms of teaching became obsolete, though they did not disappear rapidly. A book promoting new ideas, if printed, could quickly reach hundreds of readers, not just a handful. Ideas, opinions, and information moved more widely and more rapidly than ever before. Surely one reason why the humanistic culture of Italy spread more rapidly across the Alps towards the end of the fifteenth century is that books were circulating in print.

Printing also broadened the intellectual outreach of humanistic scholarship. The major interest of early humanist editors was in literary, rhetorical, and ethical texts – that is, texts related to the academic subjects defined as 'humanities'. But the techniques of textual criticism that were applicable to Cicero or Livy could be applied also to the ancient texts that were the basis of learning in the natural sciences and the professional faculties of the universities: law, medicine, and theology. Humanism did not claim to embrace all fields of learning and was not a comprehensive system of philosophy put forward as a rival to the traditional scholastic philosophy or to the professional study of law, medicine, and theology. Yet precisely because humanism implied a method of intellectual procedure rather than a comprehensive philosophy, it had certain implications that were not so modest as its rather limited scope might suggest. Modern interpretations of humanism and of its relationship to the prevailing academic culture often minimize a discord that contemporaries saw clearly. All fields of learning in the Middle Ages and the Renaissance, including professional and non-humanistic ones, were based on certain authoritative texts, nearly all of which had been transmitted from the ancient world: the *Corpus Juris Civilis* in law, Galen in medicine, the Bible and the Church Fathers in theology. Even physics, which to the modern mind rests solely on empirical observation and mathematical analysis, in that period rested on the text of Aristotle. When experience required changes, these were thought of as interpretations and explanations of what the ancient authority must have meant. No one would suggest that the ancient authority's opinion was simply irrelevant. Science (physical, medical, legal, theological) was in the text.

Humanism as a universal method

But here lay a great problem, the deeper cause of conflict between humanism and traditional learning, for the text of ancient books was precisely the field over which humanists were claiming control. Medieval scholars had been remarkably indifferent to the quality and accuracy of the texts from which they taught. Humanists could not be: criticism of texts was their speciality. Inevitably, their interest in ancient learning led them to investigate and evaluate the authoritative texts used by the three professional faculties and also, especially in the fields of medicine and theology, to broaden the potential sources by discovering works by acknowledged authorities like Galen in medicine or various Greek Church Fathers in theology, and then to prepare usable Latin translations. But when they critically evaluated the texts basic to legal, medical, and theological science, they were in effect asserting control over those fields. If a humanist editor changed the wording of a key passage or challenged the authenticity of an attribution or even the meaning of a word or phrase, he was making a prior judgement to which all specialists in the field must conform. Valla in demonstrating that the Donation of Constantine was a forgery was in effect telling canon lawyers that they could no longer cite that document as a valid part of ecclesiastical law. Perhaps the most contentious such case occurred in the sixteenth century when the Dutch humanist Erasmus observed that not a single one of the Greek manuscripts of the New Testament he had seen contained the *comma Johanneum* (1 John 5–7), the passage that theologians long had used as the most explicit scriptural proof of the doctrine of the Trinity. Hence Erasmus omitted the passage from both the Greek and the Latin texts in the first two editions of his Greek New Testament. Erasmus was fully orthodox on the doctrine of the Trinity and was not telling the theologians that they were wrong to uphold it. But he was telling them that they could no longer use this convenient passage as a scriptural proof. His purely textual (and fully justified) editorial decision certainly impinged on theology and led to frenzied accusations that he was trying to revive the ancient Arian heresy.

The source of the difficulty was that although humanism was not a philosophy, it was an intellectual method applicable to any question where authentication and interpretation of ancient texts was involved. Conflicts over this issue were few in the early Renaissance, but by the end of the fifteenth century, as humanists became more self-confident about the value of their methods, they did make claims that affected all other academic fields. They may have thought that they made no metaphysical claims, but in a sense their metaphysic was neatly concealed in their method. Many traditional scholars regarded the humanists as troublemakers, and in theology, even as heretics. These conflicts, conducted largely within the academic world, were only beginning in the later fifteenth century; but in the next century, especially north of the Alps, they gave rise to a number of heated controversies.

Humanism and religion

Although humanism may have challenged the conventional authorities of the academic world, including scholastic theologians, it was not meant to be a challenge to Christian faith or to Catholic orthodoxy. Petrarch, for example, expressed doubts about his own spiritual worthiness, but he never doubted the truth of Christianity; and his objection to the Italian scholasticism of his time was not that it was too religious but that it was materialistic and contrary to the teachings of the church, especially on questions like the immortality of the soul and the creation of the world. Salutati did endorse the active secular life for most people and followed that course in his own life, but he still revered the monastic calling. In the 1390s he and his family were adherents of a revivalist movement of pious lay people that encouraged quite traditional forms of devotion. The inherent and general irreligiosity of Renaissance humanism is a creation of nineteenth-century historians, both secular liberals (who approved) and conservative Catholics (who were aghast), but not of the Renaissance itself. It is true that humanists longed for a thorough reform of the church and voiced many criticisms of abuses. But it is a gross error to assume that late-medieval and Renaissance Catholics were like those post-Tridentine Catholics who accepted Loyola's advice never to criticize church officials in public. The pre-Reformation church was not like that. The criticisms expressed thwarted love for the church, not loss of faith. The tragedy of the pre-Reformation church was that the most deeply religious people were the most likely to be enraged by corruption and to speak out. Why would irreligious people even care?

To say that Renaissance Italian humanists were still (for the most part) religious is not to deny that they were interested in worldly things. Although the educated classes as well as plain folk were often deeply moved by revivals like the *Bianchi* movement in Salutati's Florence or the preaching of Savonarola exactly a century later, Renaissance Italians were also strongly attracted to material wealth, to power, to human love, and to family life. But though these attractions explain why most people did not become monks, they do not mean that the people were irreligious. Renaissance humanism was predominantly a culture for lay people, and specifically for the energetic, talented urban people who were making Italy the most wealthy and the most highly civilized part of Christian Europe.

Treatises idealizing family life were common in Quattrocento Italy. One of the first important Venetian humanists, Francesco Barbaro, wrote *Concerning Marriage* (1414), which repudiated the traditional ideal of poverty and defended the acquisition of wealth as the foundation of family life and of the Venetian republic itself. Later in the century, the defence of the active life of the layman, idealizing his role as father of a family and his acquisition of wealth, formed the theme of *On the Family* (1433) by Leon Battista Alberti (1404–72), who was one of the ablest humanists of the mid-fifteenth century and also an important writer on architecture and art. Though modelled on a work by Xenophon, a disciple of Aristotle, it reflects current Italian interests and explicitly upholds the superiority of an active life over a life of contemplation. Many of the same themes appear in *On Civil Life* (*c.* 1435–8) by a wealthy Florentine, Matteo Palmieri (1406–75), who unlike the exiled Alberti spent his whole career in Florence and combined an active business career with deep love of classical learning and successful participation in politics.

Such opinions can hardly be dignified by the term 'humanistic philosophy', though they certainly did express the values that prevailed among the prosperous classes that ruled Florence. This set of values is not ascetic: it regards marriage, family life, acquisition of wealth, and participation in political life as natural and good. That does not, however, justify the claim of many older historians that such views were anti-Christian. These humanist authors were practical moralists, setting forth an ethic suitable for Christian lay people. They assume that there are also transcendental, spiritual goals existing beyond the worldly ones; but these goals are to be sought through a religion that (however reluctantly at times) accepts the reality that the great majority of Christians will not be monks.

The humanists' treatises on secular life were not so much a product of their classical studies as a literary reflection of prevailing social attitudes. More closely linked to classical inspiration was the tendency of many humanist writers of the Quattrocento to glorify human nature. Here again, some historians have misinterpreted this as evidence of an inherently anti-religious spirit. Early humanists, including Petrarch and Salutati, did express some optimistic views about human nature, though they also showed awareness that all humans face death and suffering and are inclined towards sin. A much more consistent affirmation of the goodness of human nature is Lorenzo Valla's *On Pleasure*. This work has often been grossly misread as an irreligious affirmation of sensual pleasure written under the spell of Epicurean philosophy. But recent studies have shown that the real point of the book is that the conventional Christianized version of Stoicism, urging humans to reject all worldly goods and to shun pleasure, is neither realistic nor Christian, and also that the real hope of human happiness depends not on human striving but on divine grace, a view that one scholar has called 'profoundly Christian, even evangelical' (Trinkaus 1970, I, p. 103).

From the thirteenth century onward, all discussions of the human condition were dominated by one extremely pessimistic book, *On the Misery of Human Life*, written by the greatest medieval pope, Innocent III (1198–1216). Encouraged by King Alfonso of Naples, the humanist Giannozzo Manetti (1396–1459), Florentine ambassador to Naples, wrote a contrary essay praising human nature. Manetti was strongly committed to the ideal of civic humanism, was one of the most famous orators of his generation, had been active in politics, and also was admired as a pious and upright man. Like Valla, he rejected the ascetic Stoic opinion that a wise man should suppress the passions and follow only reason. Such views, he charged, were inhuman; it is unnatural and unrealistic to reject human love and passion. In Aristotle and Cicero, but also in Church Fathers like St Augustine and Lactantius, he found authority for a more optimistic assessment of human nature. Whereas the pope had dwelt on the putrefying decay and the excrement of the body as symbols of true human nature, Manetti lauded the harmony and beauty of the human body, reflecting man's creation by God in his own image. God placed man in the world and ordered him to rule it, to work and be active and free. Man's dignity is expressed in his creative actions. Manetti's treatise is not brilliant or original, but it pulls together, in a firmly Christian setting, many ideas about human dignity earlier expressed by Petrarch, Salutati, and Valla; and its optimistic judgement about human nature and about the life of the layman and citizen was widely though not universally shared by his contemporaries (Garin 1965, pp. 56–60; Trinkaus 1970, I, pp. 230–50). Later in the century, a similar theme of human dignity would be developed with quite different practical implications by the Florentine Neoplatonists.

Generational change in Florentine culture

Florentine society, which had been the most creative centre of humanism since Salutati's time, was changing during Manetti's lifetime. Although republican institutions survived, the dominance of the Medici family became more and more open between their winning political control in 1434 and their expulsion in 1494. Florentines remained proud of their 'liberty', but many members of wealthy and powerful old families were excluded from public office and even forced into exile. Manetti himself was one of these, forced into exile in 1453 because of his opposition to Cosimo de'Medici's foreign policy. His exile coincides with the virtual dissolution of the group that had made Florence the centre of humanistic learning. Many of the major figures were dying off: for example, Niccoli in 1437 and Bruni in 1444. There was even a sharp religious reaction against the enthusiasm for studying pagan authors, led by St Antonino, the brilliant but ultra-conservative archbishop of Florence.

Part of this cultural shift was a result of inevitable generational change. But there was a deeper cause. Except for professional civil servants who were migrants from other Tuscan towns (like Salutati and Bruni), Florentine humanism had been the culture of the wealthy mercantile aristocracy that dominated the political system. The republican 'civic humanism' of Bruni had been the ideological position of this group, for it justified the sharing of political power by a fairly large privileged group who thought of themselves as a proper ruling class comparable to the governing aristocracy of the ancient Roman republic. But after mid-century, the younger generation of this dominant patriciate seems to have experienced a shift of outlook. Enthusiasm for 'civic' and rhetorical values waned, and interest in spiritual, religious, and speculative questions grew. Philosophy, which the previous generation had scorned as useless in real life, now became fashionable among the leisured rich, beginning with a fashion for attendance at the lectures of Johannes Argyropoulos (1410–87) on Aristotle between 1457 and 1471. Though some scholars have conjectured that these popular lectures must have had a strongly Platonic bias, a recent study demonstrates that they expounded the philosophy of Aristotle in the traditional scholastic order. They seem to coincide with a marked shift from rhetorical and moral interests to speculative, philosophical interests on the part of the rising generation of the old ruling families.

Platonism and the quest for spiritual enlightenment

The ultimate beneficiary of this shift of interests was not Aristotelian philosophy, which was too traditional and apparently also too worldly to suit these elegant trend-setters, but the philosophy of Plato and the *LOL* Neoplatonists. The influence of Plato and his Neoplatonic interpreters had already strongly affected Christian thought in the Middle Ages, but then it was indirect, coming from the writings of authors such as Cicero, St Augustine, Dionysius the Areopagite, and other Church Fathers, and from medieval Arab philosophers such as Avicenna. Only one work of Plato himself, the *Timaeus,* was widely available in Latin during the Middle Ages. Yet Plato's ancient reputation as a philosophical rival to his pupil Aristotle was well known. When humanists such as Petrarch began attacking scholastic Aristotelianism, they often cited Plato as a countervailing authority, though they knew virtually no details of his thought. The successful introduction of Greek studies into Italy by Chrysoloras at the end of the fourteenth century changed matters somewhat, for several of his pupils produced translations of a number of Platonic dialogues.

Platonism was still a living philosophy in the Greek east, and the arrival of the distinguished Byzantine delegation to the Council of Ferrara–Florence in 1438–9 seems to have stimulated a general interest in Plato. Several self-proclaimed Platonists were among the Byzantine delegation, including Bessarion, the youthful patriarch of Nicaea, and the elderly Georgios Gemistos Pletho, whose avowal of Platonic philosophy thinly masked an anti-Christian and vaguely Platonizèd monotheism that honoured the ancient Greek gods as allegorical symbols of divine powers. Since he obviously did not advertise his most radical ideas to his new Italian friends, he made a powerful impression on the Italians he met. Many Florentine intellectuals were attracted by Pletho's claim that fundamentally all the rival Greek philosophical systems agreed with one another and that a thorough knowledge of Plato could lead to philosophical concord and a religious unity that they, unlike Pletho, conceived in broadly Christian terms. Marsilio Ficino (1433–99) later claimed that Cosimo de'Medici dreamed of creating a new Platonic Academy in Florence and so selected young Ficino and supported his preparation to become the restorer of Platonic philosophy. In reality, Ficino seems to have begun his philosophical studies independently as part of his preparation to become a physician, receiving a traditional scholastic education and failing (to his later regret) to develop the elegant Latin style typical of the humanists.

The main cause of Ficino's turning from the scholastic Aristotle to study of Plato was his distress over the tendency of Aristotelian philosophy to deny the immortality of the human soul. During his early studies, he experienced a personal religious crisis that he ultimately resolved through his conviction that Plato's philosophy had been given by divine providence to prepare the pagan world for conversion to Christianity. By about 1460 he drew a clear distinction between the philosophy he wanted to pursue, which dealt with the spiritual health of the soul and was based on Plato, and the secular Aristotelian philosophy of the universities. In 1462, Cosimo gave him a country house at Careggi near Florence; and from about that period, Ficino began giving lectures to an informal group (never a school in the formal sense) that became known as the Platonic Academy. Cosimo also urged him to translate the works attributed to Hermes Trismegistus, which were believed to represent a distillation of the wisdom of ancient Egypt. In 1463, Ficino presented Cosimo with a Latin translation of the most important of these vaguely Platonic tracts, the *Pimander*. Before Cosimo's death in 1464, Ficino had given him several other translations of works by ancient Platonists, including ten dialogues of Plato. Indeed, though Ficino was not yet an ordained priest, he reports that he ministered words of consolation from the Platonic writings to the dying patriarch of the Medici clan. Ficino continued his lectures and his work of translation, producing a Latin text of all thirty-six of Plato's known dialogues. The first edition was printed in 1484. For the first time, the full text of all surviving Platonic dialogues was available for readers of Latin. It was a superb translation, far superior to earlier versions of individual dialogues; and it remained the standard text for students of

Plato until the nineteenth century. In subsequent years, he prod¹ influential Latin translations of major pagan Neoplatonists sucn a⌄ Plotinus and of the Christian Platonist Dionysius the Areopagite.

Ficino was a professional philosopher, not a humanist, even though he did not teach in a conventional academic setting and had the social elite of Florence rather than undergraduates for his audience. His own philosophical works, such as the *Platonic Theology* and *On the Christian Religion,* applied Plato to uphold Christian doctrines such as personal immortality. His translations, treatises, and commentaries on Plato gave him a great reputation, first in Florence and eventually throughout all of Europe. His concept of Platonic love (purely spiritual, free from bodily and material desires) became a major influence on the poetry of all European literatures.

But the mere excellence of Ficino's philosophical translations is not an adequate explanation of his great impact on Florentine culture. Why did his works, why did Plato himself, rapidly become a major force in Florentine intellectual life? Plato, of course, is one of the world's greatest philosophers. But some recent studies suggest that the cultural shift in mid-century Florence was not just a movement towards Plato. It was also a movement by a large segment of the cultural elite away from rhetorical culture and the ideal of ethical commitment to the active life of family, business, and politics and towards a consciously chosen philosophical culture that devalued these things. The generation of Alberti, Palmieri, and Manetti were still disciples of Bruni and glorified the active life of the lay citizen. Hence most of that generation avoided philosophy because they thought that, except for ethics, it was useless for the life of laymen. This 'civic humanism' no longer had much attraction for the young intellectuals who came of age after mid-century. Ficino's lectures eventually became the focal point of the new outlook. Although he functioned as a humanist when he translated Plato and the Platonists, his profession was philosophy, not humanism; and he did not share either the stylistic elegance (his Latin style was quite drab by humanist standards) or the commitment to social and political action that had been typical of most Florentine humanists up to that time. His views on human nature and the somewhat similar views of associates such as Giovanni Pico della Mirandola must not be equated with 'humanism' or 'humanist philosophy' but represent a particular phase in the long history of Platonism. They are a partial rejection of earlier Florentine humanism, abandoning not only its emphasis on the active citizen life but also its devotion to rhetoric. Ficino's followers believed that rhetoric had concentrated too narrowly on philological science and on the tricks of literary embellishment. Their insistence that they were interested in *res* (real things) rather than

verba (mere words) may be one of the sources of that popular misunder-
standing of humanistic rhetoric which still makes modern readers think
of it as mere verbal decoration, mere gaseous puffery, mere style without
substance, 'mere rhetoric'.

The great advantage of Ficino's lectures over those of Argyropoulos is
that while the exiled Greek was just teaching philosophy, Ficino was
excitedly revealing to rapt audiences what he thought of as a secret
wisdom that went back to the origins of time. This wisdom embraced the
ancient philosophies of the Egyptians (the Hermetic tracts), the ancient
Hebrews (the Cabala), and the wisdom of Pythagoras (all of whose books
were conveniently lost). It then continued through Plato and later
Platonists to his own time. To him, all of these ancient sages were divinely
inspired. Their mission down to the Incarnation was to prepare the world
for Christian faith by teaching the superiority of spiritual over material
goods. Since the time of Christ, their role was to provide an armoury of
philosophical weapons for the defence of Christian belief, in particular to
provide ideas that would make Christianity credible to an enlightened
elite that could no longer be held to the faith by the sort of old wives' tales
and superstitions that the friars preached to the credulous, unenlightened masses.

What Ficino offered his hearers was a sort of elegant, gnostic, perfectly
spiritualized brand of Christianity that appealed to their own sense of
being superior to ordinary people. He conceived himself as a physician of
troubled and delicate souls, guiding them (and himself) towards a contemplative equilibrium which would free them from the depressing dis-
tractions of the everyday world and lead them towards the eternal
happiness that could be found only through the intellectual vision of
God. There can be no doubt that he thought of his philosophy as thoroughly – indeed, especially – Christian. For him, Jesus Christ was the
perfect fulfilment of all the spiritual aspirations of humanity, the goal only
partially glimpsed by pagan sages like Plato. He was particularly hostile to
the prevailing Aristotelian philosophy (the only system taught in the universities) because its rationalism tended to undermine faith, especially
faith in immortality. His preference for Plato was based on the Platonic
depreciation of the material world and the exaltation of the spiritual and
eternal. He found the same advantages in the works of Hermes
Trismegistus, the Jewish Cabalists, and pseudo-Dionysius. Being quite
without any sensitivity to the issues raised by humanistic textual critics
like Valla, he firmly believed that these other texts (all of which were products of late Antiquity) were preclassical and went back (except for
Dionysius) to the very beginnings of human civilization, in fact to a sort of
preliminary revelation that God had given to ancient sages.

The magical Renaissance

One aspect of Ficino's Platonic philosophy was his interest in magic, which was historically linked to some of the post-Platonic texts he translated, such as Hermes. While he had some interest in the kind of magic that could perform material works, he was mainly interested in spiritual magic, in which he combined asceticism, meditation, music, and astrological influences to strengthen his soul and thus to gain power over material objects, other persons, and especially himself. His spiritual magic was intended to relieve and control the spirit of melancholy that supposedly afflicted scholars like himself. Thus for Ficino the magical aspect of Platonism represented a sort of do-it-yourself psychotherapy that gave calm and power to the soul.

The foundation of Ficino's philosophy and of his magic was a hierarchical view of the universe which was based ultimately on Plato's famous doctrine of ideas but derived more directly from Alexandrian Neoplatonists like Plotinus. In this hierarchy, the highest rank was held by the uncreated and purely spiritual being, God; and all other beings were ranged in order, from the more spiritual down to the more material. The position of any particular being (animate or inanimate) in this great interconnected chain is the determinant of its true value in the total picture of reality. The various parts of the universal hierarchy are intimately and mysteriously interrelated, and the whole of being is likened to a great musical instrument on which parts tuned to the same pitch vibrate sympathetically in harmony with one another. This theory provided a supposedly rational foundation for occult pseudo-sciences such as astrology, in which the higher rank of celestial beings causes them to influence corresponding beings at lower levels.

A rational being who understands the celestial correspondences and other mysterious relations between things can use that understanding to affect and control one thing by the power of another thing that stands above it in the hierarchy. This is the theoretical foundation of magic, which in late Antiquity was closely linked with vaguely Platonic notions (in the Hermetic books, for instance). The person who understands and uses these occult connections between things is the *magus*, or magician. Since the Neoplatonic world is permeated by spiritual forces, the *magus* may be able to produce works not only by using the interrelationships between material things (natural magic) but also by summoning spiritual beings, demons. This practice is potentially dangerous, since some of the spirits or demons are good, while others are servants of Satan and evil. No one denied that attempts to conjure with the power of evil demons was a sin; but even efforts to employ good spirits were risky, for evil spirits might disguise themselves as good in order to lure souls into bondage. Ficino himself actively practised natural magic and even (good) demonic magic, though he was very cautious in expressing his beliefs, because he believed that the immense power of demonic magic would be turned to evil uses if the knowledge on which it was based fell into the hands of evil men, or into the hands of the rabble, who would easily be misled into idolatry – that is, devil-worship. Magical knowledge and practice must be confined to a small inner circle of educated, select, and pure spirits like Ficino and his intimate friends.

Ficino attributed great cosmic significance and supernatural power to human nature. In the great hierarchy of being, humanity occupied a crucial middle position, the sole point of contact between the spiritual world and the material world. Human beings, having both body and soul, had power in both realms; and humankind, as the point of connection that guaranteed the unity of creation, was especially dear to God. The *magus* has access to that power because he has prepared himself spiritually and has acquired the necessary knowledge (of astrological signs, for example) to command the powers of all created beings to do his will. This power, Ficino taught, also inheres (though not in so sublime a way) in the artist, who has a vision of God, even a kind of spiritual madness (*furor*) that inspires him to create (Wilcox 1975, p. 113). Each person faces a choice between cultivating the material and bodily side of human nature, and so falling away from God, and cultivating the spiritual side, and so becoming united with God.

Ficino's glorification of human nature repeated a theme expressed earlier in the century by humanists like Bruni, Alberti, Palmieri, and Manetti. But his glorification of man differed in that he presented it within the metaphysical framework of the Platonic hierarchy. The earlier humanistic descriptions of human nature avoided speculative philosophy and described human greatness in terms of moral excellence, solidarity with society, political commitment, and daily family and business relations – in terms of the active life. Ficino's glorification of human nature, on the other hand, defined human glory in contemplative terms and repudiated the values of everyday life. Inevitably, such a system could appeal only to a small elite of persons who had the leisure to prepare themselves for enlightenment. Ficino had little to offer to the politically disfranchised or even to solid middle-class Florentines whose economic and social condition precluded intensive study and directed their efforts to the worldly realms of family and business. His spiritual universe was elegant and aloof, and he felt remote disdain for the more traditional and plebeian spirituality promoted by the popular sermons of the friars.

The magical aspect of Ficino's philosophy was potentially harmful to his own reputation, and he was probably ambivalent himself about use of conjurations – that is, demonic magic. But there were other dangers in his intellectual system that he did not see at all. Like most forms of mystical contemplation, the effort of Ficino and his followers to purify and elevate their souls placed the emphasis on human action rather than God's action (that is, grace). It could easily lead to the kind of spiritual arrogance that often afflicts individuals and groups who think themselves to be humble but insensibly pass over into claiming to be a spiritual elite. This danger was especially acute since Ficino's followers were in fact a consciously separate social elite who despised the rabble and the crude superstitions that the priests peddled among them. The ease with which Ficino himself, though an ordained priest who surely thought himself orthodox, could slip into questionable magical practices is one example of this danger. The very foundation of his influence was his offer of a Christianized Platonism as the cultural marker that identified members of his circle as superior. Mere humanistic culture of the 'civic' type, based on Cicero and linked to the daily life of Florentine families and service to the republic, was no longer elegant enough for the splendid young aristo-crats who flocked to his lectures. Bruni had shown a broader ruling aris-tocracy how to be useful. But the new generation felt itself to be above utility. Ficino's philosophy allowed them to feel holy, yet without all the cumbersome regulations and controls of monastic life. Humanistic culture had always been elitist, based as it was on mastery of Latin lan-guage and classical learning. But the philosophical clients of Ficino were a far narrower elite. Ficino offered these young men more than just the inner spiritual calm that he himself found in his blend of Platonism and Christianity. He offered them the chance to feel spiritually superior. He was preaching 'a special esoteric form of Christianity for an intellectual elite' (Hankins 1991, I, p. 287). His brand of elegant Platonism formed a perfect addition to the culture of despotic courts, and it fits neatly into the idealized picture of the ducal court of Urbino depicted in Castiglione's *Book of the Courtier*.

Old-fashioned Marxist cultural historians like Alfred von Martin (1932), Friedrich Antal (1948), and Arnold Hauser (1952) acutely observed this affinity of despotic courts for Neoplatonism. They even suggested that at Florence the Medici deliberately promoted Platonism because its disdain for the active life drew the educated classes away from civic ideals and republican liberty. There are serious difficulties with such a reductionist interpretation of these developments. But though such crude materialist interpretations seldom stand up to close examination, they can offer useful insights. Certainly there was a striking shift in Florentine culture about the end of the 1450s, and it had its origin among young men of the most prominent families, who abandoned interest in rhetorical studies and activist values and adopted philosophical studies and contemplative ideals. The new fashion did turn attention away from authors who concentrated on moral and political decisions made by free men, and towards Plato, an author who disdained popular governments and favoured rule by a tiny elite of people who had undergone philosophical training and spiritual enlightenment.

Not all Florentine intellectuals, not even all those who clustered about the Medicean 'court', swallowed the Platonist ideal. The satirical poet Luigi Pulci (1432–84), who functioned almost as court jester in the household of Lorenzo de'Medici, sneered publicly at Ficino's pretentious otherworldliness. Lorenzo himself seems to have had a divided mind. He was eager for worldly power and wealth, but he joined the Platonist groups from time to time.

Pico and the glorification of humanity

The Medicean circle contained a number of people who accepted Ficino's Neoplatonism, including the humanist poet and scholar Poliziano and the poet and rhetorician Cristoforo Landino (1424–1504), who became an influential popularizer of Plato and Ficino. Aside from Ficino himself, the most distinguished philosophical figure in the group was the young prince Giovanni Pico della Mirandola (1463–94), though his philosophical background was independent of Ficino, based on study of scholasticism at the University at Padua and at Paris. As early as 1485, he engaged in a published debate with the prominent Venetian humanist Ermolao Barbaro, defending the superiority of philosophy to the central humanistic subject, rhetoric, which he belittled as mere play on words. Pico shared Ficino's belief in a continuous tradition of ancient spiritual wisdom that ran through the works of all the ancient sages, such as Hermes, the Cabalists, Zoroaster, and Orpheus, as well as Plato and the later Platonists. Indeed, he adopted a philosophical and religious universalism even more expansive than that of Ficino, for he thought that all religious traditions contained some truth (though not in equal degree) and that it would be possible by studying the writings of the wise men of all nations to distil from their works a common set of true doctrines on which concord of all philosophies and all religions could be built. Pico studied Hebrew as well as Greek and Latin and was especially hopeful of proving that Jewish religion, if properly understood from the books of the Cabalists (Jewish mystics believed to be ancient but really medieval in date), would fully agree with Christianity. He investigated the beliefs of all known religions, seeking a basis for universal peace and harmony. He assumed that Platonic philosophy was the key to discovering the underlying points of agreement and resolving all conflicts, and that the ultimate beliefs would be identical with a purified Christianity. Yet without intending to do so, both he and Ficino relativized all religions and jeopardized Christianity's claim to a unique status among the world's religions. When in 1486 he offered to sustain in public debate a list of 900 propositions, many of them derived from the Cabala and the Hermetic books, he was charged at Rome with heresy and found it expedient to retire to France for a time.

Pico's most famous work is the little treatise now known as the *Oration on the Dignity of Man,* published in 1496. As the modern title suggests, it does deal in part with the theme of human dignity, and both because of its inherent attractiveness and because of its brevity, it is commonly studied not only as the quintessential statement of Renaissance views on the nature of man but also as a work that expresses *the* humanistic philosophy of human nature. Neither of these judgements is sound. As for humanism, any reader of Machiavelli (to offer just one example) should be aware that Pico's poetic and glowing praise of human nature is not typical of all humanists. And while many humanists did write in praise of human nature, the union of that theme with an otherworldly metaphysic sets the works of Pico and Ficino quite apart from works on human dignity by humanists like Bruni, Alberti, Palmieri, and Manetti.

Pico adopts many of Ficino's opinions. Yet there is one significant difference, rooted in Pico's Aristotelian background. In Aristotelian philosophy, the nature of any object determines what it is and hence imposes strict limits. For example, because a newborn puppy is by nature a dog, it can never become anything but a dog. From this perspective, Ficino's decision to place humanity at one specific point in the hierarchical order of creation seemed deterministic. Man may hold an especially honourable place as the one creature that consists of both soul and body. But by being the middle link in the chain of being, man is bound and limited. His potential is determined by his nature. Pico did not accept this view. His *Oration* offers a striking alternative. Presenting a hypothetical narrative of creation, he declares that first God created the natures of all things, spiritual and material, to form a complete and perfect universe. Only then did God create man. But since the hierarchy of creation was already complete and all possible natures had been given out, he gave man no fixed place in the hierarchy and no nature at all. Instead of a nature, man – and only man, not even the angels – received freedom, the freedom to choose his own place in the hierarchy and to choose for himself any created nature. The man who makes the right choice will cultivate the spiritual part of his being and become spiritual. Of course the man who makes an unwise choice, who follows his baser instincts, will become like a beast. The true 'nature' of man is to have no nature that rigidly determines what he becomes. By his own free choice, man creates himself. Eugenio Garin has described this position well: every other created being is a *quid*, a something; man alone among all creatures is a *quis*, a someone, a person; and this is a condition he shares only with God himself. Thus he is truly made in the image of God, in a way that no other creature can be. This is an optimistic view indeed, so optimistic that one may wonder whether Pico really meant it to apply to man after the fall of Adam. But his own treatise imposes no limitation to prelapsarian times. It is important to recall, however, that this view of human nature is Pico's special blend of Neoplatonic and Aristotelian philosophy and must not be equated with 'humanism'. It must be regarded as the opinion of only this one philosopher. His view of human nature seems to leave no need at all for the action of divine grace, no need for a crucified and resurrected Saviour: it seems totally Pelagian.

Educated elites and popular culture

The cultural interests of the humanists, and still more, those of the Platonic Academy of Florence, may seem very esoteric to modern readers. Yet the elegant Florentine aristocrats who heard Ficino's lectures and the gatherings of chancery secretaries who read classical literature and perused humanistic commentaries and treatises were trend-setters, precisely because they were an elite group and hence caught the attention of all aspirants to elite status. The eagerness of the urban ruling class in most of Italy's small towns to provide humanistic Latin schools for their sons demonstrates that both humanism proper and the Platonist philosophy that was loosely associated with it penetrated the upper and middle classes of Italian cities very thoroughly. This new culture, expressed in both humanism and Neoplatonism, engaged a surprisingly broad audience. Latin was its principal medium, but this did not restrict its audience unduly. All lawyers and physicians, and the better-educated members of the clergy, and also all successful products of the new grammar schools, could read, write, speak, and understand Latin.

Furthermore, both humanistic and Platonist authors produced works of popularization and translations for the much larger group who could and did read books in the vernacular. Although the quality of literary works written in Italian seems to have declined for almost a century after the deaths of Petrarch and Boccaccio, some humanists wrote influential vernacular books that reflected the political, family, and economic interests of a broad spectrum of the middle classes. Alberti, Palmieri, and

Manetti are examples; and though Bruni wrote his much-admired *History of Florence* in Latin, an Italian translation was printed later in the century; and he himself wrote his lives of two of the great figures of the Florentine literary tradition, Dante and Petrarch, in the vernacular. Not only Bruni but Salutati before him and Poliziano and Landino after him presented vernacular public lectures honouring one or more of these great Florentine authors. The Italian poems of Poliziano, Landino, and their patron Lorenzo de'Medici expressed Neoplatonic themes in a form accessible to a broad public. Italian popular literature also retained a taste for the chivalric themes of the Middle Ages, which will be discussed in Chapter 6. Some historians interpret this flowering of chivalric culture even among the merchant aristocracy of Florence as a loss of nerve, a kind of cultural regression to pre-bourgeois values, as the republic fell increasingly under the thumb of the Medici family. Likewise the decline of commitment to the active life and the emergence of a Platonic style that emphasized otherworldly contemplation (and by implication, political submissiveness) rather than citizenship has been seen as a parallel regression to medieval conditions; and the ultra-refined and esoteric character of much Florentine art under Lorenzo de'Medici has been interpreted as another sign of the death of republican ideology and the emergence of a court culture. On the other hand, all this might just show that the culture of the ruling elites at Florence as well as in the princely states was still in touch with the common folk, among whom a romantic interest in knights and ladies, giants and sorcerers, and all the other paraphernalia of the medieval romances had never died out.

At Florence, despite the fashion for learned contemplation, chivalric literature, and even tournaments, the older civic traditions lived on. The rising popularity of the Dominican friar Savonarola, who attacked much Renaissance art and literature as pagan, shows that Florentines – not only the rabble but even many of the elite – were still drawn to the kind of popular revivalism that had attracted Salutati a century earlier. Likewise, the affirmation of the active life and republican politics by the earlier 'civic humanists' did not entirely disappear. Indeed, it was kept alive by the popular histories of Florence. Bruni's history, though written in Latin, was highly regarded, commonly compared in quality to the work of the ancient historian Livy, and was translated into Italian and published at Venice in 1476. Poggio's history of Florence, also written in Latin, carried the ideas of civic humanism and republicanism forward into the latter part of the century, and a translation by his son was printed in 1476 along with Bruni's history.

Machiavelli and the Florentine tradition

The true heir to this surviving tradition of civic humanism was another humanist historian whose career lies in the sixteenth century, Niccolò Machiavelli (1469–1527). His right to be called a humanist has sometimes been challenged, partly because he wrote all his books in Italian rather than Latin but mainly because his bleak view of human nature does not agree with the misbegotten notion that humanism necessarily implied a highly optimistic assessment of human nature. He had received an excellent classical education. After the downfall of both the Medici regime in 1494 and Savonarola in 1498, Machiavelli was named chancellor of the second chancery under the regime of the moderately reformist aristocrat Piero Soderini. Machiavelli rose to great influence as a civil servant, being sent on important embassies in Italy and abroad, administering the war to reconquer Pisa, and attempting to create a citizen army. Real control of Italy in this period had slipped into the hands of the large foreign monarchies, France and Spain, which had intervened in Italian politics and wars from 1494. In 1512, a Spanish army restored the Medici to power, though still under cover of the republican constitution. The restored regime dismissed only a few of the civil servants, but Machiavelli was one of these. He had been too close to Soderini and was too well known for his efforts to preserve the reformed, anti-Medicean republic.

Politics had been Machiavelli's life, but he never again held a position of real political influence. Without this personal disaster, he probably would never have written any of his famous literary works. Driven out of office, he did the only thing he could do to relieve his boredom and sorrow: he became the most important Italian author of the fifteenth and sixteenth centuries and one of the greatest political writers of all time. Most modern readers know of his political tracts, at least *The Prince*; but he also wrote two of the best and earliest comedies in the history of the Renaissance stage, *Mandragola* and *Clizia,* and one excellent prose tale, *Belfagor.* The only one of his political works to be published in his lifetime was *The Art of War* (1521), which was later translated into French and English and was used by many military authors.

Far more important is his *Florentine History,* written between 1520 and 1525. It draws heavily on his humanistic predecessors, especially Bruni and Poggio. He carried the story up to 1492, the death of Lorenzo de'Medici. The work clearly expresses his love for the venerable republican political tradition of the city; and when he treats Lorenzo, he cautiously and shrewdly presents the great Medici politician not as a tyrant who subverted the republic but as a wise, strong, and moderate leader who successfully sought both internal political stability and a general Italian

peace that had both vanished in the disastrous years following his premature death. Thus the *History* catered to his new Medici patrons but did so
by reinterpreting their ancestor as the wise protector of republican liberty.

For the humanists, history was closely linked to politics, and
Machiavelli's two famous political treatises, *The Prince* and *Discourses on
the First Ten Books of Titus Livius,* reflect the author's lifelong political
commitments. *The Prince,* of course, is the famous (even infamous) book,
but the two works are intimately related; and anyone who wants to understand Machiavelli's politics must read them both. Both works draw examples from Machiavelli's personal experience as a public official and
diplomat and also from his reading of history, both modern and classical.
Despite his undeserved reputation as an apologist for despotism, neither
work betrays the strong commitment to republicanism expressed in his
record as an active politician. A careful reading even of *The Prince* shows
that Machiavelli never regarded authoritarian rule as an ideal form of
government or as anything more than a transitional expedient when
society was so disorganized that a regime based on citizen participation
was impossible. Although his study of history had convinced him that
constant change is the rule of life and that no human institution lasts
forever, in the *Discourses* he demonstrated that a 'balanced' constitution in
which a strong executive, an aristocracy of wealth and talent, and the
masses of the people share power, such as he imagined the Roman republic to have been, was the most likely to combine a fair degree of social
justice with durability.

Even in *The Prince,* despite his frequent aspersions on the timidity and
selfishness of ordinary people, Machiavelli insists that popular support is a
strong ruler's only reliable foundation. His warning that while a ruler can
safely act in ways that make the people fear him, he must never act so that
the people hate him, is just one of many hints in *The Prince* that the overriding goal of any government is not the personal welfare of the ruler but
the welfare of the whole community; and this point is made even more
clearly in the *Discourses.* Machiavelli is no friend of democracy, which he
associates with disorder; but his preference for a regime in which power is
broadly distributed and is not left in the hands of a single individual or a
tightly closed aristocracy is quite clear. It is an unspoken endorsement of
exactly the type of reformed Florentine republic that his patron Piero
Soderini attempted to establish. The limitations he imposes even on a
prince demonstrate also the error of the widely held notion that
Machiavelli endorsed political immorality or amorality. Very clear moral
limits are placed on any ruler who wants to garner the popular support
necessary for survival. Cruel deeds that the prince inflicts only for his own
personal gain or pleasure are destructive of political stability because they

engender active hatred and so endanger the political system. There is a lively concern for political morality in this descendant of the moralistic tradition of civic humanism, but the moral restrictions on a ruler are not identical to the moral code by which a private individual is required to live.

The relative advantages and disadvantages of personal rule, 'narrow' aristocratic rule, and 'broad' (but not universal) participation in government discussed in *The Prince* and the *Discourses* were timely. Modern research has shown that Machiavelli's thought reflected political debates which had gone on within the Florentine ruling class since the overthrow of the first Medici regime in 1494. Where Machiavelli differs most clearly from fifteenth-century Italian political thought is in his denial that politics is a rational process and can be effectively controlled through intelligent policy. The political disasters of the foreign invasions that afflicted Italy from 1494 and gradually cost all her states their freedom had convinced Machiavelli that blind fate and overwhelming force could thwart even the most intelligent and carefully laid plans. His acceptance of the role of chance and violence in political life did not, however, persuade him that careful planning and vigorous action were useless; and the whole point of *The Prince* is that a strong and determined leader by intelligent and decisive action can bring order out of chaos. Despite the important role played by blind chance in history, following wise policies drawn from close study of history will allow the statesman some degree of control over events (about half of the time, he guessed).

The Renaissance artist: from craftsman to genius

Alongside the cultural mastery achieved by fifteenth-century Italian humanism stand the extraordinary artistic achievements of the age. The relationship of Renaissance art to humanism seems at first glance to be simple and direct, but in reality it is not. Italians of the late Renaissance regarded the flowering of humanistic studies and the flowering of art as merely two parallel examples of a comprehensive cultural renewal, a rebirth of true civilization. Giorgio Vasari (1511–74), a talented painter whose *Lives of the Artists* (1550) exerted an enduring (and sometimes misleading) influence on the interpretation of Renaissance painting, points to Giotto di Bondone (*c.* 1266–1336) as the one who 'brought back to life the true art of painting'. He explicitly likens the role of Giotto in reviving painting to the role of his Florentine contemporary Dante in restoring the art of poetry. Art historians for centuries accepted this judgement and generally interpreted it to mean that Giotto rediscovered the 'true art', the secret of ancient classical art, and that his successors gradually revealed all aspects of that art and perfected it until it reached absolute

1 Giotto di Bondone, *The Lamentation over the Dead Christ* (1305–6; post restoration). Arena Chapel, Padua (Bridgeman Art Library Ltd)

perfection in the works of the three supreme geniuses of High Renaissance art, Leonardo da Vinci, Raffaele Sanzio, and Michelangelo Buonarroti. Nearly all modern art historians would disagree, both with the judgement that the Renaissance began with Giotto (who is now defined as a late Gothic painter) and with the notion that there was one single 'true' line of development leading step by step from Giotto through the Florentine painters of the Quattrocento to the great masters of the High Renaissance.

It is significant that Vasari links Giotto's name not with Petrarch, the founder of Renaissance humanism, but with Dante, who does indeed represent a remarkable poetic achievement, but one that is firmly tied to medieval, not Renaissance, culture. Giotto and his teacher Cimabue illustrate the way in which Florence and other Italian cities bubbled over with social, political, economic, and artistic energy but initially expressed that vitality in more or less medieval forms. Giotto does mark a high point in Italian art, but it is a high point in Italian Gothic art.

So Giotto stands safely classified as a late medieval painter, drawing both on Italian adaptations of the thirteenth-century Gothic style of northern Europe and on the recent Greek or Byzantine style that flourished in thirteenth-century Italy. Yet Giotto is somehow different, and despite the justifiable decision of art historians to put him into the 'late medieval' pigeonhole, he does represent a remarkable break with earlier painting, one that the real Renaissance painters themselves admired, studied, and learned from. Medieval society regarded artists as skilled craftsmen – very clever and highly regarded ones, perhaps, but still just manual labourers plying a mechanical trade. But Giotto became famous in his own lifetime; and two and a half centuries later, Vasari was still able to collect numerous anecdotes illustrating his uncanny skill and the admiration he aroused. In the opinion of Renaissance critics, the distinguishing characteristic of good art was realism, a term by which they meant the ability to create the illusion of physical reality. But the realism in Giotto's work is not so much accuracy of individual details, a skill in which many medieval artists equalled or excelled him. It is rather a conceptual realism, a holistic and unified way of conceiving the entire work and of making all individual elements contribute to the general vision of the artist. His general patterns are simple, in the sense that all details contribute to a striking inner coherence. His human figures are massive, solid, and three-dimensional in appearance even though he had not mastered the sophisticated perspective techniques of the Quattrocento. In general, his pictures have what critics call high tactile values – that is, the figures look as if the viewer could reach into the picture and touch them. So although he is in most technical respects just an unusually great late medieval painter, the Florentine chronicler Filippo Villani, writing about 1400, had good reason to state that Giotto's paintings had equalled or excelled the paintings of the ancients because the figures in his paintings seemed alive. He attributed to Giotto the same role he attributed to Petrarch in literature: he had rediscovered the lost greatness of the ancients. There is, however, no glimmer of classical influence in Giotto's paintings; and while some of the legends preserved about him suggest the quiet self-confidence that often accompanies true genius, there is no hint that he himself claimed to have brought ancient art back to life. That is a claim made by his later admirers. His immediate successors admired his work, but they imitated the details and missed the spirit, the conceptual power on which his genius rested.

Italian art at the end of the fourteenth century was under the spell of a foreign style originally centred at the court of France. This

International Gothic style was realistic, but not in Giotto's way, for it expressed a realism of little details, of foliage and flowers and animals, of the luxurious costumes and surroundings of the aristocrats who paid the painters and who therefore populated many of the pictures. International Gothic is a court style: elegant, colourful, reflecting the luxury and elaborate etiquette of the nobility. Its human figures lack the solidity and impressive presence of Giotto's people, and the pictures generally have the clutter typical of much late medieval art, lacking the simplicity and conceptual unity that Giotto had achieved. Its best Italian representatives could produce beautiful paintings, such as Gentile da Fabriano's *The Adoration of the Magi* (1423). But at the very moment of its completion, the *Adoration* was about to be made obsolete by a new line of development that art historians classify as the true beginning of the Renaissance in art.

The Quattrocento style

As in the case of humanistic learning, it is easy but incorrect to give the impression that all the important developments occurred at Florence. While this is no more true for painting than for humanism, Florence really does appear once again as the focal point for the new creation. The three crucial figures are Florentines, and actions taken by the government and the guilds to beautify the city provided both financial support and inspiration for a remarkable outburst of artistic creativity. In 1401, the Calimala guild sponsored a competition for the design of gilded bronze doors for the north portals of the cathedral's baptistery. The winner was Lorenzo Ghiberti (*c.* 1381–1455), an accomplished artist trained as a goldsmith. His prize-winning trial panel shows some striking classical details, but such details were common in medieval art and had little or nothing to do with the growing fashion for classical literature among the educated classes. Ghiberti's style shows characteristics not of the Renaissance but of the International Gothic, and though his later work shows conscious adaptation to the success of the Renaissance style, fundamentally he remained a late Gothic sculptor to the end.

Some nearly contemporary accounts claim that one of the losing entrants in the baptistery competition of 1401, Filippo Brunelleschi (1377–1446), gave up sculpture in disgust and, accompanied by a young sculptor, Donatello (1386–1466), made a trip to Rome. The two friends spent much time drawing and measuring the city's ancient ruins and trying to rediscover their proportions. Donatello remained a sculptor and became, indeed, the greatest sculptor of the Quattrocento. But Brunelleschi became predominantly an architect. Art historians seem

2 Gentile da Fabbriano, *The Adoration of the Magi* (1423).
Uffizi Gallery, Florence (Bridgeman Art Library Ltd)

universally agreed that the statues and buildings produced by these two
prolific artists mark the real beginning of the classical realism commonly
defined as Early Renaissance style, though there is some disagreement
about the date of their journey to Rome and the decisive nature of
its impact.

The 'new' Brunelleschi, whatever his source of inspiration, did not
surface until 1417–19, when the civic authorities were facing the
problem of how to construct the gigantic dome specified by the thirteenth-century architect for the cathedral. No one since Antiquity had
attempted such a dome. Once again Brunelleschi and Ghiberti com-
peted, but this time Brunelleschi won the contract because his radical

new design avoided the cumbersome wooden scaffolding (and hence much of the expense) called for by traditional methods. His design would produce a dome remarkably light for its size and would not require heavy and costly wooden trusses needed to support a solid masonry dome. The resulting dome was (and remains) one of the supreme accomplishments of Renaissance architecture, even though its outward appearance could not be 'classical' because of the Gothic character of the cathedral. In other commissions where he could give free expression to his study of ancient structures, Brunelleschi produced buildings more expressive of Renaissance taste for the classical: in the reconstruction of the Medici parish church of San Lorenzo, in the churches of Santo Spirito and Santa Maria degli Angeli, in the elegant little Pazzi chapel, and in palaces built for the Guelf party and for the Pitti family.

Brunelleschi's companion in Rome, Donatello, returned to Florence to work under Ghiberti but early showed signs of breaking away from tradition. Both he and his more conservative contemporary, Nanni di Banco, produced impressive statues in 1411–13 for niches on the exterior of the church of Or San Michele. Nanni's group of four figures shows unmistakable signs of influence by ancient statues, but his work is still tied, in medieval fashion, to the architectural background. Donatello's *St Mark*, carved at the same period for the same church, is radically different. It is completely free-standing, in the ancient manner. It shows full understanding of the classical *contrapposto*, the asymmetrical bodily stance that makes a carved figure look relaxed, natural, and capable of moving freely. Nanni's statues have realistic classical detail, as do many medieval works; Donatello's work, on the other hand, contains no obvious quotations from classical sources but is much more deeply classical in that its basic treatment of the human form is classical. The same mastery of *contrapposto* and the same classical conception of the body appear in other works such as his *St George* and his unidentified prophet (popularly known as *Il Zuccone*, 'Pumpkin-head'). By the mid-1420s, these revolutionary sculptures had made Donatello famous. He also developed, probably under the influence of Brunelleschi, a remarkable mastery of the newly discovered principle of vanishing-point perspective, and in the progression from his early low-relief *St George and the Dragon* (1415–17) to his *Feast of Herod* (1425) to his *Ascension of Christ* (1429–30), the growth of his mastery of perspective can still be followed. Other artists felt the influence of the new treatment of perspective. Ghiberti, a conservative sculptor but one who kept up with fashion, described the perspective method in his *Commentarii* and demonstrated a sophisticated mastery of the technique in his second set of doors for the Florentine baptistery, the ones popularly known as 'the Gates of Paradise' (1435).

3 Brunelleschi, Façade of Pazzi Chapel (1429–33). Church of Santa Croce, Florence (Courtauld Institute of Art)

4 Donatello, *St George* (*c.* 1416). Bargello Museum, Florence
(Courtauld Institute of Art)

In the art of painting, the new style emerged slightly later and was the work of an artist about whom much less is known. Masaccio (1401–28) did not begin painting until about 1425 and produced only a handful of pictures; but they represent a drastic change, one viewed by some interpreters as resuming and continuing the line of development begun by Giotto. Giotto's paintings had been remarkably effective at presenting rounded figures and the illusion of three-dimensional depth on a flat surface, and a number of northern painters only slightly older than Masaccio, such as the Limbourg brothers and Hubert and Jan van Eyck, had developed 'aerial perspective', based on the increasing indistinctness of figures as they recede into the background. But no earlier painter had fully understood and applied the concept of vanishing-point perspective developed by Brunelleschi. In Masaccio's earliest dated painting, *The Holy Trinity with the Virgin and St John* (*c.* 1425), the new system of painting had already arrived. The central figures are placed within a classical-style, barrel-vaulted chapel, and the spatial relationships are expressed so perfectly that it is possible to calculate the dimensions of the imaginary chamber within which the principal figures stand. The painting also turns away from the slender, idealized human forms of the International Gothic style. With Masaccio, the complex clutter of elegantly clad, slender figures is gone. Now the conception of the picture, its composition, has been radically simplified in a way similar to Giotto's approach. The human figures have a rounded solidity reminiscent of Giotto, but even more successful in that Giotto still conceives body and clothing as a single unit, whereas Masaccio's figures, like the clothed figures in Donatello's sculpture, are conceived as human nudes covered by real fabric. The crucial importance of the nude figure, even if draped in clothing, is one of the traits of the new Renaissance style; and this importance of the nude appears even more clearly in two of the fresco panels that Masaccio executed about 1427 for the Brancacci Chapel in Florence, *The Tribute Money,* where the figures are fully clothed, and *The Expulsion from Paradise,* where the nude Adam and Eve stride forward, their faces and bodily movements displaying what may be the most complete expression of human despair in the whole history of art. Masaccio has fully mastered vanishing-point perspective, the thematic simplification of composition to create unity, and the realistic expression of the volume and solidity of the human body. In addition, in *The Tribute Money,* he has borrowed the *contrapposto* position developed by Donatello to give his human figures an appearance of energy and motion. Though his known works are few and he died too young to train disciples, Masaccio marks the almost instantaneous maturation of the new style in painting.

5 Tommaso Masaccio, *Holy Trinity, Virgin, St John and Donors*
(c. 1425). Church of Santa Maria Novella, Florence
(Bridgeman Art Library Ltd)

Brunelleschi's importance goes beyond his achievements as an architect and an engineer. Although in his time artists were still regarded as craftsmen and did not receive a classical education, his success as a technician and engineer reflects a remarkable mathematical talent which affected the work of all subsequent Renaissance artists. While at Rome, he reportedly spent much time measuring ancient monuments and calculating the mathematical proportions that underlay the harmony of Roman buildings. Perhaps during the process of making sketches of these structures, he discovered the mathematical principles on which vanishing-point perspective is founded. There is no way of determining how fully he understood these principles, but apparently he could explain them to others. At least his influence has been claimed for a small relief made (1415–17) by Donatello for the church of Or San Michele and is even clearer in a relief that Donatello made about 1425 for the baptistery of Siena, *The Feast of Herod*. Before the latter relief was done, Masaccio was already at work. Soon, increasing numbers of artists began demonstrating success in three-dimensional representation. About 1435, the classically educated humanist Leon Battista Alberti (1404–72) published a vernacular treatise, *On Painting*, that devoted considerable space to describing surfaces and the action of light and explained in some detail how vanishing-point perspective can be attained. This treatise explained – in Italian – perspective drawing in a practical way that working painters could use. Successful three-dimensional representation was no longer limited to great genius, either mathematical or artistic: it became a reasonably simple technique that any competent draughtsman could learn. In the years just before Alberti wrote the book, disturbed political conditions at Rome forced the pope to move the whole curia to Florence. Alberti was a political exile from Florence, but as a papal functionary he was allowed to live there. Thus he had an opportunity to become well acquainted with members of the local artistic community, among whom Brunelleschi's discovery of perspective drawing was spreading. His influential book on painting may have served to codify the new technique as well as to diffuse it among readers all over Italy. He addressed the introduction to *On Painting* to none other than Brunelleschi, and he mentions not only Brunelleschi but also Donatello, Ghiberti, Masaccio, and the sculptor Luca della Robbia as artistic geniuses comparable to those of Antiquity (Holmes 1969, p. 223).

Alberti himself had great artistic talent and late in life emerged as a major classical-style architect. But he was most important as a personal and literary bridge between the dominant world of wealthy aristocrats and humanists, on the one hand, and the artisanal world of artists, on the other hand. He also wrote treatises on sculpture and architecture, the latter strongly influenced by the famous treatise *On Architecture* by the Roman architect Vitruvius. His treatise on painting is also important because it makes a direct contribution to raising the social standing of the artist from craftsman to practitioner of a liberal art. A successful artist, he insists, cannot get by with manual skill alone but must have the proper intellectual equipment, including mastery of geometry (one of the traditional seven liberal arts) and also enough literary education to associate easily with orators (humanists) and poets, who will advise him on choice of mythological subjects.

Although Alberti was the only humanist who actually was a significant artist, he did not originate the relationship between humanists and art. It should not be surprising that interest in ancient literature and history stimulated the collection of ancient works of art (chiefly small statues, which were plentiful in Italy) and coins by humanists and their wealthy patrons. The eccentric Florentine humanist Niccoli was actually criticized by the schoolmaster Guarino Guarini for his interest in trivia like coins, and Niccoli's friend and financial backer Cosimo de'Medici began a famous collection of ancient coins, gems, and statuary. There were several cases where humanists advising wealthy collectors of ancient objects sought the opinion of Donatello on the artistic quality of ancient works. By the 1430s, well-connected humanist visitors to Florence not only called on Niccoli to see his rich library of classical manuscripts and his collection of antique art and coins but also went to gawk at the workshops of Donatello and Ghiberti. The veneration felt by humanists for ancient works of art was widely remarked upon; and since the new Renaissance art was regarded as a rediscovery of the principles and spirit of ancient art, a three-sided influence among ancient work, modern artist, and modern humanist was only natural. The famous low-relief sculpture of *St George and the Dragon* by Donatello may have been inspired by his familiarity with ancient engraved gems. Many years later, the helmet of Goliath in his bronze *David* bore an imitation of an antique gem. Masaccio's *Virgin and St Anne* includes a Christ Child who strongly resembles a child on an Etruscan bronze that was known at that time and still survives in the Vatican Museum. The closeness of Florentine artists to contemporary humanists also appears from their use of the ancient letter-forms for inscriptions appearing on their work. This sort of interaction was commonplace in Florence by the second quarter of the Quattrocento, and it is possible to trace the influential Niccoli's interest in ancient works of art back into the first decade of the century. While Alberti was the only full-fledged humanist among practising artists, the influential sculptor Ghiberti not only selected a classical title, *Commentarii*, for his book of memoirs but also borrowed tags of classical wisdom from Vitruvius and Pliny the Elder to create a theory of the artist as an educated man.

The creative generation of Early Renaissance artists active at Florence earned the respect of the socially superior humanists and the still more socially superior aristocrats, such as Cosimo de'Medici. In this age of civic humanism, the community itself (that is, its dominant classes) also provided the patronage that embellished the city with works of art. Patronage, even in projects for building and beautifying churches, was largely in the hands of the city government, or the great guilds which formed the basis of political power, or religious confraternities, which were usually dominated by rich and pious individuals. These were the same groups that admired and collected ancient art, provided humanistic education for their sons, and employed leading humanists in the office of chancellor and in other administrative jobs, as well as hiring humanists as publicly paid lecturers in the university. Patronage remained largely public through the first half of the century. Even Cosimo de'Medici, who was a generous and tasteful patron of both humanism and the arts, concentrated his artistic patronage on public projects, not on works for his private enjoyment. Only later, in the time of his grandson Lorenzo the Magnificent, was Medici patronage given more openly, directly, and showily – no longer mainly for public projects but for production of objects that the donor would keep for himself.

This book is not a history of Renaissance art, and it will not trace in detail the development of Renaissance style through the middle decades of the Quattrocento. Both Brunelleschi and Donatello (but not Masaccio) were long-lived and remained stylistically dominant. Along with Ghiberti, they became famous in their own lifetime – deservedly so, in view of the quality of their works and the enduring influence of their innovations. Their fame spread beyond Florence. In 1445 Donatello was invited to Padua to produce a heroic bronze equestrian statue honouring the deceased Venetian general, Gattamelatta. Similar examples in painting are numerous. In 1439 the Venetian painter Domenico Veneziano (c. 1410–61) settled permanently in Florence and fully adopted the new Florentine style. His assistant was Piero della Francesca (1420–92) from the small Umbrian town of San Sepolcro. Piero worked mostly in provincial towns of Tuscany and Umbria. His work lays great emphasis on vanishing-point perspective. The same is true of the paintings of Paolo Uccello (c. 1397–1475) and Antonio del Pollaiuolo (1431–98). Uccello, Filippo Lippi (c. 1406–69), and Donatello had all worked in Venetian-ruled territory; and Andrea Mantegna (1431–1506), the real founder of the distinctive Venetian Renaissance style, though probably trained by a Paduan master, drew inspiration from the Florentine artists. Although his

6 Piero della Francesca, *The Resurrection of Christ* (*c.* 1460). Pinacoteca,
Palazzo Communale, Borgo San Sepolcro (Fratelli Alinari IDEA)

works reveal a thorough mastery of classical forms, Mantegna's style
(especially his use of colour) also shows influence from the brilliant and
still-medieval Flemish style of painting, which was popular in fifteenth-
century Italy. A similar combination of Florentine and northern
influences appears in the work of the second great master of the Venetian
school, Giovanni Bellini (*c.* 1431–1516).

At Florence the powerful realism of Masaccio had been prettified by the
worldly friar Filippo Lippi. In many ways the austere work of Piero della

7 Sandro Botticelli, *Primavera* (c. 1478). Uffizi Gallery, Florence (Bridgeman Art Library Ltd)

Francesca, done outside of Florence, was a more genuine continuation of Masaccio's achievements than anything produced by a Florentine painter of that generation. Grace, lightness, and a strong sense of movement rather than solidity and volume characterize the work of Sandro Botticelli (1444–1510), the painter most favoured by the Florentine intellectuals who were close to Lorenzo de'Medici. His two most famous paintings, *The Birth of Venus* (c. 1480) and *Primavera* (c. 1478), show little concern with deep perspective and roundedness of figures or with the passion for anatomical structure shown by several mid-century painters. Both pictures have an aura of transcendent unreality and a sort of dreamy wistfulness that can be explained only if they are interpreted as allegorical expressions of abstract ideas fashionable among followers of Neoplatonic philosophy. The lack of physical realism, the intricate allegorical expression of abstract ideas, and the quasi-religious mood make many of his works seem almost medieval in spirit. They reflect the same shift away from the everyday world of active life that can also be seen among the intellectuals of Ficino's Platonist circle. Botticelli's Platonically tinged paintings provide a good example of how the artist at the Medici 'court' had become a member of the intellectual elite and how the ideas of that court circle penetrated into the themes and even the very appearance of the artist's works.

By the middle of the fifteenth century, the papacy had finally settled securely where it belonged, in Rome, and had outgrown the humiliation it experienced during the 'Babylonian Captivity' in Avignon and the ensuing schism, disasters followed by several decades of turbulence at Rome that forced several popes to take refuge in other Italian cities. The popes became deeply involved in political and military schemes to establish control over many outlying cities that had been virtually independent since the thirteenth century. In cultural terms, the consolidation of papal rule at Rome enabled the papacy to become a more active patron of humanistic learning and the fine arts. The efforts of Pope Nicholas V (1447–55) through his library collections and his sponsorship of translations from Greek have been mentioned previously, and the same pope conceived a grandiose plan for rebuilding the shabby and ruinous ancient city into a splendid capital of Christendom, though he was not able to carry the plan out. His successors did not lose sight of this goal, which is symbolized by the decision to build a new St Peter's basilica, begun under Julius II (1503–13) and not fully completed until the building of Bernini's great colonnade in the middle of the seventeenth century. By 1500, the centre of patronage and innovation in Italian art was shifting from Florence to Rome, even though most of the major artists were Florentines by birth or training.

This first great change, the emergence of Rome as a cultural centre, was closely bound up with a second, the French invasion of Italy in 1494 and again in 1498 to enforce the king's hereditary claim to the thrones of Naples and Milan, followed by a countervailing Spanish invasion in 1495. The result was a long series of wars between France and Spain, fought largely on Italian soil, that ultimately brought all of Italy except the Papal State and Venice under direct or indirect foreign rule. The old tradition of communal liberty and republican institutions had not fared very well in the fourteenth and fifteenth centuries, but the true realities of power were made clear in 1512, when Spanish and papal troops restored the hegemony of the Medici in Florence. The outward forms of the republic survived until 1532, when the Medici transformed the city into a duchy. Only Venice retained full political independence and a republican form of government; and the late-blooming Venetian Renaissance, in the arts as well as literature, became a tool of ideological defence against threats of conquest and domination by the papacy and foreign monarchies, somewhat as civic humanism had done at Florence in the early Quattrocento.

The age of the great masters

These changes meant that the patronage of art as well as humanistic scholarship was increasingly in the hands of authoritarian regimes. Even Venice, though a republic, was a remarkably authoritarian one. Rome, the other new cultural centre, was in principle the most authoritarian of all. This political situation by no means weakened the cultural hegemony of Italy, at least not at first. In the fine arts, the most mature and highly developed phase of Renaissance art was supported by the popes and other despotic rulers. Italy in the High Renaissance produced many talented artists, but three great masters dominated the scene: Leonardo da Vinci (1452–1519), Michelangelo Buonarroti (1475–1564), and Raffaele Sanzio (known in English as Raphael, 1483–1520). The architect Donato Bramante (1444–1514) and the Venetian painters Giorgione (1478–1510) and Titian (1488–1576) are sometimes added to this list of supreme geniuses. But despite the wide range of ages represented, all of the artistic works generally recognized as products of the High Renaissance were produced between 1495 and 1520, with the exception of the long-lived Titian. Michelangelo also lived much longer, but from the mid-1520s his style underwent a significant change that is now commonly defined as an early example of a post-Renaissance style that critics call Mannerism.

The achievements of the three principal artists are so great that even to list them would be useless. Each of their major works by itself would have made the reputation of another artist. Leonardo, trained at Florence by Andrea Verocchio, one of the best of Donatello's successors, was essentially a painter; but he spent much of his career working as a military engineer for the duke of Milan. His paintings are notable for his masterly use of *chiaroscuro*, contrast between light and dark forms, rather than lines, to delineate figures. His *Last Supper* and *Mona Lisa* would surely be contenders for recognition on any list of the most famous paintings ever made. He continues the characteristic Renaissance mastery of vanishing-point perspective and the practice of radical simplification, stripping away the multitudinous details typical of medieval art. As *Mona Lisa* shows, he was able to avoid prosaic depiction and idealize a portrait while still maintaining a sense of unique individuality and psychological depth. Leonardo was also fascinated by the study of nature, and his notebooks contain remarkably well-informed anatomical drawings and sketches of machines, though since they were not published until centuries later, they had no demonstrable effect on either art or natural science at the time.

Michelangelo, on the other hand, thought of himself as essentially a sculptor but also painted and designed buildings. More than any other Renaissance artist, he embodied the conception of the artist as inspired by divine genius, an idea derived from the Neoplatonic philosophy fashionable in Florence during his youth. His essential task was the creation of men – images of men, that is. He conceived his chisel as setting free the human form imprisoned within a block of marble; and the human form, especially the nude male, was the only subject he regarded as worthy of representation. His marble *David* (1501–4) so impressed the people of Florence that they changed its location so that it could stand in front of the city hall as a symbol of the republic. He undertook a vast programme of sculpture for the tomb that Pope Julius II planned for himself but completed only a few of the pieces because the pope insisted that he stop and fill the ceiling of the Sistine Chapel at Rome with the vast array of frescoes that probably make this work of this self-proclaimed sculptor the greatest cycle of paintings in the history of art. Individual panels, such as the *Fall of Man* and *The Creation of Adam,* would be in contention with a handful of Leonardo's works for designation as the greatest painting of the Renaissance. His frescoes in the Sistine Chapel exemplify the heroic, idealized view of man that is typical of High Renaissance art. Another gigantic and only partly complete sculptural commission was the work he did on tombs for the Medici family at Florence. By the time he did this work in the 1520s, his artistic style had changed dramatically. The conflicting religious passions in his world and his own soul gave to his great fresco *The Last Judgment* (1534–41) a tense dynamism that marks his abandonment of the poised High Renaissance style. Michelangelo was also an architect, designing the Laurentian Library to house the Medici family's vast collection of books, and the *Campidoglio*, a complete reshaping of a public square at Rome. He also took over and recast the design of

8 Leonardo da Vinci, *The Last Supper* (1495–97; post restoration). Santa Maria delle Grazie, Milan (Bridgeman Art Library Ltd)

9 Michelangelo Buonarroti, *David* (1501–4). Galleria dell'Accademia, Florence (Bridgeman Art Library Ltd)

10 Michelangelo Buonarroti, *The Creation of Adam* (1510; post restoration). Sistine Chapel, Vatican City (Bridgeman Art Library Ltd)

the new St Peter's basilica at Rome, which had originally been designed by Bramante, had then been supervised by Raphael, and was transformed into something like its final form by Michelangelo. The colossal dome that he created for St Peter's established the domed structure as the standard form for public buildings throughout Europe.

In differing ways, Leonardo and Michelangelo embodied the Renaissance artist as an inspired and almost super-human force whose ego could be endured only because of his undeniable genius. The third and youngest of the three High Renaissance masters, Raphael, was a less dazzling personality, but perhaps for that reason he was the most steady and prolific producer of paintings. He was not a Florentine but an Umbrian from Urbino, trained by Perugino, another Umbrian painter, but one closely in touch with Florentine art. Raphael was almost exclusively a painter, best known for his many gentle, idealized, and yet highly individual madonnas. Yet he also had the crucial Renaissance skill of defining and organizing complex themes in simple and orderly fashion, a skill best represented by his *School of Athens* (1510–11), painted in the Vatican palace. Finally, he was a remarkably talented portraitist, cultivating a genre not much practised by earlier Italian masters. His *Pope Leo X with his Nephews* (*c.* 1518) creates an elegant image of his patron and yet also conveys a subtle sense of the power and dignity, but also the arrogance and self-indulgence, of this Medici prince become pope.

These three artists have for centuries been venerated for their remarkable works. Yet they are equally important to the cultural historian because with them the artist had completed his social migration from humble craftsman practising a contemptible manual art to universal genius, companion of princes, inspired creator of the image of man, and hence somehow mystically linked to the Creator himself.

The humanistic and artistic achievements of Renaissance Italy reached their peak in the early sixteenth century. But the disastrous wars that began in 1494 made the peninsula a battlefield and ended by making all of Italy except Venice and the Papal State directly or indirectly subject to some foreign ruler. Italy's cultural hegemony outlived her freedom; and Italian painting, sculpture, and architecture remained vital and productive, though a remarkable stylistic change, marking the shift from High Renaissance style to Mannerism, became evident by the 1520s, the same decade in which the brutal sack of Rome (1527) by the army of the emperor Charles V demonstrated that not even the pope could defy the overwhelming power of the king of Spain. The Renaissance (in a Mannerist mutation) lived on; but increasingly, as the sixteenth century grew older, regions north of the Alps began disputing the cultural hegemony that Italy had exercised since the late thirteenth century.

4   Crossing the Alps

Although Italy in the fourteenth and fifteenth centuries was a distinct society with a distinct culture, sharply different from the rest of Europe, it was closely linked to transalpine Europe by religion, politics, and trade. Not only people but also ideas and books passed back and forth across the Alps. During the fourteenth century, many of the mercenary troops who conducted Italy's wars were foreigners, especially French and English. Large colonies of Italian merchants were established in northern commercial centres such as London, Paris, Lyons, and the cities of Flanders and Brabant. The clergy were important carriers of cultural influence, both northerners going to Rome to conduct lawsuits in the church courts, seek dispensations, or petition for appointments, and Italians going north as papal legates, collectors, and appointees. Other carriers of ideas were university teachers and students. A few of these were Italians going north to study (almost exclusively theology, at Paris) or to teach in northern schools and universities; but far more numerous were the northerners coming to Italian universities. From the thirteenth century, Italian faculties of medicine and law were regarded as the best in Christendom, and a doctorate in law or medicine from Bologna, Padua, or another Italian university provided a clear competitive advantage when students returned home. Until after 1450, few northern students came primarily to study humanistic subjects; but Italian law and medical science had some connection with humanistic studies. When transalpine students returned north, they not only carried both ideas and books with them but also in many cases gained influential positions that enabled them to become patrons who promoted humanistic learning. The great wealth of Italy, the elegant and densely populated cities, even the self-defined and self-proclaimed cultural superiority of the Italians, could not help but impress (and sometimes offend) visitors from less 'advanced' regions.

Northern societies lacked the large and populous cities, the self-governing communes, and the urbanized nobles and wealthy merchants who provided the social basis for both humanistic culture and the new art of the Quattrocento. In the north, the royal courts and the feudal aristocrats set the tone for society. The kings and aristocrats, much like their barbarian ancestors of the fifth and sixth centuries, disliked cities and preferred rural life; and their rather simple literary tastes favoured traditional courtly themes of war and love, not classical learning. Even the wealthy and ambitious townspeople conformed to the tastes of the court and the aristocracy. The educated portion of the clergy still favoured the scholastic theological learning of the universities. While in France, England, and Spain the royal courts eventually did adopt humanistic culture, large portions of central and eastern Europe, notably Germany, lacked effective centralizing institutions that might become vehicles for its diffusion.

Nevertheless, northern society did contain elements that eventually favoured reception of humanism. There were wealthy merchants who had to be literate and were likely to have dealings with travelling Italian businessmen. The universities did give some limited attention to Latin grammar and rhetoric, and the letters of some humanists such as Filippo Beroaldo were collected and used as models in that practical side of rhetoric which taught students to compose proper Latin letters. Most important of all, in countries that had a relatively strong monarchy, the functionaries who staffed the law courts and administrative offices had to be educated. These were headed socially by lawyers, and hence in all countries but England by a professional group that had studied either Roman law or canon law, the law of the church. The church in all northern countries was headed by bishops and abbots who possessed great wealth and much leisure; and though these wealthy clerics were drawn mainly from the feudal aristocracy and therefore often inclined to war, politics, hunting, and drinking rather than to spirituality and learning, some of them had travelled or studied in Italy and acted as patrons of humanistic learning. Germany lacked a powerful royal court, but some of the larger territorial princes were beginning to build their own semi-independent states and, pursuing a conscious policy of cultural patronage, aspired to educational autonomy by founding new universities. In western Germany, many of the larger towns had become *de facto* independent. Towns like Nuremberg, Augsburg, and Strasbourg were ruled by an exclusive oligarchy of wealthy merchants and landlords, not so rich or sophisticated as those who ruled the Italian cities, but somewhat similar. They traded with Italy, sometimes sent their sons to study there, and often found the Italianate culture of humanism more attractive and more useful than the scholastic culture of the universities. A good example is the influential Pirckheimer family of Nuremberg. Willibald Pirckheimer (1470–1530) was the first of this family to become known as a humanist, but his father and grandfather as well as Willibald had studied law in Italy.

The quest for native origins

Nationalistic scholars of the early twentieth century tended to minimize Italian influence and to search for native sources of the new learning. They were right in one sense, for humanism would never have been attractive unless native culture and society had been predisposed to receive it. Yet the basic elements of northern humanism were imported from Italy, though in each country the local people refashioned the borrowings to suit local needs.

Those who wish to find a native, non-Italian matrix for the growth of northern humanism have followed several strategies. The most influential is the work of a number of German and Dutch scholars who claimed that certain native movements dedicated to stimulating personal religious commitment among lay people not only ignited a religious revival but also (rather surprisingly, one might think) encouraged the study of pagan Latin literature as an alternative to the spiritually uninspiring teachings of scholastic theology. The prime example is a popular religious movement founded by Geert Groote (1340–84) and known as the Modern Devotion (*Devotio Moderna*). Groote underwent a religious conversion and became an itinerant preacher to the impoverished and spiritually restless people of Dutch towns, urging his hearers to seek God's power in their own souls and to express their faith in lives of religious devotion, strict moral rectitude, and service to the needy. He attracted a band of devoted followers who pooled their resources and lived a common life, supporting themselves by copying books and doing manual labour. After his death, his followers continued their life as a religious commune of lay people. Their communities, the Brethren of the Common Life and the Sisters of the Common Life, were not religious orders and involved no permanent monastic vows. But Groote also encouraged monastic life, and a group of his followers founded a monastery at Windesheim that became the centre of a reformed branch of the Augustinian Canons. Groote was a highly educated man. But after his conversion he repudiated the intellectualism of scholastic philosophy and theology and discouraged his followers from seeking university degrees. This reaction against the arrogance and unspiritual rationalism of the academic world forms a recurrent theme in the most famous book related to the Modern Devotion, *The Imitation of Christ*, which is attributed to Thomas à Kempis (1379–1471), a monk in one of the Windesheim monasteries.

Despite this anti-intellectualism, a number of historians have identified the Modern Devotion as the agency responsible for the diffusion of humanism in and near the Low Countries. Because their writings often expressed hostility to scholastic learning, these modern scholars have assumed, on the basis of very little evidence, that the Devotionalists were promoting humanistic studies. Hence 'the schools of the Brethren of the Common Life' have been repeatedly cited as channels through which humanism entered north-western Europe. These historians have assumed that the Brethren functioned somewhat like an order of teaching brothers in the post-Tridentine Roman Catholic Church. In reality, neither they nor any other group in the pre-Reformation church had such a mission. Localized studies of schools both in Italy and in northern Europe have shown that in this period, most pre-university schools were financed and largely controlled by laymen or were conducted by ecclesiastical corporations (such as cathedral chapters). The sharpest critic of the older view, R. R. Post, regarded 'the schools of the Brethren of the Common Life' as a myth. Though Post may have gone too far, his basic thesis that the Brethren were not educational reformers is valid. They did conduct some schools, but education was not one of their original goals and never became their major activity. They were communities of humble and pious souls, many of them literate but few of them really learned. They did not send their members to the universities and hence did not qualify them to become teachers in Latin grammar schools. Their principal activities seem to have been the copying and sale of vernacular Bibles and devotional books, and providing hostels for boys who came to attend school in some of the Netherlandish cities. In their hostels they do seem to have conducted review exercises for the boys who boarded with them. But they were rarely teachers in the schools even though they assisted the schools by providing decent housing and helping their boarders review their lessons.

Most of the so-called 'schools of the Brethren of the Common Life' were owned by local governments or church corporations and employed laymen or secular priests as teachers. The most famous example is St Lebwin's school in Deventer, where not only Erasmus but many other prominent humanists received their grounding in Latin grammar. The school was owned by the canons of the cathedral, not by the local Brethren. The humanistic headmaster under whom the school reached its peak, Alexander Hegius (in office 1483–98), was not a member of the Brethren, nor were most of the teachers he employed, though he did employ one member, Johannes Synthen, to teach grammar and collaborated with him in publishing (1488) an influential commentary on the traditional textbook of Latin grammar, the *Doctrinale*, which mitigated some of the defects that humanist critics had found in the *Doctrinale*. A necrology of members of the local Brethren house was kept, and while there are gaps in this record (Synthen is not listed), the surviving biographies show brethren whose occupations were cook, tailor, brewer, baker, rector, and confessor of the Sisters' house; not a single member is listed as teacher. Hegius himself was deeply religious, and St Lebwin's was permeated by a piety that left its mark on many former pupils, including Erasmus; but the school was not an activity of the Brethren.

The true origin of northern humanism is much more complex. The task of understanding it is complicated by a fact well known but often left out of account, that some interest in Latin language and literature had always been an integral part of medieval culture. But as the universities developed into major centres of advanced study during the twelfth and thirteenth centuries, the study of Latin grammar and rhetoric was narrowed and the study of dialectic or logic was emphasized in order to create the rather narrow liberal-arts curriculum of the thirteenth and later centuries, when study of the liberal arts was rigorously pruned to focus effort on those skills, chiefly in logic, that were conducive to success in the three higher faculties of theology, law, and medicine. It is often hard to tell whether a particular instance of classical interest in the fourteenth and fifteenth centuries represents the first beginnings of penetration by Italian humanist culture or a twilight glimmering of medieval interest in the classics.

One early example is the interest in ancient literature, history, and mythology among a handful of English friars active at Oxford and Cambridge between about 1320 and 1350. The principal modern study concludes that their classicism was an outgrowth of efforts to improve the friars' effectiveness as preachers. There is not the slightest hint of a desire to abandon medieval traditions of learning or to dream of a comprehensive revival of ancient culture. This is clearly an application of classical texts in the spirit of medieval learning, not a harbinger of the Renaissance. Much the same can be said of the substantial interest in Roman literature and in Petrarch's works evident among some French clergymen of the fourteenth century.

Modern historians have wasted their time looking to a handful of English friars, or the Brethren of the Common Life, or Petrarch's French friends as the origin of the English, Dutch, or French Renaissance. The true source of their own national Renaissance lay over the Alps, in Italy. This does not mean that in some almost physical sense the Renaissance flew over the Alps and was planted in the north. In each northern country, only those parts of Italian humanism that seemed useful for local needs took root and grew. The problem with which historians struggled was to find the agencies through which Italian influences were received, refashioned to suit local needs, and broadly diffused. As already suggested, there were many such agencies, including the international movement of goods, people, and ideas occasioned by trade, diplomacy, university study, and the administration of the church.

The role of schools and universities

The principal mechanism, however, was the most obvious of all: the schools and universities. More than a century of scholarship proves that in country after country, the first humanists were teachers who had studied in Italy and who returned to their homeland eager to spread 'good learning' there.

Each major northern country had precursors, persons influenced by Italian humanism who do not quite mark the beginning of native humanism. In France at the end of the fourteenth century, for example, the cultural leader at the court of King Charles V (1364–80) was Nicolas Oresme, a scholastic philosopher in the medieval tradition who produced translations of Aristotle's *Ethics* and *Politics* from Latin into French. In the next reign, Jean de Montreuil (1354–1418), who became royal chancellor, knew and admired the Florentine humanists Leonardo Bruni and Niccolò Niccoli and revered Petrarch. He collected an outstanding library and gathered a group of disciples. But he was among those assassinated in the violent *Putsch* of 1418, when the Burgundian court faction seized control of the government.

An even earlier but still more questionable claim for the genesis of northern humanism has been put forward for Germany. The central figure is the emperor Charles IV (1347–78), who was also king of Bohemia. He made his court an active cultural centre. But the art, literature, and scholarship of the imperial court were distinctly medieval. The imperial chancellor, Johannes von Neumarkt, showed some interest in the antipapal revolutionary Cola di Rienzo (1313–54) and corresponded with Petrarch. In his own letters Neumarkt tried to follow the classical style of Latin favoured in Italy, and he created a new set of classical-style form letters for use in the imperial chancery. The emperor himself met Petrarch in 1354. Yet this relationship with the first major Italian humanist was only an incident in a cultural policy that remained essentially medieval.

A more academic venue is sometimes claimed for the prehistory of humanism in Spain. Spanish students frequently studied law in Italy. Yet the evidence for Spanish humanism in the first half of the fifteenth century is ambivalent. The most prominent literary figure in that period, the marquis of Santillana (1398–1458), used classical rhetorical devices and cited classical authors. But since he could not read Latin and was dependent on texts available in Spanish or Italian, it is hard to take him seriously as a humanist. His friend Juan de Mena (1411–56), often cited as a co-founder of the Renaissance in Spain, could at least read Latin and had studied in Italy, but he is more properly seen as an early figure in the rise of a national literature than as a humanist. His principal work, the

Laberinto de fortuna, cites classical authors but is most strongly influenced by Dante, and like Dante reflects an essentially medieval view of the world. Much closer to real humanism was Alonso de Cartagena (1384–1456), bishop of Burgos. He made a number of translations of Cicero into Spanish. Yet his intellectual habits were resolutely scholastic. He criticized Leonardo Bruni's new translation of Aristotle's *Ethics,* arguing that a translator of Aristotle must be guided by what his philosophical reason dictates rather than by what the Greek words indicate. A real humanist would regard the original Greek text as authoritative, but Cartagena favoured making the translation philosophically 'correct' even if the actual Greek words suggested something else. His idea of textual authority and his assumptions remained medieval.

Early fifteenth-century England also provided a number of admirers of Italian culture whose failure to generate a real humanism demonstrates how unready England was to assimilate humanist learning. If social rank alone were enough, humanism should have flourished there long before the Tudor period. Poggio Bracciolini, the famous discoverer of lost manuscripts, lived in England for several years and enjoyed the patronage of Cardinal Henry Beaufort. Just a few years later, Humphrey, duke of Gloucester (1391–1447), uncle of King Henry VI, used his wealth and rank to foster humanistic studies. He employed two Italians as Latin secretaries, collected a large library of classical and humanistic books, corresponded with Italian humanists, and encouraged one of his secretaries, Tito Livio Frulovisi, to write a laudatory biography of his brother Henry V. If patronage alone could have made humanism grow in England, Humphrey should have been able to do so. Another influential patron of humanists was John Tiptoft (1427–70), earl of Worcester. He spent some time in Padua and probably studied law there. He became friendly with several Italian humanists, studied for a time at the famous humanistic school of Guarino at Ferrara, and collected an outstanding classical library. Tiptoft himself made translations of Latin authors into English but is important primarily as a patron, not only of Italian humanists but also of English scholars like John Free, who probably was his secretary at Padua. Other powerful patrons of the new learning included William Grey (d. 1478), bishop of Ely, and Robert Flemmyng, both of whom studied theology at Padua and humanities under Guarino at Ferrara.

Several Englishmen of lower social rank also studied in Italy and developed interest in humanism. Thomas Bekynton (1390–1465) became secretary to Henry VI and introduced a more classical Latin style into official letters. John Free (1430–65), a protégé of Bishop Grey, who supported him in his studies at Ferrara, also studied medicine at Padua and lectured on classical subjects there. But he died at Rome in 1465 without ever returning to England. Yet another English pupil at Ferrara was John Gunthorpe (d. 1498), who also studied at Padua and Rome. He became chaplain to Henry VI and was frequently employed as an ambassador by both Henry and Edward IV. He is of special importance because his rise to high office and his success in retaining favour at court through the dynastic changes from Henry VI to Edward IV to Richard III to Henry VII shows that command of classical learning and a distinguished Latin style were beginning to be seen as a necessary attribute for certain high officials. Yet none of these English figures is more than a precursor of a true English humanism. The prevailing culture remained medieval.

Looking more broadly at the countries surveyed, the same general point is clear. By the early or middle decades of the fifteenth century, individuals from the privileged and educated classes of transalpine Europe were becoming aware of the new culture, but most of them fitted their new knowledge into a world-view that remained traditional. Only a few caught the inner spirit as well as the outer details of humanistic learning. Only a few shared the common humanistic conviction that medieval culture had been mere barbarism and that a whole new civilization must be created through rediscovery of classical civilization.

The age of itinerant humanists

By the second half of the fifteenth century, however, humanism was no longer an oddity, and the humanist programme of 'restoring good letters' began to take hold in the north. Germany was probably the first to develop a real humanist movement. After a long period of political, social, and territorial disintegration, the country began to feel the stirrings of national revival, and humanism became closely linked with this spirit. The task of actively introducing humanistic studies into the German academic world began (in a very small way) with the teaching of a number of itinerant humanists, often called 'wandering poets'. Peter Luder (1415–72), who had studied at Heidelberg, was one of the first of these. He went to Italy about 1434, studied humanities under Guarino at Ferrara, and spent nearly twenty years in Italy before returning home in 1456. He lectured at several German universities, beginning with Heidelberg, on what he called *studia humanitatis.* His public announcement of his first lecture grandly declared his intention to restore the ancient purity of the Latin language, which had fallen into 'barbarism'. But though he received a hearing in the university, he did not gain a permanent position there. Subsequently he lectured at Ulm and the universities of Erfurt and Leipzig. In 1462 he returned to Italy, where he completed a doctorate in medicine and then was hired by the city of Basle as lecturer on both poetry and medicine in its new university, but also as town physician. He occasionally served as diplomatic representative for Duke Sigismund of the Tyrol, and in 1470 he lectured at Vienna. The brevity of Luder's stay at these universities has been attributed to his excessive drinking, his many love affairs, and scholastic hostility to the new learning. In fact, the most likely reason is simply the smallness of the market. Since such special lecturers normally depended entirely on fees paid by their auditors, and since such lectures were not part of the curriculum leading to any university degree, a semester or two of lecturing probably provided as much classical scholarship as the market could absorb.

Luder was not the first lecturer on classical literature at a German university. For example, the scholastic philosopher Georg Peuerbach, a noted writer on astronomy, lectured on Latin poets at Vienna between 1451 and 1461; and at Heidelberg, there were lectures on some classical authors about 1450. But Luder's long period of study in Italy, his appearance at several universities, and his ability to arouse interest in the task of restoring classical learning in Germany, all combined to make him an influential figure despite his modest talents and small literary production. There were several other 'wandering poets', both Italian and German, but all of them remain obscure figures. Germany also developed a number of active translators of classical literature into German, work that does not represent great scholarship but probably did much to spread interest in classical culture. Examples are Niclas von Wyle (1410–78), town clerk of Esslingen and director of a private school for young nobles, and Albrecht von Eyb (1420–75), who had studied at Erfurt, Pavia, Bologna, and Padua, and had earned the coveted double doctorate in Roman law and canon law.

None of these earliest humanists appears to have had a particularly creative and critical mind. They were, however, talented enough to realize that Italy had created a brilliant new culture, and each of them worked more or less consciously to spread the new culture in Germany. But this early generation did produce one figure of real intellectual stature, Rudolf Agricola (1444–85). He was the only member of the pioneering generation who was specifically remembered and honoured by the humanists of the next century. His one major book, *On Dialectical Invention,* though it did not appear in print till 1515, became one of the crucial textbooks promoted by those humanists who eventually succeeded in reforming scholastic education in its most important subject, dialectic. Its author was born in Frisia and educated at Erfurt, Cologne, and Louvain. Interest in the classics drew him to Italy in 1468, and he lived there for more than ten years. His initial studies at Pavia were in law, but he developed a local reputation there for outstanding mastery of Latin. In 1474, he moved to the

University of Ferrara, which had a reputation for excellence in humanistic subjects. He returned to Germany in 1479 and became city secretary at Gröningen in his native province. Since this position left him little time for study, his friend Johann von Dalberg, chancellor to the Elector Palatine at Heidelberg, secured for him an appointment at court that allowed him to lecture in the university when he wished but did not impose any mandatory duties. He became a trusted adviser of the electoral prince, but during a trip to Rome in 1485, he fell ill and died at the age of forty-one. He wrote very little, but his works did include a biography of Petrarch that pointed to the poet as the person who had begun the restoration of good learning. Thus he had a clear conception of the humanist idea of a rebirth of civilization.

Agricola's *On Dialectical Invention* was the most influential manual of logic from its first publication in 1515 down to the middle of the sixteenth century. It is important because it presented to students the humanists' emphasis on probable argument and persuasion rather than absolutely certain conclusions as the kind of reasoning most useful in everyday living. Like the Italians, Agricola emphasized the value of Cicero and Quintilian as the best guides to dialectic, and he criticized Aristotle's logic, though he did not wholly reject it.

In the Netherlands, a simplified and more classical approach to the teaching of Latin grammar developed. It is not at all clear that Italian influence had much to do with this. It may simply have been the result of a talented teacher working within the medieval grammatical tradition. The teacher was Antonius Haneron (1400–90), who was educated at Paris, not in Italy, and who taught Latin grammar for about a decade at the new University of Louvain. He wrote a number of widely used handbooks on grammar. His presentation of grammar was deliberately simple and direct, suited to students' real needs, and free of the elaborate logical explanations for forms and constructions that were typical of medieval handbooks. In addition, he drew his examples almost exclusively from classical authors. This simplified approach to teaching Latin was continued for much of the fifteenth century by another teacher at Louvain, Carl Maneken (Carolus Virulus, 1413–93). Figures such as these two were not really humanists, but they do represent an approach to teaching grammar that repudiated the medieval system of viewing logical reasons rather than usage as the basis for linguistic practices.

Humanists as marginal figures

Such efforts to improve the quality of written and spoken Latin were not viewed as subversive at Louvain or the various German universities, as the wide acceptance of Haneron's manuals demonstrates. Many Italian-educated humanists returned home and taught in northern universities without experiencing any difficulties. But teachers of grammar held a clearly subordinate position in the universities. Most teachers in the arts faculties of universities were also candidates for professional degrees in theology, law, or medicine. They had no seniority and little influence in university governance. Humanists were often allowed to offer courses of lectures on classical authors, though there was always some opposition, especially if the pagan writers were regarded as 'obscene', like Martial or Ovid. But there were seldom fixed salaries for such teaching, and masters received nothing but modest fees paid by those who attended. Such humanistic courses formed no part of the statutory requirements that students must satisfy in order to qualify for degrees. So even if at times there was lively student interest in classical literature, most students could not afford to devote much time or effort to what was a purely extracurricular subject. The official curriculum had place for only limited attention to grammar and even less to rhetoric. Within the traditional liberal-arts curriculum, logic, which was useful for academic disputations in the liberal arts and in the higher faculties, received the greatest attention, a practice that had elicited complaints as far back as the twelfth century but had nevertheless come to prevail everywhere.

In both grammar and rhetoric (indeed, in all statutory subjects), the teacher did not have free choice of either the textbooks used or the topics covered. University statutes everywhere required the use of precisely those manuals that humanists disdained as examples and propagators of medieval 'barbarism'. In grammar, for example, most universities required the antiquated *Doctrinale,* a collection of rhymed verses composed in 1199 by Alexander of Villedieu. This book had the virtue of being thorough, and because it was in a singsong doggerel, it was easy to memorize. Its greatest advantage was that it introduced students to the concepts and vocabulary presupposed by the manuals that later in a student's career would teach the far more important subject of dialectic. Thus even the grammar book prepared students to excel in the study of logic and become skilled in the academic game of formal disputation which most humanists despised. The *Doctrinale* based its presentation of grammar not on usage by ancient authors but on supposedly logical reasoning. Furthermore, it provided no examples to illustrate how the rules being memorized worked in practice. Although it was easy to memorize, it was virtually impossible to understand without the assistance of a detailed commentary or a highly skilled teacher, or both. Indeed, even conservative masters of grammar were aware of this defect; and nearly all working copies, including many printed editions, contained 'hundreds of pages of close, logical glosses'. Yet even these commentaries generally drilled students on Aristotelian logical concepts and terms and provided no literary examples at all. Eventually the humanists killed this book, but until after 1500 it was so widely used and they were so lacking in seniority and influence that they hardly dared to complain openly about it.

Though humanists did find employment as teachers in the faculties of arts, they had no opportunity to change anything or to take any but the most indirect actions towards fulfilment of their dream of reviving classical learning and making the study of classical literature and rhetoric, rather than logic and speculative philosophy, the foundation of the programme leading to the BA and MA degrees. The new Italian approach to grammar and rhetoric was known north of the Alps. Valla's *Elegances*, the most sophisticated product of Quattrocento grammar, was widely consulted by German humanists, and so were a number of new Latin grammars by Italian authors who had abandoned speculative grammar and based their presentation of Latin on the usage of the best classical writers. One example was the *Rudiments of Grammar* by Niccolò Perotti, an excellent and teachable manual written in 1468, printed at Rome in 1473 and at Strasbourg in 1476. In 1482, Bernhard Perger, an educational reformer at the University of Vienna, published an adaptation of Perotti's book for use by German students. He offered his book as an acceptable starting-point, while still conceding that the *Doctrinale* should be retained for more advanced study.

Town and chapter schools

Since the rigidity of university statutes and the tight control by elderly professors in the higher faculties impeded efforts of humanist teachers to reform grammar, certain pre-university grammar schools seem to have played an influential role in early efforts to spread humanistic educational practices. The history of Dutch and German Latin schools in the Renaissance is still unwritten. Many towns had created grammar schools to educate the sons of well-to-do and ambitious families. By the fifteenth century, most boys attending these schools were not destined for the priesthood but were preparing for university study leading to lucrative secular careers. In the earlier period, such schools used a traditional medieval textbook such as the *Doctrinale* in the higher forms. They rarely devoted significant time and effort to study of literary works, and of course they taught no Greek since there was no practical use for that language. But such schools did not have the rigid statutes, the venerable academic traditions, and the weight of institutional inertia and vested interest that impeded change in the universities. Their institutional structure was simple. Normally, a single master was in charge, with authority to hire (out of his own pocket) such few assistant teachers as he might need. As masters of arts returned from study in Italy or elsewhere, fired by a desire to improve the teaching of Latin and to make the curriculum more classical and more literary, there were no serious institutional impediments to a modest degree of curricular change, though obviously a wise schoolmaster would not depart so far from the norm as to alarm the town council or the cathedral chapter that hired him.

The most famous humanistic school in the Germanic language area was St Lebwin's school at Deventer. While Alexander Hegius was headmaster (1483–98), it was the most famous school in the Low Countries, noted for its excellent instruction in Latin. It reached the remarkable enrolment of 2,000 boys by the end of Hegius' career. Influential humanists who received part or all of their basic schooling there included Hermann von dem Busche, Ortwin Gratius, Mutianus Rufus, and Erasmus. Almost nothing is known about Hegius' early life or education, but it seems certain that he never studied in Italy or even visited there. He wrote a considerable number of Latin poems and other works on literature and education. He was deeply religious, a close friend (but never a member) of the Brethren of the Common Life at Deventer, and his school gave much attention to development of the students' spiritual life as well as to perfecting their Latin style.

Hegius was a cautious humanist, by no means ready to throw out all traditional practices. But his school may have been the first north of the Alps to teach Greek, and he encouraged pupils to write Latin verse. He was also an outspoken critic of the *modistae,* the teachers of the logical or speculative grammar that dominated university instruction. He warned that study of the logical basis of linguistic practice does not give boys a usable command of grammar, and he observed that Italian teachers of grammar did not waste their pupils' time on such useless things. This shift from logical proof to actual usage as the governing authority in grammar had long been a principal characteristic of humanists' grammar-teaching in Italy.

There were other important grammar schools that taught in the new manner at Münster in Westphalia and Sélestat in Alsace. The latter school, under the talented teacher Ludwig Dringenberg (1410–77), educated many important Alsatian humanists, including Jakob Wimpheling and Beatus Rhenanus. Dringenberg was largely traditional in outlook, but he was hostile to speculative grammar. Under his successor, Crato Hofmann (in office 1477–1501), the humanistic tendency of the school became even more pronounced.

Growth of humanism in Germany

By the end of the fifteenth century, there were humanists (some of them with Italian experience, others totally home-grown) in all German universities, but nowhere had they significantly changed the nature of degree requirements or even seriously tried to do so. A growing number of town schools and chapter schools were under the control of headmasters who took some limited steps to modernize their curriculum. Some rulers were beginning to favour employment of men with the new classical education for positions in their civil service. At the same time, the wealthy patrician families of the more important towns favoured a humanistic education for their sons. Like-minded humanists, many of whom had met in a progressive grammar school, a German university, or even in Italy, kept track of each other's accomplishments, corresponded to share information, ideas, and inspiration, and gathered to read or discuss ancient literature or their own works.

These early humanists were often cautious about breaking with tradition. One of the most conservative, Jakob Wimpheling (1450–1528), was nevertheless a powerful influence in attracting others to humanistic studies. He was an ardent German (or, perhaps better, Alsatian) nationalist and prided himself on never having set foot in Italy, France, or even the neighbouring German province of Swabia. Although sharply critical of corruption in the church, he was a very conservative Catholic, critical of the church only because it failed to live up to its own ideals. In his treatise on education, *Isidoneus Germanicus,* he emphasizes the importance of religious indoctrination but also sounds many humanist themes, such as a demand for simplification in the teaching of grammar and an emphasis on developing ability to speak and write good Latin rather than on the logical presentation of grammar. He opposed those clergymen who wanted to ban pagan authors from Christian schools. On the other hand, he clearly divided pagan literature into acceptable authors (Vergil and Cicero, for example) and authors unacceptable because of the bawdiness of their language or their subject (such as Ovid and Catullus). Although he had earlier been somewhat critical of scholastic philosophy and theology, in a book written against his own former pupil, Jakob Locher, who had questioned the value of scholasticism, Wimpheling firmly upheld scholastic learning. He tried to strike a balance between old and new, but as a younger and bolder generation of humanists arose and then the Protestant Reformation divided the humanists, his position became increasingly difficult. By the end of his life, he was a man whom time had passed by. In his earlier career, however, in the 1480s and 1490s, he was an important influence in favour of humanistic culture. His Latin play

Stylpho (1480) was the first dramatic work of German humanism. His historical writings also had a lasting influence. His *Germania* (1501) proved that Alsace had been inhabited by Germans since the time of the emperor Augustus and hence that France had no claim on it. His *Epitome rerum Germanicarum* (1505) was a short history of Germany, a rather uncritical blend of myth and genuine history, which tried to show that Germany had a history as ancient and as full of achievement as any other country.

Wimpheling's contemporary and friend Johann Reuchlin (1455–1519) was also deeply religious and generally conservative on religious questions, but he was a far abler person, one of the great scholars of his generation. The bitter controversy over Jewish books in which he later became involved usually dominates biographies of him, but his intellectual formation and his fundamental ideas place him in the generation of Wimpheling. Reuchlin received his arts education at Freiburg, Paris, and Basle and then studied law at Orleans and Poitiers before becoming legal counsellor and judge for the count of Württemberg and later for the Elector Palatine. In the service of these princes he made three extended trips to Italy.

Reuchlin was a mature man when he first saw Italy in 1482. He became acquainted with Lorenzo de'Medici and his splendid library in Florence, and also met Marsilio Ficino, Pico della Mirandola, and the famous Venetian humanist Ermolao Barbaro. By 1492, and perhaps earlier, he began the study of Hebrew, first under a Jewish physician to the emperor and then with a noted Jewish scholar in Rome. In 1506 he published the first successful grammar of Hebrew. Reuchlin was also the first German to acquire a really thorough command of Greek. Thus he was northern Europe's first genuinely trilingual scholar. His command of all three scriptural languages, Latin, Greek, and Hebrew, became the programmatic ideal of the following generation of northern humanists and also of the early Protestant Reformation.

Although Reuchlin held influential positions as legal counsellor to German rulers, by temperament he was a scholar. His principal interests were in the field of religion, which he wanted to revive by making ancient Greek and Hebrew learning known to Christian readers. He fully shared the conviction of his Florentine friends Ficino and Pico della Mirandola that the thought of Plato and the Neoplatonists (including occultist and magical texts like the Hermetic treatises) contained profound insights into spiritual life. Exactly the same approach motivated his study of Hebrew language and Jewish religious writings. His study of the esoteric and mystical writings known as the Cabala convinced him that this ancient wisdom was thoroughly harmonious with both Platonism and Christianity. He assumed that the cabalistic books transmitted a secret revelation given by God to Moses, whereas in reality they originated in medieval times and were derivative from late Roman Platonism. He was, in fact, an important link between the occultist elements in Florentine Renaissance thought and the humanism of northern Europe. His cabalistic writings, *On the Wonder-Working Word* (1494) and *On the Cabalistic Art* (1517), may strike modern readers as a byway, a dead-end, but in Reuchlin's time and for at least a century afterward, they attracted many intelligent and learned theologians.

Far less conservative than both Wimpheling and Reuchlin was Conrad Celtis (1459–1508). Celtis was more assertive and worldly, but precisely because of his lesser respect for tradition, he did much more than either to spread humanism throughout Germany. Born the son of a peasant, he ran away and enrolled as a poor scholar at the University of Cologne. After his BA degree he moved to Heidelberg, where he became an admirer of Rudolf Agricola, and then to Erfurt, Rostock, and Leipzig. In 1487 he published a short manual on versification that won for him the honour of being crowned poet laureate by the emperor Frederick III. In 1487 he began a two-year visit to Italy, where he met Battista Guarini, the son and successor of the great schoolmaster Guarino, at Ferrara. At Florence he met the Platonic philosopher Ficino; at Rome, the famous antiquarian Pomponius Laetus. From Italy he brought back the idea of fostering humanism in Germany by founding informal 'academies' or sodalities of persons who wished to promote the growth of humanistic studies. He also brought back very ambivalent feelings about the Italians, whose scholarly achievements he admired but whose arrogant sense of superiority he resented. He taught and studied at several universities, and his inaugural address at Ingolstadt urged his hearers to bring glory to the German nation through scholarly achievement.

Although he possessed the ability to inspire young Germans with his dream of reviving high culture in Germany, Celtis was an indifferent professor. He neglected his duties both on account of his personal habits (such as heavy drinking and the love affairs reflected in his poems) and on account of his constant pursuit of new and better jobs. But his founding of humanist clubs at Ingolstadt, Heidelberg, Vienna, and several other cities strengthened humanism as a self-conscious movement.

As professor of poetry at Vienna from 1497, Celtis also attracted the attention of the emperor Maximilian, who quickly realized that the linguistic talents, literary knowledge, and leadership abilities of young German humanists could be helpful in the dynasty's effort to spread Habsburg influence throughout Europe. Maximilian presented himself to those humanists (and through them to the educated classes of Germany) as the restorer of German national power and the universal claims of the

'Roman' emperors. He even founded a special institute, the College of Poets and Mathematicians, headed by Celtis and dedicated to the study of two aspects of the liberal arts, literature and mathematics, that were given short shrift in the traditional university curriculum. Celtis was also influential for his Latin dramas and poems. While most humanist poets produced metrical prose rather than real poetry, Celtis had genuine poetic talent and became an important influence on later humanist poetry. His strongly nationalistic spirit enhanced his influence. Celtis was no intellectual giant, and his achievement was further limited by his irregular life-style. But his eloquent oratory, his facile verse, his enthusiastic dream of cultural leadership and political power, caught the attention of a whole generation of young Germans. Even his unstable flitting about from one university to another served to spread his message widely. His success in organizing many humanist sodalities provided a network of local and regional centres from which humanism was diffused throughout Germany. The practice of maintaining connections between these centres through correspondence meant that by shortly after 1500, German humanism was no longer limited to a few scattered and isolated individuals but was becoming a true intellectual movement, able to find patrons among German princes and urban patricians, even able to claim a growing place within the universities.

German humanism has received special attention from historians because of its close association with the origins of the Protestant Reformation. But humanism also developed in other countries of northern Europe. The same general pattern emerged as in Germany: increasing penetration of the universities by humanists, but in subordinate positions and without significant curricular change; the gradual rise of humanist scholars to influential positions as headmasters of Latin grammar schools; and the emergence of a number of outstanding individuals whose growing fame and social prominence mark the transition of humanism from being an eccentricity of scattered individuals to being a movement of well-placed scholars having significant influence on the culture of university students and the urban elites.

Early French humanism

In the case of France, the traditional story is that humanism was the result of the invasion of Italy by King Charles VIII in 1494. Yet French interest in Italian culture went back as far as the time of Petrarch. The greatest single impediment to acceptance of Italian influence was national sentiment. The new Renaissance outlook implied the contemptuous rejection of the whole Middle Ages as a period of barbarism. Yet in all the northern countries, the roots of the nation itself lay in the medieval period; and a total repudiation of the medieval heritage was especially difficult for the French because France had been the very centre of medieval civilization. French intellectuals who did not want to repudiate their own national heritage found it awkward to embrace all aspects of Italian humanism. They borrowed from it with increasing frequency from the late fifteenth century (and well before 1494), but they borrowed selectively, choosing only those elements that contributed to traditional fields of interest, such as moral philosophy and theology.

The most famous centre of higher learning in France, the University of Paris, came out of the turmoil of English and Burgundian occupation badly disorganized. Despite its universal claims, it never regained the international stature it had held in the past. Many of the Paris colleges were in decay, their revenues diminished and their membership depleted. While the monarchy offered little in the way of financial help, it clumsily intervened in intellectual matters that the court hardly understood, such as the rivalry between the 'ancient' or 'realist' way of teaching philosophy and the 'modern' or 'nominalist' way. When effective reforms did occur at Paris, it was only within particular colleges. Thus the Collège de Navarre under the puritanical Jean Raulin and the Collège de Montaigu under another puritanical theologian, Jean Standonck, both underwent drastic reforms based on strict internal discipline. At both places, serious academic work resumed, but their academic programme was strictly traditional. Erasmus, who spent a miserable year as a resident of Montaigu when he first came to study at Paris, found the intellectual fare as tasteless as the foul food which, he charged, permanently undermined his health.

Yet despite the conservatism of Raulin's and Standonck's reforms, humanist influence did seep in. As far back as 1458, the university appointed Gregorio Tifernate, an Italian who had studied in Greece, to a chair of Greek. This was not a permanent position, but when Johann Reuchlin came to Paris as a young student, he was able to find former pupils of Tifernate to teach him Greek. Much more lasting was the influence of Guillaume Fichet (1433 to after 1480), who received his early education at Avignon, where Italian humanism had exercised influence since the time of Petrarch. At Paris he taught the scholastic subjects of logic and theology but also gave evening courses on classical authors. A trip to Italy in 1469–70 increased his interest in the new learning. Having become librarian of the Sorbonne, he helped to bring in the German workmen who in 1470 established the first printing press in France. His humanistic interests were reflected in the output of this pioneering shop: Sallust, Florus, Valerius Maximus, Cicero's *De officiis,* and works by modern humanists such as Lorenzo Valla's *Elegances* and

Fichet's own *Rhetorica*. Fichet was still essentially a scholastic philosopher, but he was open to the value of humanistic learning. In 1472, however, he entered papal service in Rome.

The central figure among French humanists after Fichet's departure was Robert Gaguin (1423–1501), a Trinitarian monk. About 1457 he came to Paris as a student of canon law. He travelled widely on business for his order, and after his election as general of the order in 1473, he was also sent on diplomatic missions for the French king. He had been attracted by Italian scholarship during his trips there. Around him coalesced a little informal academy of enthusiasts for ancient literature that included not only members of the arts and theological faculties of the university but also royal officials and legal counsellors in the Parlement of Paris, the country's supreme judicial court. Gaguin was also an influential author, publishing French translations of Caesar and Livy as well as his own history of the origins of the Franks (1498). He encouraged the literary efforts of the young Erasmus. Erasmus' first two published works appeared in the preliminary matter of two of Gaguin's books. Thus Gaguin introduced the future prince of humanists to the literary world of Paris at the end of the fifteenth century.

Fichet and his successor Gaguin were not isolated figures in Paris, not even within the faculty of arts at the university, although intellectual life there remained predominantly scholastic. Interest in humanistic books became significant. The output of Parisian publishers reflects growing interest in Italian humanism. Important works by Italian humanists were published there as early as the 1470s, including Lorenzo Valla's *Elegantiae*, the major guide to classical Latin usage; Gasparino Barzizza's collection of model letters, used for the study of rhetoric; Agostino Dati's *Elegantiolae*, a guide to elegant (that is, humanistic) Latin style; and Niccolò Perotti's *Rudimenta grammatices*, the most successful and probably the best of the new textbooks of Latin grammar. Valla's book, the most intellectually sophisticated of the lot, was printed at Paris in 1471, concurrently with the first edition at Rome. About 1490 Guy Jouenneaux (*c.* 1450–1505) published an adaptation of Valla's book for the French market. The publisher Josse Bade, who had a remarkably good sense of the market for books, was one of the Paris publishers who reprinted Jouenneaux's adaptation. The humanists did not gain influence without making some concessions. Jouenneaux's book and even Dati's *Elegantiolae* were simpler and less overtly hostile to traditional scholastic learning than Valla's book; and they were republished more frequently. Language books written in the medieval rhetorical tradition, such as the *Synonima Britonis*, an alphabetical list of words and synonyms, continued to sell well at Paris (and hence to be reprinted) into the first decade of the sixteenth century.

Within the body of the university itself, interest in humanistic learning surfaces from time to time in the lives and writings of individuals but is difficult to trace in general terms, partly because the records of the Paris faculty of arts are not well preserved. Both individual cases and the history of some of the university's colleges prove that humanism attracted a following and that the university was by no means closed to new influences although the official programme of instruction remained traditional. Even the exceedingly conservative Collège de Montaigu was open to humanist influence. In 1508–9 its principal, the theologian Noël Béda, who in the 1520s led the conservative attack on the humanists Lefèvre d'Etaples and Erasmus, ordered that students in the most advanced level of grammar should study the works of Jouenneaux and Dati and both the ancient grammar by Donatus and the humanistic one by Perotti (Moss, p. 42). Béda's regulation calls for these textbooks to be used in conjunction with the traditional versified grammar, the *Doctrinale* of Alexander of Villedieu, which humanist educational reformers despised. In all levels of grammar, students at Montaigu were expected to read short passages from one ancient prose author (probably Cicero) and from one poet, though the poet selected must not be one of those (Martial, parts of Ovid) whose books Béda prohibited on moral grounds. The general curriculum for the BA and MA degrees at Montaigu remained thoroughly traditional. After they finished grammar, students at Montaigu would hurry on to the study of the *Summulae logicales* of Petrus Hispanus, a book written in the inelegant shoptalk of medieval philosophers and theologians, which was the traditional authority used for the study of logic.

A significant by-product of Gaguin's humanist circle was a cautious effort to reform scholastic philosophy by replacing the defective thirteenth-century Latin translations of Aristotle with new versions made by Italian humanists. The crucial figure in this humanistic reform of Aristotelian philosophy was Jacques Lefèvre d'Etaples (*c.* 1460–1536), the first really great figure of French humanism. His initial goal was to expound the main ideas of Aristotle simply and directly, without giving attention to the many scholastic commentaries that had accumulated. In 1490 he wrote a straightforward explanation of the ideas presented in the first six books of Aristotle's *Metaphysics,* the only portion of that work that was taught at Paris. What makes it notable is its focus on Aristotle's main doctrines and its omission of the scholastic commentaries. Beginning in 1492 with a paraphrase of Aristotle's works on natural philosophy, he published a series of commentaries, paraphrases, and translations of other works of Aristotle, thus creating a fresh approach to the university's official philosophical authority.

But secular philosophy was not enough for this deeply pious scholar, who found Plato and the texts associated with Platonism even more attractive than Aristotle. In 1491–2 and again in 1500 and 1507 he travelled to Italy in order to learn more. The Venetian humanist Ermolao Barbaro, whom he met at Rome, was a major source of his plan to purify the Aristotelian tradition. At Florence he met both Marsilio Ficino and Pico della Mirandola and learned at first hand about ancient Neoplatonism and the Hermetic literature, which like them he regarded as sources of an ancient tradition of wisdom that both supplemented and confirmed Christian teachings. His religious concerns also led Lefèvre to study and publish the works of the Catalan mystic Ramón Lull and Dionysius the Areopagite, a sixth-century Greek Christian author whom both medieval and Renaissance thinkers mistakenly thought to be a first-century Athenian philosopher converted by the Apostle Paul himself. French scholars like Lefèvre found Dionysius especially attractive because they also confused him with St Denis, the patron saint of France. By the end of the century, Lefèvre had begun to attract a following of younger men who shared both his interest in humanism and his hunger for religious enlightenment. Within another decade, Lefèvre would extend these interests still further into the study of religion, producing a series of influential biblical studies. By that time also, Lefèvre had become the most famous French humanist and had begun to attract the patronage of powerful individuals in church and state as well as the growing hostility of conservative theologians who regarded him as a danger to traditional religion. There is little evidence that humanistic studies had made an impact at the level of grammar schools in France, though they certainly did so during the sixteenth century. Despite the important connections of Gaguin's humanist friends with the court, humanism probably had penetrated French society less deeply by 1500 than in Germany and the Netherlands.

The rise of humanism in England

England in the late fifteenth century has commonly been regarded as unusually advanced in the development of humanism. Yet much of this reputation rests on the fame of Thomas More; on the rather inflated reputation of John Colet, whom recent research has shown to be a humanist only in a very limited sense; and on the undisputed reputation of their mutual friend, the Dutch humanist Erasmus. The late fifteenth century did produce a number of English scholars who travelled to Italy for study and were attracted by humanism. Colet was one of these, being recorded at Rome in 1492. He seems to have stayed in Italy for three or four years, visiting Rome, Padua, and Florence. He was strongly attracted to Florentine Neoplatonism but apparently never succeeded in meeting Ficino. While in Italy, Colet studied the Church Fathers and especially the Neoplatonist philosophers, since this supposedly pious philosophy harmonized very well with his religious interests. Thus Colet was deeply influenced by his Italian studies, but those studies were exclusively religious and largely Neoplatonic and did not embrace ancient Latin and Greek literature either then or in the famous school he founded.

Other Englishmen of this period who studied in Italy were more open to secular studies and hence to the full range of humanism. One of these was Thomas Linacre (1460–1524), who went to Italy in 1487, studying Greek and Latin at Florence under Demetrius Chalcondyles and Angelo Poliziano, living for a time at Rome, and taking a doctorate in medicine at Padua in 1496. Linacre helped with the first Greek edition of Aristotle's works (5 vols., 1495–9) at Venice by the press of Aldus Manutius before returning to England in 1499. In England his connections were not with the universities but with the royal court, both as tutor to the royal children and as physician to King Henry VIII. Later in his career (1518) he was the founder of the Royal College of Physicians, and in his will he left endowments to found professorships in medicine at both universities. His scholarly publications included Latin translations of Greek medical and scientific authors and works on Latin grammar. Both through them and through his friends at court, he became an important figure in the development of English humanism. A somewhat older humanist was William Grocyn (d. 1519), who spent two years (1488–90) in Italy, studying under Poliziano at Florence and meeting the printer Aldus Manutius at Venice. Back at Oxford by 1491, he offered that university's first regular lectures in Greek. He was a close associate of Colet in 1499, when Erasmus met both of them there. In 1496 he received an ecclesiastical living in London. He delivered lectures in St Paul's that challenged the apostolic date of Dionysius the Areopagite, but he was generally conservative on religious questions and a pronounced supporter of Aristotle against the Platonists. Another Italian-educated humanist of this generation was William Latimer (1460–1545), educated at Oxford and at Ferrara, where he took the doctor of arts degree in 1502. He spent a second period in Italy, at Rome, in 1510–11 and in 1513 became tutor to the king's cousin Reginald Pole. Through Pole he was an important influence on a younger generation of English humanists who clustered about Pole at Padua in the 1520s and 1530s. Another influential product of Italian schooling was the grammarian William Lily (1468–1522), who studied at Rome, became first high master of the reorganized St Paul's School created by Colet, and wrote a simple and widely used Latin grammar. Lily began the process of quietly transforming the school from Colet's narrow focus on Christian authors into one of the most influential centres for the diffusion of humanistic studies in Tudor England. Though all of these scholars had connections with one or both of the English universities, they were also active in London and at the royal court, thus constituting a talented and well-connected group of Italian-educated humanists in the English capital. These men stand at the threshold of an age when humanism set the cultural style for the capital and the court.

Sir Thomas More (1478–1535), by far the most famous English humanist, was a figure of the second generation, not one of the founders. Although he studied briefly at Oxford, his humanistic interests developed during the years spent studying and practising law at the Inns of Court in the first decade of the new century. The capital and the royal court, far more than the universities, were the centres of the careers of all those who were the real founders of Tudor humanism, men such as Linacre, Grocyn, Latimer, and Lily; and Grocyn and Linacre instructed More in Greek. A shared enthusiasm for Greek language and literature was one of the foundations of the famous friendship between More and Erasmus. More's own humanistic studies found early expression in vernacular poems inspired by Petrarch's *Trionfi* and by a pseudo-Vergilian Latin epigram published by the German humanist Sebastian Brant. They are also reflected in his English translation of the *Life of John Picus, Erle of Myrandula*, written by Pico's nephew Gianfrancesco Pico. In this book More takes the elder Pico as the model of a learned Christian layman, just at the moment when More himself decided, after much soul-searching, not to become a monk but to marry and pursue a secular career. Despite his deep piety, one of the strongest classical influences on him was the biting, irreverent, and anti-religious satirist Lucian, some of whose dialogues he translated from Greek to Latin about 1505, when he and his house-guest Erasmus engaged in spirited competition to capture the spirit of Lucian in forms intelligible to readers of Latin. Though More justified his work on Lucian by referring to the author's criticism of human vice and folly, the true value of Lucian for him was the author's skill at laying bare the essential ambivalence of the human condition, torn (as More himself was) by the contending imperatives of worldly and spiritual goals.

This theme appears repeatedly in More's Latin epigrams, written between 1509 and 1519, and also in his literary masterpiece, the Latin dialogue *Utopia*. This book is not only a living example of Plato's influence but also a major work of political philosophy. It is also one of the handful of humanistic works still read (in translation, of course) today. Taken as a whole, *Utopia* deals with one of the central issues of all humanist thought, the moral responsibility of the educated man to participate in the world of politics and public affairs. Written in 1515 and 1516 and first published late in 1516 at Antwerp with the assistance of Erasmus, it was the foundation of More's substantial reputation among continental humanists. Erasmus secured prefatory letters of praise from other humanists but provided no public endorsement of his own. Perhaps his caution stemmed from its unconventional social and political ideas, but more likely he was embarrassed by his English friend's rather uneven Latin style, which was not quite up to the standards expected of the very best continental humanists (Marius 1984, pp. 238–41).

More's later career as a royal councillor changed the nature of his writing. From the mid-1520s he emerged as one of the principal English opponents of Luther. Yet the original foundation of his public career was not theology, nor even his mastery of English common law, but rather his reputation for classical learning and his skill at delivering extempore Latin orations at the formal reception of foreign ambassadors and other state occasions. The tragic circumstances of his martyrdom by Henry VIII have given dramatic emphasis to More's importance in the history of English humanism but have also created the false impression that his death destroyed the movement, which continued to flourish and was effectively co-opted into royal service by the most brilliant of early Tudor politicians, Thomas Cromwell.

English universities: change masked by immobility

The English universities were slow to embrace the new learning, but neither of them was so resistant to humanism as formerly was thought. As early as the decade 1454–64, a Milanese monk named Stefano Surigone lectured at Oxford on humanistic subjects. In the 1480s Cornelio Vitelli, a humanist who had failed to catch on as a teacher at Paris, enjoyed better success there, lecturing on grammar at New College and giving private lessons in Greek. At Cambridge the Franciscan friar Lorenzo Traversagni, though employed to teach theology, lectured on rhetoric and ethics between 1472 and 1482 (Leader 1988, p. 242). Probably not long after, Caius Auberinus, another Italian humanist, settled in Cambridge, where he was described as a *poeta* and earned part of his living by composing official letters sent in the name of the university to high-ranking officials. This is significant evidence that ability to write Latin in the new humanist style was beginning to be regarded as a practical and useful skill. Auberinus also received payments for lecturing on 'Terence' (a generic term for advanced grammar, not necessarily limited to the works of the Roman comic poet). Native Englishmen also received payment for courses on 'Terence' in the 1490s, including John Fisher, the future bishop of Rochester. These are all cases of individual efforts, but they show that both foreign visitors and Englishmen were able to promote humanistic subjects at both universities. Fisher is also important because of his ties to the royal family. From 1498 he was chaplain to Lady Margaret Beaufort, mother of King Henry VII and a generous patron of humanist educational efforts.

Although both universities retained a largely medieval curriculum throughout the Tudor age, already in the fifteenth century both were undergoing subtle changes. An important development that masked the degree of curricular change was the growing importance of the colleges, including a number of new ones, as centres for teaching, thus providing a venue where instruction could be less formal and less traditional than in the lectures specified in university statutes. Many of the major changes in the content of teaching occurred quietly and privately within certain colleges, without being reflected in any direct way in the statutes, thus creating a false impression of immobility and rigid conservatism that makes it hard to understand how such benighted universities could have educated so many humanists. In the medieval English universities, colleges had been limited to postgraduate students seeking degrees in the higher faculties. At Oxford the foundation of New College in 1379 marked an important departure by providing some places for undergraduates. This meant that instruction in undergraduate subjects had to be provided. The founder of New College, William of Wykeham, devised the practice that eventually became the universal solution to this need: the more senior scholars, students in the higher faculties who had already completed the liberal-arts programme, taught the undergraduates and were paid for doing so. In the second half of the fifteenth century, the new Magdalen College included thirty undergraduates supported from the endowment. It also added three salaried lecturers in theology, moral philosophy, and natural philosophy and provided that these lectures were to be open to all members of the university, not just members of Magdalen. Senior fellows were paid an additional fee for each undergraduate whom they tutored. Another innovation is that the statutes of Magdalen provided for acceptance of up to twenty additional undergraduates known as commoners, who were not supported from the endowment but paid for their own room and board and also for instruction by tutors selected from the senior fellows. Bishop William Waynflete, the founder, also attached to his college a grammar school to provide grounding in Latin grammar for boys who were not yet prepared to enter the university. Magdalen College School from its beginning emphasized the new kind of grammar-teaching based on reading of classical authors.

This growth of humanism in newly founded Oxford colleges accelerated in the sixteenth century, with Brasenose College (1512) also providing for fee-paying undergraduates taught by tutors who were studying theology, and for one salaried lecturer assigned specifically to teach undergraduates. Corpus Christi College (1517) included endowments for twenty undergraduates. In addition to tutors, undergraduate learning was advanced by the provision of three salaried college lecturers whose courses would be public (open to all members of the university), in the subjects of humanity (rhetoric), Greek, and theology. The theological lectures were intended for the senior fellows, and the statutes specified that the lecturer was not to expound the *Book of Sentences* (the medieval scholastic textbook) but was to expound the Scriptures, aided by the writings of the Latin and Greek Fathers. The lecturer for humanity was required to teach specific classical authors and also two of the major products of recent Italian humanism, the *Elegances* of Valla and the *Miscellanies* of Poliziano. Brasenose and Corpus Christi, of course, belong to the new century, but they are evidence of the growing importance of the colleges at Oxford, as well as clear evidence that humanistic studies were infiltrating the university even though the university statutes showed no evidence of change.

At Cambridge, King's Hall (1317) accepted undergraduates from its beginning, long before there was any influence by Italian humanism; and for purely financial reasons, other Cambridge colleges began accepting pensioners (youths who paid for room and board and also for tutoring by senior fellows) from the late fourteenth century. In 1436 Cambridge acquired a new college, originally called Godshouse and in 1506 reorganized as Christ's College. Although small, it was significant in that the founder's aim was to remedy the country's lack of competent masters of Latin grammar. Because it was conceived as principally an undergraduate centre, Godshouse also provided a salaried lecturer to teach the undergraduates, the first collegiate lecturer at either university. There were several other new collegiate foundations at Cambridge in the middle and later fifteenth century, including the ambitious scheme begun by Henry VI for King's College (1441). In most of these foundations, the provision of more competent teachers of grammar and preparation of better-educated parish priests were declared goals; but in the beginning, there was nothing specifically humanistic about them. At the very end of the century, the foundation of Jesus College, with undergraduate as well as graduate fellows and with a clear commitment to preaching and to the teaching of grammar, foreshadowed the important Cambridge foundations of the sixteenth century, especially because the patrons (including Lady Margaret Beaufort) were all wealthy laymen and all close to the growing humanist circle at the royal court.

The informality and flexibility of teaching in the colleges allowed humanism to develop almost unobserved at both Oxford and Cambridge. Within the general structure of both universities (and also in continental universities), only the three higher faculties traditionally depended on salaried or beneficed professors. Teaching in the faculties of arts was performed partly by advanced candidates for arts degrees and partly by a requirement that recently graduated masters of arts must remain at the university for a year after graduation and teach the courses required by the degree curriculum, without salary (but with the right to collect a fee from each hearer). This system of mandatory teaching was known in England as 'necessary regency'. It suffered from two defects. First, it assumed that all masters of arts were equally competent to teach all subjects – that there were no specialists. But this assumption was not valid for the new courses in humanistic grammar and rhetoric and in classical literature, which most prospective teachers were not prepared to teach. In the case of Greek or Hebrew, 'necessary regency' did not work at all: most masters of arts were not qualified to teach such subjects. This weakness of 'necessary regency' probably distressed only those who wanted significant curricular change, but the second defect of the system affected everyone. Many masters of arts simply were unwilling to teach, even though as a condition of receiving their degrees they had sworn to do so. After graduation with the MA degree, they wanted to get on with their future careers. At both universities by the fifteenth century, congregation (the governing assembly) faced a growing number of petitions for relief from the obligation to teach; and with increasing frequency the university granted such exemptions, usually in return for payment of a fee. The whole system was breaking down in practice. Either the required lectures were not given at all or they were given in superficial, desultory fashion. Yet neither university abolished this increasingly farcical system. The actual task of offering whatever required lectures could be provided devolved on those few who were remaining in the university after graduation in arts and on an aggrieved minority who could not afford the fees and fines levied on those who did not teach.

A partial solution to this problem was the transfer of more and more liberal-arts teaching to the colleges, both through the use of tutors and through the use of endowments or fees to provide salaried lecturers. But the public courses of the university still constituted the core of the requirements for the BA and MA degrees, and hence there had to be provision of sufficient lectures to allow undergraduates to qualify for degrees. The ultimate solution was to provide salaried professorships in arts. Oxford was slow to adopt this practice, even though fines and fees paid by those seeking exemption from teaching provided a possible source of revenue. Not until the second half of the sixteenth century did this simple, fair, and moderately effective practice come into use.

Cambridge faced the problem earlier and more directly. A statutory reform enacted in 1488 created salaried positions for three masters who would offer public lectures on arts subjects. Two of the subjects to be taught, logic and philosophy, were traditional; but the third, intended for students in their first two years at the university, was to be on books of 'humanity', that is, grammar and rhetoric. This change meant a reduction in the emphasis on logic, which formerly was taught during the first two years of study. In 1495 another new statute referred to the 'humanity' course as 'Terence', a term that implied teaching any classical literary texts. The cost of these three professorships was assessed on the heads of houses (colleges and hostels); and the Italian humanist Caius Auberinus, who had been teaching at Cambridge since 1483, was the person chosen to deliver the first 'Terence' lectures, with John Fisher holding the chair the following year.

By the beginning of the sixteenth century, therefore, humanistic studies had established a limited but real and growing presence at both universities, and at Cambridge but not at Oxford had even benefited from modest statutory changes that officially recognized the teaching of humanism. All of these lines of development would continue during the new century.

Education and public office

Closely related to the growth of humanistic studies at the two universities is a significant change in the status of public officials. Since its beginnings in the twelfth century, the top level of the monarchy's administrative officers had been members of the clergy, partly no doubt because in principle (if not always in reality) clergymen were free of the temptation to use their governmental positions to benefit their children, and also because clerical officials could be rewarded with ecclesiastical appointments at the expense of the church rather than from the royal treasury. At the outset, even more important was that the clergy constituted the only pool of educated manpower. By the later Middle Ages, however, lay noblemen and wealthy merchants were usually literate, though generally only in the vernacular. During the fifteenth century, ambitious laymen were seeking administrative office and were fully aware that they needed an education (not just vernacular literacy) to qualify. Throughout that century, educated lay officials became more numerous, though men in clerical orders still predominated. The Signet Office, founded by Richard II (1377–99), consisted only of laymen from its beginning. In addition, officials involved in English foreign relations, especially with the Italian states and the papacy, by the fifteenth century had to command a Latin style humanistic enough to avoid public embarrassment. So there was a strong tendency for ambitious social climbers, including youths from noble and gentle families, to seek a humanistic education. The increasing flow of commoners and pensioners into the colleges of both Oxford and Cambridge reflects these desires, and so does the tendency of collegiate tutors to read the works of classical authors and recent Italian humanists with their paying pupils. By the late sixteenth century, a whole unofficial curriculum had grown up in the colleges, embracing even modern languages and literatures, dancing, and swordsmanship, for young gentlemen who needed the gloss of education more than its substance.

Spanish humanism and public office

In Spain, the interest in Italian Renaissance literature reflected in the works of men like Santillana, Mena, and Cartagena continued to develop along two tracks, a vernacular one appealing to aristocrats and a parallel Latin one followed by university graduates who sought the career opportunities open to *letrados* (men of education) in the newly unified Spanish monarchy. The vernacular tradition found its greatest expression in the comedy *La Celestina* (1498) by the Salamanca law student Fernando de Rojas. The more learned and more classical direction is represented by Alfonso de Palencia (1423–90), who was encouraged in his youth by Cartagena and educated in Italy (*c.* 1447–53). His writings included a compendium of ancient Spanish place-names, several Spanish translations of ancient authors, a Latin–Spanish dictionary, and an unprinted history of contemporary Spain.

By far the most widely known Spanish humanist of the late fifteenth century was Antonio de Nebrija (1444–1522). Educated at Bologna and skilled in both classical Latin and Greek, he was the intellectual equal of any Italian humanist of his time, and just as skilled as they at promoting his own claim to be the restorer of true learning. Although he became royal historiographer in 1509, he spent most of his life as a university teacher at Salamanca and Seville, and later at Alcalá. His most influential work in his own lifetime was a Latin grammar (1481) that with remarkable ease supplanted the old medieval books. Though this grammar proved too old-fashioned to suit later generations, it was important because it abandoned the medieval practice of explaining grammar in terms of logical inferences rather than from classical literary usage. In the long run, an even more important product of his scholarship was his *Arte de la gramática castellana* (1492), the first systematic and scholarly grammar of any modern European language. He also applied his linguistic skills to the study of the Bible, a risky undertaking that led to the seizure of his notes by the inquisitor-general in 1506. Cardinal Ximénes de Cisneros, a powerful patron of humanistic studies, intervened to secure their release and eventually gave him a research appointment at the new University of Alcalá so that he could help with the famous Complutensian Polyglot Bible being edited there under the cardinal's patronage. Nebrija was a far more philologically advanced textual critic than his peers on this project; and while Cardinal Ximénes heard out his objections to the conservative tone of the edition under preparation, and even allowed him to publish separately his textual notes on the Bible, his pleas that the Latin text must be revised on the basis of the Greek and Hebrew originals were ignored.

The emergence of a unified Spain in the later fifteenth century created a need for well-educated royal officials. The first rulers of the unified monarchy, Ferdinand and Isabella, as well as their successors Charles V and Philip II, recognized this need and promoted higher learning. Until then, universities had played only a limited role in Spanish life; but after unification they became the sole source of the *letrados* or educated officials who dominated all aspects of administration except the military. In the century following unification, twenty-seven new universities were founded, bringing the total to thirty-three. After 1493, appointment to the highest administrative offices was restricted by law to those who had studied civil or canon law for at least ten years. Thus the Spanish universities were directly linked to the recruitment of high-level civil servants. In the late fifteenth and early sixteenth centuries, this royal interest was favourable to humanistic studies, though study of law benefited most directly. The link between university education (at least partly humanistic) and high office became typical of most northern countries in the sixteenth century, but in Spain its foundations had already been laid by 1500.

5   Triumph and disaster

By the beginning of the sixteenth century, the programme of humanistic studies and the dream of a renewal of 'civilized' learning and literature and an end of 'barbarism' had established themselves to some extent in all the major countries of western and central Europe. But the new learning, often viewed with suspicion because of its Italian origins and its reverence for pagan literature, had by no means become dominant north of the Alps. Its marginal and subordinate position was accurately reflected in the life of the universities (see Chapter 4). There were some masters in every faculty of liberal arts who criticized traditional textbooks and aspired to modify the curriculum leading to arts degrees in order to de-emphasize logic and give greater attention to humanistic studies. These men were able to offer lectures on classical authors and private lessons in Greek from time to time. A genuine and spontaneous interest in the new learning was growing up, and even in such a notoriously conservative university as Cologne, many students managed to lay the foundation of a mastery of classical Latin and ancient literature, even of Greek, that enabled them to become prominent humanists in later decades. Most humanists were perfectly content to work quietly on the margin of university life, teaching the works of classical or modern humanistic authors, and eventually working their way into more important positions as heads of colleges or attaining far more important positions in one of the three higher faculties that dominated the institutions and offered virtually the only stable, salaried or beneficed professorships.

Demands for a new education

But from the first decade of the new century, some humanists were becoming more outspoken and voicing openly their desire for a fundamental change in the liberal-arts curriculum, seeking to de-emphasize logic and disputations and to give much greater attention to classical Latin grammar, rhetoric, moral philosophy, and the reading of ancient authors. This development brought open conflict into academic life, as tradition-minded senior faculty, who controlled all universities, resisted the pressure for change. One modern study of German universities has concluded that while these conditions produced many controversial tracts, virtually all of the controversy moved in one direction: there were many humanist tracts conducting an active polemic against conservative opposition to humanistic studies, but virtually no countervailing attacks by conservatives against humanism. On the other hand, the traditionalists had little reason to engage in polemics. The curricular requirements they favoured were already embedded in the statutes of the university. Furthermore, academic etiquette forbade public agitation, or even public discussion, of matters determined internally by the faculty; and every person who matriculated took an oath promising to obey the rector, deans, and other academic officers. Anyone who publicly criticized the institution would be perceived to have violated this oath and might be subject to fines, arrest, and in extreme cases expulsion. When humanists eventually did carry their criticisms and demands for educational reform outside the private world of the faculty and began exerting external pressure through the ruling prince or city council, such action was bitterly resented (as it still would be in any faculty today); and faculties made formal or informal reprisals if they dared. Even more bitterly resented, perhaps, was the humanist who used his access to the new printing press to publish works that brought internal conflicts out into the open.

Historians of German humanism have noted a significant generational difference among humanists, with each of the three generations becoming more assertive and less amenable to tradition than its predecessor, culminating in the generation of radical young humanists who were swept into the early Reformation movement in the 1520s. In the case of the universities, earlier humanists had been junior, marginal, and powerless figures, barely tolerated by the older men who controlled the institutions. But by 1500, the new generation of young humanists had in mind a rather comprehensive programme of curricular reform for the faculties of liberal arts. They were no longer willing to see the subjects they wanted to teach regarded as non-essential frills, nor to endure their own inability to gain power, influence, and decent incomes because their subjects were excluded from the official programme for degrees.

Criticism of the traditional concentration on logic and training in dialectical skills, including the emphasis on participation in the formal disputations that were a significant part of the degree requirements, had been at least implicitly present in the lectures of pioneering humanists such as Peter Luder, but early humanists generally found it wiser to extol the benefits conferred by study of their subjects than to challenge the value of traditional subjects. Even the more outspoken young humanists of the early sixteenth century, though they dared to demand curricular reforms, did not intend to destroy all of the traditional scholastic programme, merely to make it less heavily focused on logic and more oriented towards linguistic and literary study.

Certain demands were voiced by nearly all would-be reformers. The first of these was for abandonment of the standard medieval manual of Latin grammar, the *Doctrinale*. Fifteenth-century humanists such as Hegius had objected to the speculative, logical kind of grammar associated with use of this book but had not demanded its abolition, seeking merely to supplement it with commentaries that emphasized the usage found in classical authors rather than logical explanations for the grammatical forms. An attempt to teach students to write better, more classical Latin through use of new manuals such as the *Rudiments of Grammar* by Niccolò Perotti might seem innocent enough, but in fact the existing system of grammar-study in universities was an integral part of a highly articulated curriculum in the liberal arts. Traditional modal (logical or speculative) grammar was designed not only to teach boys Latin but also to impart at the beginning of university study a thorough grounding in the terminology and categories basic to the dialectical method on which advanced academic study was founded. The traditional grammar courses introduced young students to the Aristotelian terms and concepts that were required in their future courses in logic and in the disputations that constituted a major portion of the arts curriculum and prepared them for similar academic exercises in the three higher faculties of law, medicine, and theology. A student who learned grammar from the book of Perotti would write a more classical Latin style and would probably be more familiar with ancient literature, but he would not be adequately prepared for his subsequent study of scholastic logic and philosophy (Heath, pp. 15–16, 18, 31).

At first the senior faculty simply ignored the movement for reform of grammar. But at Tübingen, outspoken agitation against the *Doctrinale* by the humanist lecturer Heinrich Bebel aroused opposition among conservative masters, and in 1505 the faculty required all masters to teach grammar from the *Doctrinale*. Similar efforts to block the spread of new humanistic grammars occurred about the same time at Freiburg-im-Breisgau and Leipzig; and in another blow at innovators, Cologne and other universities took steps to require use of the old textbooks and also to restrict or even ban lectures on poetry.

Poetry was a second issue of university reform, because another widely voiced demand of the younger humanists was for one or more regularly salaried lectureships on poetry, a subject that implied study of classical Latin literature. They also demanded creation of permanent university chairs (that is, salaried positions rather than positions dependent on student fees) in rhetoric, moral philosophy, and even history, and also in Greek. Instruction in these topics (except for Greek) was by no means rare and went back to the time of wandering poets like Peter Luder. But such instruction was sporadic, non-statutory, and remunerated poorly and irregularly. Now reformers demanded that such humanistic lectures be supported by permanent salaries. This would have meant that the humanistic subjects become part of the regular university programme, not just marginal frills. It might well imply that the statutes should be changed to require all degree candidates to attend such lectures. It certainly implied the untraditional employment of specialists, rather than the traditional system under which arts faculties presumed that all masters were equally qualified to teach all subjects.

A third demand of reformers at this period was the replacement of the traditional Latin translations of Aristotle by new translations made directly from the Greek in fifteenth-century Italy. This demand, like the demand for new grammar textbooks, did not seem very radical at first sight. Who, after all, could object to getting his Aristotle in more accurate form? But it had disquieting implications for the conservative academic mind. It raised the danger that some mere grammarian, fluent in Greek but perhaps unskilled in the intricacies of Aristotelian philosophy, would determine the meaning of the fundamental texts on which all serious scientific and philosophical discourse was based, a concern already expressed in the criticism of Leonardo Bruni's Aristotelian translations by the Spanish theologian Alonso de Cartagena (see p. 108, above).

Conflict over educational reform

These demands for educational reform in the liberal arts were partly successful. Even before the turn of the century, the emperor Maximilian had appointed the humanist Bernhard Perger as superintendent of the University of Vienna and had backed his efforts to enforce reform through governmental pressure, taking advantage of the university's need for legal exemptions and financial assistance. But stubborn obstruction by senior faculty members impeded the success of even modest reforms, such as a salaried lectureship in rhetoric and poetry, and adoption of Perotti's Latin grammar; and in 1500, Perger resigned his superintendency. As noted in Chapter 4, Conrad Celtis, the lecturer in humanities, in 1501 was made the head of a special College of Poets and Mathematicians in order to make his position in the university independent of control by the four traditional faculties. But despite some early successes, the new college faltered and faded away. Even at its peak, it constituted a kind of academic ghetto in which the two liberal-arts subjects most neglected in the usual curriculum, humanities and mathematics, were taught to a handful of students. Those who completed the literary courses were entitled to be crowned by the emperor himself as laureated poets. But what this really meant was that since their course of study did not cover the statutory subjects required for the BA and MA degrees, they were ineligible for any recognized university degree. The whole reform effort at Vienna foreshadows the experience of the new century, foretelling both the obstructionist tactics used by the faculties to thwart reform and the reliance of reformers on external political pressure.

Other German universities, notably Cologne and Heidelberg, were even more recalcitrant and rarely did more than provide for the occasional temporary appointment of a salaried humanist or, more frequently, authorization of unsalaried lecturers who tried to live from whatever fees they could levy on those who attended their courses. A few universities – Basle in 1464, Freiburg in 1471, Tübingen in 1481, Ingolstadt in 1476 – did provide for a salaried lecturer in poetry or rhetoric; but in the cases of Tübingen and Ingolstadt, this was done at the demand of the ruling prince and directly or indirectly at his expense. Leipzig and Erfurt, though they lacked salaried lectureships in rhetoric, seem to have been more successful than most of the others in promoting humanistic study, and Leipzig even made study of rhetoric a requirement for the MA degree. But the change at Leipzig was part of a complicated set of reforms pushed through in 1496 at the insistence of the duke of Saxony. The two new universities founded in eastern Germany, Wittenberg (1502) and Frankfurt an der Oder (1506), each had a salaried humanist lecturer from the beginning. Apparently by that time, a new university needed to provide some regular instruction in poetry and rhetoric in order to attract students: humanistic study had become fashionable. Yet the degree requirements at both universities remained fully traditional. All the subjects required for degrees were based on traditional scholastic texts, and no humanistic courses were required for degrees.

Individual masters of arts who tried to introduce change found little success. At Cologne in 1509, when young Hermann von dem Busche prepared to teach grammar using the *Ars minor* of the fourth-century Roman grammarian Donatus (a textbook used throughout the Middle Ages), a more conservative humanist, Ortwin Gratius, led the opposition on the grounds that this short manual was too elementary for university study. At Ingolstadt in 1506, not even strong pressure from the Bavarian government could force the faculty to drop use of a thirteenth-century modal grammar book and adopt the humanistic manual of Perotti. At the new University of Frankfurt, the faculty did agree to make rhetoric and grammar (based on a modern grammar rather than the *Doctrinale*) mandatory for students, and it granted official status to courses on poetry though apparently not making them requirements for degrees. But it also provided that these new courses should be taught by regular masters of the faculty, not by the two salaried humanists hired by the ruler. The lectures of these two men were listed separately from courses in the faculty of arts and were not even taught in the building of that faculty but rather in the faculty of law, a symbolic but very real demonstration that the faculty regarded these governmental appointees as outsiders.

At Leipzig between 1502 and 1511, Duke George of Saxony attempted a reform of his university. A serious effort, complete with surveys of faculty opinion and reports to the government by deans, did end the total exclusion of younger (and hence pro-humanist) masters from any voice in the governance of the faculty and gave them a better chance to teach humanistic subjects that were popular and hence produced more income from fees. In 1503 the duke himself financed creation of a salaried lectureship in poetry. But the senior faculty remained hostile to curricular change. The most common complaint elicited by the initial survey of opinions was not lack of humanistic courses but the high price of beer. In 1508 the faculty restricted the use of new translations of Aristotle and new manuals of grammar and logic, and the dean of the arts faculty bitterly charged that the reforms had led to a decline in academic standards. After nearly a decade of effort, the government accepted a compromise that left the young reformers with a few modest gains but also left the old curriculum intact and the conservative senior faculty in control.

A new development evidenced by the struggle at Leipzig was the emergence of a conscious hostility to humanism on the part of many of the senior professors. About the same period, in 1508, the theological faculty of Cologne formally condemned the teaching of pagan poets and certain modern poets (the Italian humanists) in the schools. It attempted to discourage humanistic curricular reforms in its traditional feeder schools, such as the cathedral school at Münster, by warning that students who had not studied the traditional textbooks would not be adequately prepared for university study. A similar mentality is shown in efforts of some Leipzig professors to persuade the duke of Saxony to restrict the study of poetry. A number of outspoken humanists were forced to leave their university positions. In some of these cases, other issues were involved, such as Hermann von dem Busche's indiscreet public remarks and notorious drunkenness; but the faculty's desire to get rid of humanistic troublemakers was a common theme. The conservatives did not go so far as to abolish all humanistic instruction, since parts of it were related to traditional academic studies. They were aware that courses in popular humanistic subjects attracted undergraduates, and since arts faculties were dependent on fees from students, they could not afford to forbid all humanistic teaching. But they were determined to contain it within strict limits and to make sure that both the teachers and the courses were subject to the authority of the faculty.

A wave of humanist triumphs

In the long run, however, the conservative scholastics were playing a losing hand. With the passage of time, the young masters who favoured greater attention to humanistic studies became senior masters. From about 1515, a gradual rise in the number and status of humanists began to produce tangible results and real reform at several German universities.

Erfurt and Wittenberg led the way. Erfurt is a good example of how humanism could gradually win the upper hand. Humanism had fared better there than at most other universities. By about the turn of the century, the rectors of all five of the colleges of the arts faculty were men who showed at least some sympathy for humanism. From about 1506, a talented and aggressive circle of humanist poets coalesced, led from outside the city by a highly respected humanist, Mutianus Rufus (1470–1527), who had studied at Erfurt, taught there briefly, taken a doctorate in law at Ferrara, but in 1503 accepted an ecclesiastical sinecure near-by at Gotha and thereafter devoted himself to a secluded life of classical scholarship. He produced no publications at all but nevertheless won a great reputation based on his active correspondence with other humanists throughout Germany. From about 1510 partisans of humanistic reform began winning the upper hand in elections to positions in the faculty of arts, though the electors carefully avoided putting into office any of the outspoken group closely linked to Mutianus. One old textbook of logic was abandoned, and some minor changes were introduced in the teaching of both logic and grammar. The elected faculty council in 1515 authorized use of new humanistic translations of Aristotle and also decreed that lecturers should deal with the text of Aristotle, not the traditional scholastic commentaries. The council also approved the replacement of the elementary Donatus with *Donatus Improved*, the work of an Italian humanist, and the abandonment of the *Doctrinale* in favour of a grammar by a humanist of Tübingen, Johannes Brassicanus. Several other medieval textbooks were replaced by humanistic or classical works in the same period. Though the official structure of the curriculum was not changed, these reforms marked a significant advance for humanism at Erfurt.

The reforms of 1515 by no means satisfied the younger masters of arts. The changes left the arts curriculum a patchwork of old and new, in which the elementary subjects like grammar and rhetoric no longer prepared students to advance to the study of logic and philosophy that would still dominate their final years of study. In 1518 the respected and moderate humanist Maternus Pistoris was elected dean of the arts faculty. About this period also, three influential teaching positions in the largest college were filled with outspoken humanists. In 1519, the faculty's board of electors chose as rector the young humanist Jodocus Jonas, in part perhaps because at that very time he was in Louvain to meet Erasmus, the scholar most admired by young German humanists. Indeed, all three electors were sympathizers with humanism, a clear indication of the power of humanism within the institution. Led by these three, the general faculty created a commission of eight to consider reform.

The reform plan that they proposed, though still preserving elements of the old philosophical tradition and retaining Aristotle as the central text for philosophical subjects, was strikingly original. In liberal arts, there would now be seven salaried professorships, in the fields of Latin grammar, moral philosophy, dialectics and physics for undergraduates, dialectics and physics for MA candidates, mathematics and metaphysics, rhetoric, and Greek. Logic and metaphysics, the heart of the old curriculum, were still required for degrees, but the real revolution was in the addition of the central subjects of humanism – grammar, rhetoric, and moral philosophy – as required subjects. Also revolutionary was the abandonment of rotation of teaching assignments among the masters of arts. The seven salaried positions were to be held by specialists, each of whom concentrated on his particular subject. While from a modern perspective, it is obvious that the reform preserved much of the medieval programme, to contemporaries it seemed revolutionary. In his letters, the new rector, Jonas, described the new system in terms of the ideals of Erasmus, who had become the cultural hero of this generation of German humanists.

Efforts to carry out this reform continued during 1520 and 1521. Unfortunately for the reformers, their continuing ability to dominate the election of rectors and deans did not automatically translate into completed reforms. Erfurt was a municipal foundation, without a princely patron to call on for help; and the disastrous economic condition of the city meant that the city council could not provide extra money to finance the seven salaried professorships. A further difficulty arose out of the incipient Protestant Reformation. Almost all of the younger humanists and most of the students, initially at least, identified Luther's reform programme with the programme of Erasmus and with their own plans for reform of the university. When Luther passed through Erfurt in April

1521 on his way to the famous hearing before the emperor at the Diet of Worms, the poet Crotus Rubianus, elected rector for the 1520–1 winter semester, led a large and enthusiastic delegation to escort him into the city, where he was hailed as a heroic figure. But this welcome was the work of the young. Most of the senior professors in the higher faculties had already decided that Luther was a dangerous heretic. Thus the university and the entire city were bitterly divided. Rioting by the students and legalistic obstruction by the city council thwarted the efforts of the papal legate, Johannes Eck, to publish the papal bull excommunicating Luther; and attempts to excommunicate some clergy who had joined in welcoming Luther produced a violent riot directed against the persons and homes of many priests. Months of disorder followed. Then in the autumn of 1521 plague struck the city. The combination of financial weakness, violence, and plague caused virtually all of the young masters of arts to leave town; and though many of them hoped to return, few did. The young scholars who represented the living element in the university, including all of the notable local humanists, were gone forever. The faculty who remained were mostly the older men, holders of ecclesiastical prebends that provided financial support for the three higher faculties. Enrolment at all German universities collapsed in the mid-1520s, but while some universities revived after a few years, Erfurt never did. Though they were not in any sense the cause of the decline, the ambitious humanistic reforms of 1519–21 foundered amidst the collapse of the whole institution.

Luther and academic reform

By contrast, the humanist breakthrough at the University of Wittenberg not only endured but became a model for many other German universities. Two causes explain the difference. First and most important, the ruler of Electoral Saxony initiated the whole reform, carefully ensured that something was actually accomplished, and deployed not only his power but also his money to guarantee success. Second, the reform gained immeasurably because Martin Luther demonstrated qualities of leadership that quickly made him the unchallenged though unofficial leader of the academic community. The Elector in 1516 ordered his close adviser Georg Spalatin to investigate the university's resources, teaching activities, and productivity in terms of degrees granted. This demand gave the faculty an opening to put forward their own programme for change and also for increased financial support. Luther emerged as the leader of those who urged significant reform in directions already proposed by humanists.

Martin Luther was most assuredly no humanist. Still, he had belonged to an undergraduate generation for whom some exposure to the delights of classical literature and the aspirations of humanist educational reformers was unavoidable. He himself lamented that because of his old-fashioned education he had not developed the elegant Latin style that was becoming fashionable. Even so, his own letters in the early part of his career teem with stylish allusions and quotations drawn from classical sources. During the second decade of the century, Luther was working out a striking new approach to Christian theology that from the end of 1517 precipitated a great religious upheaval, the Protestant Reformation. As a child of a Renaissance generation, he inevitably conceived his new Evangelical theology as a restoration of the original and ancient Christian doctrines expressed in the writings of the early Church Fathers but above all in the Bible. Quite accurately, he sensed the affinity between his desire to restore true and ancient Christian doctrine and the desire of his humanist friends to restore ancient language and literature. Long before he had developed his new theology, indeed even before he had completed his doctorate, he had also come to share the humanists' disdain for the scholastic philosophical and theological tradition in which he had been educated. He also realized early that the philological–historical approach to the study of the Bible and the Church Fathers that was emerging in the humanistic scholarship of Lefèvre and Erasmus was the key to a deeper insight into the meaning of Christian revelation. He himself learned Greek well enough to consult biblical and patristic texts in that language; and he learned some, though not nearly so much, Hebrew for study of the Old Testament. Early in his teaching career he began using the New Testament commentaries and paraphrases of Lefèvre; and when Erasmus' edition of the Greek New Testament came off the press in the spring of 1516, Luther promptly bought a copy, discarded his old teaching notes, and began using the Greek Bible as the textual foundation of his lectures. Although he never exactly became a humanist, he used humanistic scholarship, and he most assuredly did cease to be a scholastic.

The attack on scholasticism

When the Elector's pressure to reform Wittenberg presented the opportunity, Luther became the deliberate and relentless executioner of scholasticism, not only in theology but also in the liberal arts. His effectiveness was magnified by the close and trusting relationship he had established with Spalatin, the Elector's adviser. As early as 1516, he had concluded that Aristotelian rationalism was no aid to the understanding of Christian theology, which must be based instead on a close textual study of the

Bible, guided by the linguistic procedures of Erasmian humanism. In 1516, 1517, and even 1518, Martin Luther really had no comprehensive plan for reform of the church. But he had a well-defined, forcefully stated, and radical plan for the reform of his own university; and he realized that the reform of theological education he had in mind could not advance unless accompanied by an equally drastic reform of the curriculum in the liberal arts. Although Luther was not a humanist, he certainly knew how to use the language of humanist educational reformers. His letters to the electoral court expressed his desire 'to destroy barbarism everywhere' and ultimately to reform all universities.

By the spring of 1518, just when Luther's famous attack on indulgences was beginning to attract attention to him as a religious reformer, he was already leading the Wittenberg faculty towards a comprehensive series of curricular reforms so fully dominated by humanistic ideas that they help to explain why humanists everywhere in Germany embraced his religious ideas without even considering the possibility that they might be heretical. New, permanent, and salaried professorships of Greek and Hebrew were to be founded alongside the existing humanistic course in Latin grammar. There would also be new lectures on the *Natural History* of Pliny the Elder (for natural philosophy, replacing Aristotle) and Quintilian (the ancient rhetorician), and new courses on mathematics. Outmoded courses on Aristotle, Petrus Hispanus, and Guillaume Tartaret would be abolished. Although Aristotle proved indispensable for some subjects, even these courses were to be of the new humanist sort, based on modern translations by Italian humanists, focused directly on the original text, and stripped of the traditional emphasis on the medieval commentaries. A prominent humanist, Johannes Aesticampianus, was hired to teach the new course on Pliny. The electoral government readily provided the additional funds required to bring the new professorships into being – precisely the kind of support that the Erfurt reformers lacked. The Elector Frederick wrote in person to the senior figure of German humanism, Johann Reuchlin, begging him to help find men qualified to teach the new languages. Reuchlin responded by sending his own great-nephew, Philip Melanchthon, who was dismayingly youthful but had been carefully educated under his uncle's guidance, to fill the chair of Greek.

This was a brilliantly successful appointment. Melanchthon's inaugural lecture at the end of August 1518 was a stirring manifesto in favour of humanistic educational ideals; and as Luther became increasingly preoccupied by religious controversies, Melanchthon became not only his theological supporter but also his expert on educational reform. He travelled widely and advised German towns and princes on the transformation of schools and universities into institutions that were both Lutheran and humanist. He wrote a great number of textbooks and manuals that may not have been intellectually creative but (perhaps for that reason) provided teachers and students with books well suited to the social and intellectual conditions of the time. His books were so successful that in fields like rhetoric and natural philosophy they were adopted even in Catholic parts of Germany.

Wittenberg is not commonly called a 'trilingual college', a title usually reserved for the *Collegium Trilingue* at Louvain, founded at almost the same time. Yet Wittenberg by the end of 1518 was at least as fully trilingual in programme as Louvain or the College of San Ildefonso at Alcalá in Spain (founded in 1508). Indeed, Wittenberg had a considerable advantage over Louvain, since its new language courses were an integral part of the curriculum in the faculty of arts, while at Louvain the Trilingual College was a separate institution whose connection to the university at large soon became a matter of controversy and whose courses were not readily acknowledged as qualifying students for regular academic degrees.

Despite these successes, Luther did face many problems in carrying out his reforms. It was easier to introduce new programmes with new money than to abolish old ones and reallocate resources. The old courses on Aristotle's logic and physics continued to be taught in double offerings, since Wittenberg had always offered students the choice of studying those subjects in either the Thomist style, using textbooks and teachers favourable to that tradition, or the rival Scotist style. Luther aspired to abolish the old as well as introduce the new subjects; and in the autumn of 1518 he urged that the required course in Aristotle's *Ethics* (which he had reluctantly taught in 1509) should be made optional, that a study be made of ways to incorporate the new courses into the degree requirements, and that in order to save money and avoid duplication, the traditional parallelism of Thomist and Scotist courses should be abolished, with the teacher who had been teaching Thomist logic assigned to lecture instead on a humanistic subject, the *Metamorphoses* of the Roman poet Ovid. In this way, the sacrosanct courses in Aristotle's logic and physics would still be offered so that students could qualify for degrees, but with half the teaching effort; and the whole programme in liberal arts would become more linguistic and literary in nature, exactly what humanist reformers desired. Luther was even able to persuade faculty colleagues to petition for permission to stop teaching their customary courses and to develop new teaching specialities in the humanities. The university's most prominent Thomist and Scotist theologians joined with Luther in petitioning for the abolition of the separate Thomist lectures. The combination of electoral power and money with Luther's leadership carried most of his proposals through to adoption.

Luther did not immediately get all that he wanted. In his own faculty, theology, he conceded that since entering students did not yet have adequate training in Greek and Hebrew, the traditional textbook, Peter Lombard's *Book of Sentences*, should be retained for the time being, though the Bible should immediately become the primary object of study. In general, the years 1519–21 were not favourable for additional academic reforms. Both Luther and the electoral government were preoccupied with the religious and political consequences of Luther's emergent religious movement. But Melanchthon succeeded in introducing some modest additional reforms in 1521. Much of the medieval curriculum survived until the 1530s, when the university was drastically reorganized under a new ruler. Nevertheless, by the summer of 1521 Wittenberg had been changed from a scholastic and Catholic university into a humanist and Evangelical one. Education in the faculty of arts was no longer based predominantly on logic and philosophy but on ancient languages and literature. Luther made it quite clear that the motive behind his adoption of humanistic education was his conviction that the scholastic method of applying Aristotelian philosophy to Christian theology was a ruinous mistake and had inevitably given rise to the unsound theology of the late medieval church. Yet he achieved far more for the realization of humanistic educational reform than any of his contemporaries, even Erasmus.

Reception of his religious doctrines was eased by his leading role in academic reform. For the young Dominican friar Martin Bucer, already an admirer of Erasmus, who heard Luther debating in favour of his new theology at Heidelberg in April 1518, and who had an opportunity to speak privately with Luther about the educational reforms at Wittenberg, Luther was just like Erasmus – even better, perhaps, since 'what Erasmus merely suggests, [Luther] . . . teaches openly and frankly'.

Before the end of the sixteenth century, and at many places before Luther's death in 1546, the Evangelical religion and Wittenberg-style university reform would triumph at Heidelberg, Leipzig, Rostock, Greifswald, Tübingen, Frankfurt an der Oder, and new Protestant universities like Marburg and Jena. Some German universities held out for Catholic orthodoxy: Cologne, Freiburg-im-Breisgau, Ingolstadt, Mainz, and Vienna; but even these were affected by the swing towards humanism. The ones that yielded most reluctantly to the new educational fashion suffered a long period of decline, and many of the Catholic universities that came back from that decline (Cologne, for example) did so only after mid-century, when their liberal-arts faculty was partly or wholly taken over by the new Jesuit order, which had developed its own strictly orthodox version of the humanistic educational programme.

The press and public controversy

This chapter has dwelt on humanist penetration of the universities because remarkably little attention has been given to the mechanisms by which the new culture made its way into transalpine Europe. The schools and universities clearly were the principal way. Despite the numerous and much-discussed controversies that did break out in the early sixteenth century, humanistic culture entered the north of Europe more truly through quiet and gradual penetration of education than through the fanfare of public controversy. It is true, however, that some public clashes did occur and that some of these attracted much attention among the educated classes and shaped popular attitudes that generally favoured the new and discredited the old education. There is virtually no anti-humanist polemic in early sixteenth-century Germany. Nevertheless, the rather one-sided polemical literature at least created the image (even among contemporaries) of embattled humanists bravely fighting against reactionary scholastic theologians and monks.

Germany was the scene of a number of controversies that attracted the attention of the Latin-reading elite. In these controversies, the emergent humanist sodalities developed a heightened self-awareness and established networks of literary friends, linked by social visits and by an active correspondence, that made humanism a real force in German culture. German humanists gradually discovered the potential of the printing press for shaping public opinion. Almost from its beginning, the printing industry had employed humanists as editors and translators and as authors of tracts, poems, dedications, and polemics. Although most humanists still supported themselves as teachers in schools and universities, the print-shop became an alternative focus for their careers and hence also for both learned and popular culture. The universities eschewed open controversy and, being organized as self-contained corporations, conducted decision-making and disagreement mostly in private. That, indeed, is why there was no anti-humanistic polemic: it was contrary to the etiquette of the academic establishment to conduct debate publicly.

In the early sixteenth century, however, some humanists with connections to the printing industry discovered that they could continue arguments outside the academic world and could appeal to a broader public opinion by writing tracts, poems, songs, and satires for publication. Not only academic decisions but also the policies and actions of ecclesiastical authorities could be called into question by use of the press. Thus the press became a medium for public discussion of academic and ecclesiastical issues. Humanist controversialists invented this practice, but Martin

Luther was the first to discover and exploit the truly revolutionary potential of appealing to public opinion through the press.

This use of the press began with a number of controversies in the academic world, none of them of much intrinsic interest except to the parties involved. Close study of several of them suggests that the real issues were complex and that the divisions did not coincide with the lines dividing humanists from scholastic academics. The incidents do demonstrate that in the first decade of the century, humanists were still outsiders, not taken seriously by most of the academic community. What is most significant about these petty quarrels is the tendency of both sides to resort to the press.

The deeper issues raised by this practice of turning to the press to continue academic controversies outside the academy became clear in a conflict that took place in Cologne between 1507 and 1508. The Italian jurist Peter of Ravenna joined the law faculty of Cologne in the summer of 1506. He formed close friendships with local jurists and humanists, both in the university and among the local elite that dominated the city council. Early in 1507, however, the theological faculty moved to censure him. In his lectures, Peter had criticized the local practice of denying Christian burial to condemned felons and leaving their bodies displayed on the gallows even when they had been penitent and had been absolved by a priest. Rulers who followed this practice, he charged, were guilty of mortal sin. The theologians called a hearing before the whole university and charged that his teaching was scandalous, unheard of, and 'offensive to pious ears'. A faculty commission warned him that if he continued to teach such doctrines, publicly or privately, in speech or by writing, further disciplinary measures would be taken against him. The exact motives of this bitter attack remain unclear. Peter was not speaking as a humanist (though he did have interest in humanistic studies) but as a jurist qualified in both civil and canon law. He also spoke as a pious Italian Catholic who found the abuse of felons' bodies offensive and contrary to the legal rights of penitent sinners. He conceived the quarrel as a conflict between himself as an expert in canon law and a presumptuous theologian, Jakob von Hochstraten, whom he regarded as grossly ignorant of the laws of the church. He also believed that envy of his fame and popularity contributed to the attack. Very probably, a major cause was resentment by German academics of an Italian who presumed to criticize local custom.

Peter's response to the faculty commission's threat was to restate his opinion in a revised edition of his highly regarded textbook on canon law. When he then faced a published attack by the Dominican theologian Hochstraten, he also refuted that attack in an appendix to an edition of his popular dictionary of legal citations. Eventually Peter realized that he had no future in Cologne and moved to the University of Mainz in April 1508. The truly significant point about this inherently minor conflict is Peter's resolute and effective use of the printing press, and his appeal to the entire educated world beyond Cologne, in his defiance of the university's demand for unquestioning submission. He had discovered a secret – the power of the press to transfer a conflict from the forum of the university to the forum of educated public opinion. It was a way that others soon learned to follow.

The Reuchlin scandal

These limited and petty local conflicts were eclipsed by the famous Reuchlin case. Overfield has demonstrated convincingly that this controversy was not, as earlier historians thought, a confrontation between German humanists and a regressive, unenlightened scholasticism, even though its central figure, Johann Reuchlin, was the outstanding German humanist of his generation. The real issue was anti-Semitism. The conflict grew out of the efforts of a fanatical Jewish convert, Johannes Pfefferkorn, to enforce an imperial mandate (1508) for the confiscation of virtually all Hebrew books. Although Pfefferkorn secured the backing of conservative Cologne theologians, including the Dominican inquisitor, Jakob von Hochstraten, the attack was directed against the Jews, not against humanism. The archbishop of Mainz, however, raised questions about the legality of Pfefferkorn's actions; and he and the emperor Maximilian sought expert opinions. Reuchlin, who was Germany's leading expert on Hebrew language and religious literature, was one of those consulted. All of the opinions except Reuchlin's favoured confiscation, but in 1511 the emperor overruled the majority and withdrew the mandate he had given to Pfefferkorn. Reuchlin himself was by no means free of anti-Jewish prejudice, but he did believe that Jewish religious literature contained knowledge of great potential value to Christian theologians and could even provide support for efforts to convert the Jews through persuasion. But his major objection to Pfefferkorn's project was based on law. Both as residents of the German empire and simply as human beings having rights under natural law, the Jews had a legal right to their property, including their books, and to continued existence as a religious community. His most telling objection to Pfefferkorn's campaign was that it was contrary to natural justice and to imperial law.

Infuriated by his defeat, Pfefferkorn in 1511 published a slanderous book in German, *Hand-Mirror,* in which he attacked Reuchlin personally, charging that he had harmed the church and aided Jewish perfidy because he had been bribed by rich Jews. Probably unwisely, Reuchlin replied in kind with a vernacular book, the *Eye-Mirror*. A Cologne theologian then published his own attack on this book. A series of replies and rebuttals followed. Although Pfefferkorn continued publishing, the Cologne theological faculty now took over the leading role. They secured an imperial order suppressing Reuchlin's books, and also issued formal condemnations of the *Eye-Mirror* by their own faculty and by the theological faculties of Louvain, Mainz, Erfurt, and Paris. Though himself a party to the dispute, Hochstraten, acting as inquisitor, now summoned Reuchlin to appear before his own inquisitorial court to answer charges of heresy. A protracted legal case followed. Reuchlin appealed from Hochstraten's court to Pope Leo X, and in 1514 the German bishop to whom the pope had remanded the case for adjudication issued a definitive ruling in Reuchlin's favour. The Cologne theologians appealed to Rome, however; and in 1520, when Martin Luther's teachings had changed the attitude at Rome concerning German affairs, the curia issued a condemnation of the *Eye-Mirror*. Reuchlin was not declared a heretic, but his opinions were condemned as dangerous, and he was forced to pay the very substantial court costs. To this judgement, as an obedient Catholic, he submitted promptly.

At no point in this lengthy legal process, accompanied by a flood of bitter pamphlets and tracts, was the value or lawfulness of humanistic studies an issue. The issue always was whether Reuchlin had harmed the church by being unduly favourable to the Jews. The leading figures of German humanism were mostly silent, partly because they shared the anti-Jewish prejudice of the Cologne theologians and partly because they did not want to become involved in a nasty squabble. Erasmus, who was now the most famous of all European humanists, remained cautiously silent, partly because he personally doubted the value of the Talmud, the Cabala, and indeed of Hebrew studies in general, and partly because his own programme of gradual religious reform through scholarship and education might be compromised by his involvement in this contentious wrangle. He did intervene to the extent of writing private letters to two influential Italian cardinals, expressing admiration for Reuchlin's character and also sorrow that such a good man's old age was troubled by this regrettable quarrel, hoping that the whole dispute could just be silenced. Even Reuchlin himself, though denying that the *Eye-Mirror* was full of improprieties, conducted his own defence mainly by collecting and publishing two volumes of letters that were really testimonials to his good character.

The 'obscure men': radical satire

But not all humanists felt so uninvolved. Many humanists – even Erasmus and Mutianus Rufus – were deeply offended by the Cologne theologians' unrelenting attacks on a man whom they regarded as both learned and good. A few humanists resented these attacks so bitterly that they concocted a myth – a myth that has dominated interpretation of the whole incident ever since – that the attack on Reuchlin was part of a conspiracy by scholastic theologians to destroy the whole humanist movement and to thwart any serious effort at religious reform. The principal expression of this myth was a scurrilous satire, *Letters of Obscure Men*, first published anonymously in 1515. This satire pretended to be a collection of letters from various (mostly fictitious) scholastic theologians and monks to Ortwin Gratius, a Cologne humanist who had sided with the theologians and had translated several of Pfefferkorn's tracts into Latin. These suppositious correspondents often bear ridiculous and derogatory names, names that imply base social origins or depraved moral habits ('Piggy', 'Honeylicker', 'Winefull', 'Shitloader', 'Bottleclinker', 'Sheepmuzzle') or else names that simply sound ridiculous to the German ear (Gowk, Unckebunck, Grapp, Kutz, Stompff). They comment on the Reuchlin case and while so doing show themselves and their friends the Cologne theologians to be ignoramuses, sycophants, and immoral hypocrites. The letters also refer to earlier controversies involving humanists such as Peter of Ravenna, leaving the impression that all such conflicts were parts of a conscious plan to persecute humanists everywhere. The letters betray a laughable incompetence in logical reasoning and offer a humorous parody of the scholastic style of Latin that the humanists long had ridiculed.

These scurrilous, obscene, and coarsely humorous letters were actually the work of a cabal of radical young humanists. Three men were the chief conspirators. The Erfurt-educated poet Crotus Rubianus may have originated the whole concept of a series of fictitious letters and is thought to be the principal author, perhaps the sole author, of the original collection issued in 1515, which is marked by light, playful humour and mostly avoids derogatory reference to actual persons. Crotus had the aid of the humanistic knight Ulrich von Hutten, who is generally thought to be the author of the seven new letters added to the second edition in 1516 and of nearly all of the extensive second part added in 1517. These letters are more aggressive, more libellous, more clearly intended to discredit all scholastic theologians. They often use the names of real individuals. In particular, they assiduously drop the names of many real humanists (including Erasmus) who are claimed as defenders of Reuchlin. Thus they associate the whole humanist community with Reuchlin's cause, to an extent far greater than was actually true. A few of the letters in Part Two are by a different hand, probably Hermann von dem Busche. All three of these humanists were close friends and all three had spent part of their careers in Cologne. Their satire is all the more devastating because they knew both the university and the individual targets of their satire from first-hand experience.

The furore over Reuchlin did make many humanists suspect that a concerted attack on humanistic studies was being plotted. It also further extended the use of the printed pamphlet to shape public opinion. While many of the related publications were in Latin, both the *Hand-Mirror* and the *Eye-Mirror* came out first in German, foreshadowing a tendency for controversies among the learned to spill over to a broader, less sophisticated reading public. The *Letters of Obscure Men,* which was not translated, must have confirmed the resentment and suspicion that many humanists felt against the smug arrogance of the academic establishment and the claim of conservative monks and theologians to hold the power of defining heresy in accord with their own interests. The *Letters of Obscure Men* did worse than attack the conservatives: it made them seem ridiculous and contemptible. To be laughed at is far more dangerous than to be denounced, and the anarchical disrespect expressed in the *Letters* may help to explain why many German humanists paid no heed to the early warnings from the theologians of Cologne, Paris, and Louvain that Martin Luther was a dangerous heretic.

The issue of church reform

It has been impossible to discuss either the spread of humanistic educational reform or the emergence of public controversy without referring to the Protestant Reformation. In fact, the growing influence of humanism in northern Europe came to be closely linked with the issue of reforming the institutional church and arousing a deeper, more genuine spirituality among the general population. This reformist movement led to the Protestant Reformation, whose principal leaders were nearly all either humanists or theologians influenced by humanism; but it led just as surely to the Catholic Reformation of the later part of the sixteenth century.

The need for reform of the church had been widely acknowledged for more than a century before the outbreak of the Protestant Reformation late in 1517. Calls for reform were often voiced by Italian humanists, but a specific reform programme was not part of Quattrocento humanism, nor did most of the reform agitation of that century have a clear connection to humanism. It is therefore usual, and probably correct, to regard greater concern with religious reform as a distinctive characteristic of northern humanism. A close look at the pioneers of northern humanism suggests, however, that religious reform did not hold a central place among the concerns of transalpine humanists until after 1500. Figures like Peter Luder and Conrad Celtis, with their secular goals and irregular life-styles, do not reflect a humanism that was directly concerned with reform. In France, the most important academic and spiritual reforms at the end of the fifteenth century were the work of puritanical moralists like Jean Standonck, whose intellectual connections were with a very conservative and traditionalist scholasticism, not with humanism in any form. The early leader of Paris humanists at the end of that century, Robert Gaguin, was certainly a distinguished monk; but he did not relate his scholarship in any special way to reform of the church or a general spiritual revival. Much of his career involved diplomatic missions for the French king, and his literary work concentrated on French translations of Caesar and Livy and the composition of a history of the Franks, not on religious texts or the study of Christian Antiquity. The greatest classical scholar in early sixteenth-century France, Guillaume Budé, appears to have had no connection with the movement for evangelical reform that grew up in the 1520s. Until the 1530s, his scholarship dealt with Roman law, Roman coinage, Roman material culture, and Greek philology.

Secular themes also dominated the scholarly writings of most of the early English humanists. Linacre's career was in medicine and the editing of medical texts; the other famous early names in English humanism were scholars of classical languages and literature, not religious reformers. Even Thomas More, though a deeply religious man, dealt exclusively with pagan authors or with political and social issues in his humanistic works. His publications dealt with religion only in the 1520s, when he emerged not as a humanist but as an outspoken Catholic opponent of Lutheran heresy. The one great exception is John Colet, but his religious interests, while undoubtedly dominant, took a direction that identifies him as hardly a humanist at all. His idea of reforming religion through better education was akin to the ideas of some humanists; but his particular educational reforms showed hostility to most classical literature; and his reformed St Paul's School became humanistic only because the first headmaster and his successors were able gradually to subvert Colet's original curricular prescriptions.

The invention of Christian humanism

In short, there was not necessarily an intimate connection between humanism and the agitation for spiritual renewal and for reform of the institutional church. That connection had to be invented, and it was invented during the opening decades of the sixteenth century. But it was not inevitable, and even after 1500 a number of major northern European humanists had little or no relation to the reform movement. The true programme of Christian humanism, which conceived humanistic studies as an essential part of religious renewal and concentrated on both pagan and Christian Antiquity as a source of inspiration, was essentially the creation of two men, the French humanist Jacques Lefèvre d'Etaples (*c.* 1460–1536) and the Dutch humanist Desiderius Erasmus of Rotterdam (*c.* 1467–1536), with Erasmus being by far the more important.

Lefèvre was the earlier of the two to achieve widespread reputation. His development in the 1490s as a humanistic interpreter of Aristotle and his attraction to Florentine Neoplatonism have been discussed in Chapter 4. These Platonic interests led him to the works of the late patristic author known as Dionysius the Areopagite, who was mistakenly thought to be a contemporary of the Apostles. This allegiance in turn led Lefèvre towards a growing interest in all patristic literature. In 1499 he published an edition of Dionysius' works, and the volume also contained the first published Latin texts of the genuinely early patristic authors St Ignatius and St Polycarp. Other patristic editions followed. All of these works attracted him as sources of spiritual wisdom, suitable for bringing the worldly modern church back to the purity and power characteristic of the ancient church and thereby causing a veritable Renaissance of Christianity.

Beginning about 1508, these religious interests took a strong turn towards study of the Bible. In 1509 Lefèvre published the *Fivefold Psalter*, a parallel edition of several ancient Latin texts of the Psalms. This publication was widely hailed in both France and Germany, and it was one of the first products of the new biblical humanism to be used by Martin Luther. Lefèvre and his closest disciples also turned to the New Testament, publishing commentaries on the Gospel of John and on the Lord's Prayer, and above all, the Epistles of St Paul. The commentary on Paul was based on the traditional Latin text but was paralleled by a new Latin translation made by Lefèvre from the Greek. This challenge to the traditional interpretation of Paul's epistles attracted much attention following its publication in 1512. Young and progressive theologians, even men trained in the scholastic way like Luther, drew heavily on this work until the far more impressive researches of Erasmus pushed it off the market.

The attractiveness of Lefèvre's scholarly work on the Psalms and the Epistles of St Paul was not based on profound critical insight or remarkable linguistic skill, qualities in which both Erasmus and his younger French contemporary Guillaume Budé far surpassed him. Rather, it was based on his talent for setting aside the technical jargon and abstruse issues of traditional theologians and presenting a simple, direct, and credible explanation of what the biblical author had in mind. He avoided all reference to scholastic authorities, and the relatively few learned citations he offered were to Church Fathers like St Jerome and St John Chrysostom and to certain medieval mystical authors. The principal goal of exegesis was to uncover the inspired religious message that the biblical author had intended to communicate – a goal quite close to that declared by Erasmus in the famous introduction to his edition of the New Testament. In many respects, Lefèvre was rather muddled in his efforts to set forth a new way of interpreting Scripture, but he tried to understand each biblical passage in terms of its textual and historical context, and he flatly rejected the traditional method of extracting statements from their original setting and then determining what they meant through philosophical analysis with little or no attention to what the author might have intended. Ever since Petrarch, humanists had denounced this scholastic approach as sophistical and intellectually dishonest.

Even in the hands of the mystical and rather cautious Lefèvre, this new approach to interpretation of Scripture had a potentially subversive implication for current religious doctrine and practice. He emphasized the importance of faith and grace and minimized the importance of traditional works of religious merit. He and his followers rejected not external actions like veneration of relics, pilgrimages, and the cult of the saints, but the actions of clergymen who claimed a magical power for these outward acts and promoted a sterile, formal piety while neglecting the inner, spiritual reality that the external acts were supposed to symbolize. Lefèvre did criticize some traditional beliefs that he found unsupported by either Scripture or the Church Fathers, for example, certain legends about St Anne. Conservative preachers and theologians, mostly from the mendicant orders, promptly accused him of spreading heresy, though there was nothing heretical at all about his questioning those traditions, and the church subsequently abandoned them.

Faced with bitter personal attacks, Lefèvre left Paris in 1521 and participated in an attempt by his patron and disciple, Guillaume Briçonnet, bishop of Meaux, to use the bishop's authority to reform the diocese and cut back on certain superstitious observances. Unfortunately for the reformers at Meaux, their reform got out of hand. Radical agitators influenced by the Reformation in Germany committed acts of iconoclasm in the churches, and thus seemed to justify complaints by the local mendicant friars that the bishop was recklessly stirring up heresy and disorder. Both Lefèvre and Bishop Briçonnet had been sheltered from such attacks by King Francis I and his intellectual sister Marguerite d'Angoulême. But the captivity of King Francis for more than a year after the battle of Pavia in 1525 removed this protection. Bishop Briçonnet was formally charged before the Parlement of Paris and fined for permitting the spread of heresy. Henceforth he carefully refrained from reform activity. Lefèvre fled over the border to Strasbourg for several months, and he spent the rest of his life in semi-retirement away from the centre of power in Paris. His own rather ambivalent position, in some respects closer to Protestantism than that of Erasmus, is typical of the evangelical and reformist humanism he inspired among his admirers. That is why those followers are rightly labelled 'evangelicals' rather than Protestants, though many later French Protestants (John Calvin among them) came out of this vaguely evangelical reform movement.

Erasmus: the apogee of reformist humanism

While Lefèvre was the major figure who turned French humanism towards religious renewal, his contemporary Erasmus was the most intellectually brilliant, the most broadly learned, and the most influential European humanist of his generation. Though he became the most admired person of his age among humanists and reformers, he also became the most feared and attacked figure among those who sought to maintain the status quo. His fame spread everywhere, causing, for example, a veritable craze for Erasmus among young Spanish humanists in the 1520s; but he had an especially powerful impact in Germany. Even though quite unintentionally, his programme of religious reform set the stage for the rapid spread of Luther's religious message, which at the outset was perceived by almost all except Erasmus and Luther themselves as virtually identical with the views of Erasmus. Erasmus himself had little or no sense of nationality and found the strident German nationalism of humanists like Ulrich von Hutten repugnant. But the other great leaders of German humanism were unsuited to leading a religious reform. Reuchlin was so wrapped up in study of exotic religious texts like the Cabala that he had no appeal outside an exclusive intellectual elite. Mutianus Rufus, despite his excellent contacts throughout the country and contempt for the cultural know-nothingism of many of the friars, was a non-participant who might cheer, complain, meddle, and whine from the sidelines but who never – not even once in his life – chose to exert leadership. Germany had no royal court that could have acted as a focal centre for either humanism or religious reform.

More than any of his contemporaries before Luther, Erasmus had discovered an alternative mechanism that allowed him to project his own reform programme and his own self-invented image into the consciousness of all educated Europeans, but above all the intellectually leaderless Germans. This mechanism was the printing press. Many other humanists, of course, worked for publishers and used the printed book to advance their ideas and their reputations. But Erasmus made the great publishing firm an alternative to the court and the university for the building of influence and reputation. Occasionally, when all else failed, he taught briefly at universities or acted as tutor to wealthy youths, but the print-shops were the real centre of his career: first Josse Bade of Paris; then Aldus Manutius of Venice; but above all Johann Froben of Basle, who published or reprinted virtually every one of the books on which Erasmus' gigantic literary reputation was built. Froben employed many other humanists as authors, editors, and proofreaders, many of them men of impressive learning and intellectual power. But Erasmus from the very outset of their collaboration was the star. As early as 1514, on his first trip up the Rhine from the Netherlands to Basle to confer with Froben, Erasmus found to his amazement that he was welcomed in every city as Germany's greatest literary figure – a rather startling experience for a Hollander who was never very certain that he was a German at all.

The later fame of Erasmus has almost concealed the obscurity of his origins – rightly so, since Erasmus himself invented and carefully shaped his public image. Born about 1467 at Rotterdam, the second son of a priest and a woman of Gouda, Erasmus always felt sensitive about his origins. His father sent his sons to the excellent grammar school of St Lebwin at Deventer, where Erasmus studied briefly with the famous humanist headmaster Alexander Hegius. The death of their parents from plague left the brothers under the charge of guardians who decided that the monastic life offered the only secure future for two illegitimate boys of small inheritance. Erasmus later felt that he was put under undue pressure to make irrevocable monastic vows for which he felt no genuine calling. In his later years, he secured papal dispensations releasing him from his vows as a monk and permitting him to live as if he were a secular priest.

While still in school, he had already developed a passionate attachment to the beauty of Latin language and literature. In the monastery, despite his later complaints about hostility to good letters (that is, humanistic studies), he not only managed to continue his studies but also found kindred spirits. He and the other monastic humanists felt themselves to be an island of enlightenment amid a sea of monkish anti-intellectualism, or 'barbarism', as Erasmus called it in a book he began writing in the monastery but did not publish till many years later, his *Book Against the Barbarians* (1520). In these years, he wrote classical-style Latin poetry; and while some of the poems deal with religious devotion, they do not reflect the deep, meditative piety that lay at the roots of his monastic order and of the school at Deventer.

The way out of the monastery was Erasmus' growing reputation for classical learning and an elegant Latin style. In 1493 he was appointed secretary to Hendrik van Bergen, bishop of Cambrai, who expected to be made a cardinal. Since such a promotion would require a trip to Rome,

Bishop Hendrik needed a secretary skilled in the humanistic Latin fashionable in Italy. Erasmus' departure was not meant to be more than a temporary assignment. In the event, however, he never rejoined his monastery. Political problems blocked Bishop Hendrik's appointment as cardinal, and hence Erasmus' trip to Italy fell through. He eventually secured permission to go off to Paris and study for a doctorate in theology, aided by a small pension from the bishop.

Erasmus entered the theological faculty at Paris in 1495 and remained there until 1499. He detested the intellectual narrowness, the professional arrogance, and (in his opinion, at least) the uselessness of the prevailing methods of theological study. Yet he spent four years there; and while it is likely that he soon drifted away from serious pursuit of the theological curriculum, he must have attended lectures and disputations regularly during his first year, when he resided in the strict Collège de Montaigu. He never completed a Paris doctorate, but his own letters for the period reflect his participation in theological study, and the usual conclusion that he learned nothing about theology there is unjustified. His subsequent career in theological faculties at Louvain and Cambridge suggests that he may have completed the first degree, the baccalaureate, before leaving Paris.

But there were humanists at Paris, and Erasmus eventually sought them out and gained their friendship. The most important of these early friends were the humanistic monk Robert Gaguin, who gave Erasmus his first opportunities to publish prefatory letters appended to two of Gaguin's books, and the Italian-born court poet Fausto Andrelini. Gradually Erasmus worked his way into the world of humanist poets and scholars. He published one slender volume of Latin poems in 1496 and had other poems tucked into the appendices of other men's books. In this company, Erasmus seems to have been just another young neo-Latin poet, with his interests focused on the secular literature of the ancient Romans and their modern Italian imitators. The major literary work he produced during and just after this period, the first edition of his *Adages* (1500), was a collection of 818 proverbs and sayings, mostly from Latin literature, with his own comments (often satirical and humorous) added. This early edition was a far cry from the impressive learning of its later editions, but it confirmed his reputation as a man of learning and wit.

Since Bishop Hendrik's financial subsidy began to falter, Erasmus had to support himself by tutoring sons of wealthy families. The most important of these was William Blount, Lord Mountjoy, who in the summer of 1499 invited him home for a visit to England, where he spent the balance of that year. He enjoyed England greatly and had his first taste of the lifestyle of the English aristocracy, a sharp contrast to the crabbed, poverty-ridden life he had endured at Paris. He met many humanists already mentioned above: John Colet, William Grocyn, Thomas Linacre, Thomas More, and even the future King Henry VIII. With such contacts, England seemed a most alluring place. Erasmus almost gave up for a time his longing for study in Italy. For the first time in his life, he was treated as a person of importance – a published author, an associate of prominent figures like Gaguin and Andrelini.

Erasmus' love affair with England began with this first visit in 1499. On this foundation, biographers have built a complex theory claiming that the visit transformed him, intellectually and spiritually, from a rather aimless young Latin poet into a dynamic, purposeful fighter for spiritual renewal of Christendom through recovery of both classical and Christian Antiquity. John Colet, whom Erasmus met at Oxford and who was then lecturing on the Epistles of St Paul, has been put forward as the man who gave Erasmus a sense of his real mission in life. But a recent study of Colet, based on the documents rather than on genial speculation, makes this story implausible. Colet was friendly and helpful, and during Erasmus' lengthy third period of residence in England from 1509 to 1514 the two men did become close, though the basis of their intimacy was Erasmus' participation in Colet's refounding of St Paul's School in London. Colet was a narrow and difficult man, though also in many ways an impressive one. His approach to interpretation of the Bible was radically different from that later developed by Erasmus, and there is clear evidence that while Erasmus tried to be polite to an interesting and potentially useful patron, he was capable of coolly (though privately) exposing Colet's limitations as an interpreter of the Bible. So the idea that their encounter at Oxford in 1499 revolutionized Erasmus' life is just a myth. If anything in England changed the course of Erasmus' life, it was probably not any one person but acquaintance with Italian-educated Hellenists such as Linacre and Grocyn.

In any case, upon his return to the Continent, Erasmus began working furiously at the mastery of Greek – a goal he could not have acquired from Colet, who not only never learned Greek but never really understood how essential it was for true competence as a classical scholar and biblical exegete. Erasmus progressed rapidly. By the summer of 1501, he was working on a verse translation of two plays by Euripides, a very difficult author. Ultimately he became the ablest Hellenist of his generation. His visit to Italy between 1506 and 1509 permitted him to perfect and polish his mastery of both the language and its literature, a mastery best expressed in the famous second edition of the *Adages*, published at Venice in 1508 by the press of Aldus Manutius. There, working directly in the print-shop, associating daily with the greatest team of classical scholars ever assembled, experts in both Latin and Greek (including native Greeks as well as Italians), who were constantly suggesting Latin and Greek maxims to consider for his collection, he created a new edition that became a major force in sixteenth-century intellectual life. His collection ballooned from a paltry 818 maxims to 3,260, drawing heavily for the first time on Greek sources, and each one accompanied by a pithy essay that explained the meaning of the passage, set forth its literary connections and parallels, and often added wry, humorous comments on contemporary religion, politics, and society. This book functioned as an amusing and thought-provoking collection of short essays, as a guide to the study of both Latin and Greek language and literature, and (perhaps most attractive of all) as a ready-reference tool for generations of humanists who needed apt classical quotations in order to appear more learned than they really were. The revised *Adages* became a major factor in the rapid spread of Erasmus' reputation throughout Europe.

The experience of studying and working in Bologna, in Rome, and especially in Aldus' shop at Venice was immensely important for the maturation of Erasmus. He studied and learned from the Italians, of course, especially in perfecting his mastery of Greek. But the most important lesson he learned was to value himself. He soon found that although his Italian and Greek comrades could offer him rare texts and specific pointers on matters of grammar and style, he was their peer, not their pupil. He came to realize that although certain individuals might surpass him in knowledge of some particular area of learning, he was more broadly learned, more stylistically sound, and certainly brighter than anyone else. He learned that while Italy still had much to teach northern humanists, it was no longer incomparably superior, no longer justified in its conventional disdain for northern 'barbarians'.

It is clear that Erasmus' studies after his first visit to England gradually became more and more directed towards issues of religious reform, making him the very embodiment of the association between humanistic learning and the desire for spiritual renewal that is often labelled 'Christian humanism'. Northern humanism did become focused on religious questions to a degree not typical of Italian humanism, but this shift of emphasis was not inherent in the soul of northern people. It was deliberately created by a handful of persons. Erasmus' life and writings express better than those of anyone else what has come to be known as the 'biblical humanism' or 'Christian humanism' of the early sixteenth century. They not only express it; essentially they created it. Humanistic learning became the major weapon in the battle for religious reform and spiritual renewal.

Yet Erasmus' plunging into the study of Greek did not necessarily imply an immediate commitment to study of the Bible and religious authors, for much of his early Greek study was directed towards pagan texts more obviously linked to his interests in secular Latin literature. He still worked at editing secular Latin authors like Cicero, and his early translations from Greek were of pagan authors, not only Euripides but also Plutarch and the bitingly anti-religious Lucian. Yet he also undertook a long-term project of editing the works of his favourite Latin Church Father, St Jerome, the greatest scholar among the ancient Latin Church Fathers. Shortly after his return from England in 1500, he began to write a commentary on St Paul but soon gave it up because (unlike Colet) he realized that it was impossible to go very deeply into study of the New Testament without a sound mastery of Greek.

Erasmus spent most of the period 1501–5 in the Netherlands. His shift away from a purely classical programme of studies is evident during this period; indeed, he spent the years 1502–4 in Louvain as a student of theology. Also in this period he formed a close friendship with Jean Vitrier, a reformist Franciscan friar who repeatedly got into trouble because of his sermons attacking the corruption and moral laxity of clergy and his criticisms of superstitious excesses in the cult of saints. He seems to have stimulated Erasmus' interest in the Bible and in the writings of Origen, the greatest theologian among the Greek Church Fathers. Vitrier's influence is obvious in a book that Erasmus wrote in 1501, the *Handbook of a Christian Knight* (usually known from its Latin title as the *Enchiridion*), especially in the basic idea of this book: that the true essence of religion is an inner spiritual experience which then must be expressed in a life of constant struggle against worldliness in which the believer is sustained by God's gifts of prayer and knowledge. For such a religion, study of Scripture provides the one truly necessary form of knowledge. Here Erasmus' characteristic concept of religion as a personal, spiritual experience first found expression. The *Enchiridion* is really a guide for the practice of Christian living by a layman. Its first publication, at Louvain in 1504 as part of a collection of short treatises, did not attract much attention; but it eventually caught on, being reprinted as part of another collection in 1509, six times within collections in 1516 and 1517, and then as a separate short book in 1518, after which it became a best-seller, one of the most popular religious books of the sixteenth century, published not only in the original Latin but also in Dutch, German, French, Spanish, Czech, and English. Although many modern readers have found the book dull and repetitious, and although later in the century conservative Catholic critics tried to suppress it on account of its emphasis on individual spiritual experience and its neglect of the external forms of Catholic piety, it was the first clear statement of an ideal that underlies everything that Erasmus wrote about religion. Its publication marks a declaration of faith and is one of the clearest signs of Erasmus' redirection of his own efforts towards religious issues. Already in the *Enchiridion* Erasmus directs the believer towards study of the Bible and the Church Fathers and away from attention to scholastic theologians. While Erasmus, unlike some later Protestants, did not urge total abandonment of ceremonial acts of piety, he thought them largely useless and even harmful to souls unless they were accompanied by the proper internal attitude and were seconded by a life of moral earnestness and Christian service. This conception of religion proved immensely appealing to reformist, evangelical Catholics until conservatives gained control of the Catholic reform movement following Erasmus' death in 1536. It also had obvious attractions for many Protestants and probably helped to ease the passage of many readers from traditional Catholic practices to Protestant faith – precisely why Erasmus, despite his lifelong profession of Catholicism and his open break with Luther in 1524, became unacceptable in the Catholicism of the next several centuries. The same general approach underlies his other popular works on religion, such as his brilliant social, political, and religious satire *The Praise of Folly* (1511) and many parts of his ever-growing collection of informal dialogues, the *Colloquies* (1518; first expanded edition 1522), which were widely used in schools as a textbook of Latin conversation and thus became by far the most widely diffused of all his writings.

This growing concern with religion and emphasis on the Bible received a stimulus from an important manuscript discovery that Erasmus made in 1504. He found a little-known work, the *Annotations on the New Testament*, by Lorenzo Valla, the most brilliant of the Italian humanists. Gifted like Valla with a keen critical sense, Erasmus realized that even in the case of a sacred text, a skilled grammarian's judgement on the meaning of the original words must take priority over any theologian's interpretation of any passage. He also saw that careful study of the Greek text would allow a scholar to correct errors that had crept into the Latin Bible. As heir to the philological insights of Valla, whose printed works he had long admired, he realized more fully than any of his humanist predecessors that in order not only to correct textual errors but also to get more directly at the meaning intended by the biblical author, scholars must apply to Scripture the same critical approach that had already proved fruitful in the restoration and interpretation of the secular texts of ancient literature. In short, he realized that the philological skills he had acquired as a humanist must be married to the task of interpreting the Bible. This meant not only close study of the still-unprinted Greek New Testament but also careful attention to biblical quotations and interpretations contained in the works of the earliest Church Fathers. It even meant that the whole body of patristic literature, especially the little-known Greek

Fathers, must be edited, critically annotated, translated into good Latin, and published.

Erasmus edited Valla's *Annotations,* which were published at Paris by Josse Bade in March 1505. The publication of Valla's notes was the prelude to a career devoted to editing and improving the text of the New Testament and the Fathers, an activity that Erasmus made into his principal scholarly work for the rest of his life. To him as a Christian humanist, the Bible and the Church Fathers were just as much a product of ancient civilization as the pagan classics, and of course were even more valuable because rooted in religious truth rather than pagan error. His original intention probably was to prepare a corrected Latin translation of the New Testament, with notes explaining the changes he proposed. What he eventually achieved was not just a new Latin text and a set of commentaries but also the first published Greek text of the New Testament, and subsequently a series of paraphrases in which he restated in his own words the meaning of each book of the New Testament except Revelation.

Although a residence of several months in England (1505–6) and his long-delayed stay in Italy (1506–9) seem to have been devoted in large part to study and translation of secular texts, Erasmus had now found his true identity and his life's work. He had linked humanistic scholarship with the achievement of a characteristic type of religious reform, Christian (or biblical) humanism. Though Lefèvre followed a similar path, Erasmus had a far clearer understanding of his reform programme and a far broader and more enduring influence. His Italian experience, in addition to maturing his command of Greek and establishing his confidence in his own learning and intellectual capacity, also negatively affected his perception of the worldliness and corruption of the church. Even though he depended on Pope Julius II for the dispensation that made it possible for him to create a scholarly career free from his monastic vows, the sight of the armour-clad pontiff riding triumphantly into the conquered city of Bologna confirmed both his outspoken opposition to war, expressed in a number of his works, and his conviction that the ecclesiastical hierarchy was scandalously corrupt.

The accession of Henry VIII to the English throne in 1509 caused Erasmus, at the urging of his English friends, to leave Rome and hasten back to England, where he spent nearly all of the period 1509–14. During this third period in England he also drew much closer to John Colet, collaborating with him in planning the new St Paul's School and writing textbooks for its use. Though he and Colet had very different ideas about the contents of an ideal school curriculum, they both based much of their hope for a reform of religion on the education of a new elite of men prepared spiritually and intellectually to occupy positions of leadership in both the church and secular society, and thus gradually and peacefully to improve religious life and to develop a more just society.

On his long journey from Italy to England, Erasmus sketched out his famous satire, *The Praise of Folly*, which provides much sharply critical commentary on contemporary society, both secular and ecclesiastical, but is especially directed against theologians, monks, and worldly prelates who are driven by hunger for money and power rather than truth and justice. Erasmus' idealized conception of an inward, spiritual Christianity, based on the Bible and expressed in moral action, was here joined with his literary artistry and his native wit to produce one of the greatest satires in world literature. His *Folly* became immensely popular but rapidly became the object of attack by religious conservatives who regarded it as irreverent if not even heretical. The book was a powerful statement of his idea of what was wrong with the contemporary church. Both the tenor of his criticism and his prescription for renewal through a return to the ancient sources of inspiration struck a responsive chord among contemporaries. Idealistic young humanists consciously became followers of Erasmus and shared both his discontent with the condition of the church and his dream of recapturing the original spirit of Christianity through return to the ancient sources. His programme suited the opinions of humanists in many parts of Europe who agreed with him that traditional scholastic learning was a hindrance to the recovery of ancient wisdom and to effective reform of schools and of the whole church.

Erasmus' hopes of lucrative preferment under Henry VIII were never realized. He was finally reduced to accepting appointment as a teacher, a means of support that he always avoided except in dire necessity. His new position was at Cambridge University. Though most of his biographers emphasize his activity as a teacher of Greek, it is almost certain that Bishop Fisher also arranged for him to hold the Lady Margaret professorship of divinity and that he lectured on theology as well as Greek. He did not enjoy his stay there (1511–14), but he was given a free hand, being allowed to lecture on the letters of St Jerome, which he was currently editing, rather than on the scholastic textbooks. At Cambridge he acquired a number of devoted English disciples who spread his influence as they rose to positions of power in the English church and state throughout Henry VIII's reign. Despite his grumbling, Erasmus threw himself into his scholarly work and laid the foundation for many of the important publications that came out during the years that followed.

The dream of a 'Christian Renaissance'

In 1514, Erasmus left England. He spent most of the next seven years in his native Netherlands, where he was now distinguished enough to be

appointed honorary councillor to the future emperor Charles V. The
Basle printer Johann Froben had undertaken publication of several of his
works, and in order to supervise the printing, in September 1514 he travelled up the Rhine from the Netherlands to Basle. This trip up the Rhine
marks the beginning of a period when Erasmus was the acknowledged
intellectual hero of nearly all northern humanists. Especially in Germany,
a country he had neither known well nor cared about, he found himself
lionized as a national hero, the man who had finally given Germany the
intellectual leadership of which earlier German humanists had dreamed,
and also the man whose sharp criticism of ecclesiastical corruption and of
obsolete scholastic theology made all eyes turn to him as the future leader
of church reform and a Renaissance of the spirit of the early church. This
was also the period when the *Enchiridion* emerged from obscurity and
began to be reprinted frequently. Several of his books in this period set
forth his ideal of a 'philosophy of Christ', by which he meant not a
complex system of theology but rather a loving trust in Christ as Saviour
and a manner of living that truly reflected this trust. Works like *The Praise
of Folly*, which was also frequently reprinted, made it clear how utterly
unchristian and useless he thought much conventional religious practice
to be.

A growing band of enthusiastic followers embraced his dream of a spiritually renewed Christendom and dismissed the attacks of his conservative critics as the work of mindless obscurantists and self-interested
hypocrites. The enthusiasm grew to such a pitch that Erasmus came to
believe that even the morally corrupt and terminally worldly hierarchy of
the church could be won over through persuasion and education, and that
the whole church could be reformed peacefully from within through
actions led by the hierarchy. It was an exalted vision of spiritual and social
regeneration, expressed repeatedly in many publications and hundreds of
private letters. It involved nothing less than a Renaissance of Christianity
to go along with the Renaissance of classical civilization.

Furthermore, though it now may seem too idealistic to be believed, this
dream was taken seriously. Erasmus knew that he faced bitter opposition
on many issues. But he also knew that he had supporters, not only idealistic and powerless young students but also many of the best men of his age.
He knew – and carefully advertised – that his most zealous English supporters were the two most learned and most devout of the English
bishops, Archbishop Warham and Bishop Fisher. He knew that at royal
courts, even at the papal curia, there were men of goodwill who shared his
concern about the corrupt state of Christendom and his idealistic dream
of a spiritual and social regeneration through humanistic education,
through reverent study of the Bible, and through the capture of existing
centres of secular and ecclesiastical power. Erasmus believed that the

leaders of Christendom could be won over to a programme of gradual, peaceful, orderly, and fully Catholic reform.

Everyone who counted, friend and foe alike, knew that Erasmus was at work on revision of the Latin Bible. This project, modest in its beginnings, grew rapidly into a plan to publish a new Latin translation of the New Testament, accompanied by the still-unpublished Greek text and by a set of notes. Erasmus intended his work to be a study Bible, not a replacement for the old Vulgate in the liturgy of the church. It is quite possible that the conception of a bilingual publication came from Johann Froben, who was a shrewd man of business as well as a sincere promoter of humanistic learning, and who saw the advantage of beating to the market the huge polyglot Bible being prepared by the Spanish scholars of Alcalá. Froben made sure that news of the forthcoming Greek New Testament was spread widely.

The year 1516 was the most brilliant and achievement-filled of Erasmus' life, all as a result of Froben's publications. The nine-volume edition of the writings of the greatest biblical scholar among the Church Fathers, St Jerome, included four volumes of letters edited by Erasmus himself. He also completed an important edition of the Roman Stoic philosopher Seneca. But far surpassing everything else was the New Testament (March 1516), including the first printed Greek text to be put on the market. Shrewdly, but fully in harmony with his own reformist goals, Erasmus dedicated this edition to Pope Leo X, who warmly accepted the dedication and urged Erasmus to hasten to Rome and put his talents at the service of the Holy See. Erasmus was delighted to have the pope's endorsement and not at all bashful about citing it against all who attacked his new Bible as subversive and heretical. But he had no desire to become the captive pet scholar of a papal curia that he regarded as both corrupt and corrupting. Though he received many additional invitations from Pope Leo and his successors, he never returned to Rome after his departure in 1509.

Publication of the Greek New Testament, seconded by the massive edition of St Jerome, capped Erasmus' rise to international fame and to the intellectual leadership of all those who longed for a sweeping reform of the church and who looked to humanistic scholarship and education as the way to attain this goal. Delegations from German town councils and from the University of Erfurt came to the Netherlands to honour him. In fact, Erasmus soon found the crush of uninvited admirers positively oppressive: he had become a celebrity, perhaps the first celebrity in European history. To have written a letter to Erasmus became a badge of honour for young humanists; to have received even the briefest note in reply was enough to establish a young scholar's reputation.

Erasmus' New Testament, despite the defects stemming from its pioneering nature and the limited number of manuscripts available, became the foundation of all subsequent scholarship on the New Testament until the German founders of modern biblical philology achieved the modern system of defining and tracing manuscript families in the early nineteenth century. Both in Latin and in Greek, Erasmus had a remarkable sensitivity to nuances of style and to the relationship between a particular ancient text and its specific point in time and place. Many of his proposed textual emendations were confirmed decades and even centuries later as better manuscript sources came to light. Judged fairly and by the standards of his own time, Erasmus fully deserved the reverential respect accorded him by nearly all humanists of his century.

Yet there were hostile critics. A few of them were even humanists. Lefèvre d'Etaples objected heatedly to Erasmus' reading of a passage in the Epistle to the Hebrews, even though Erasmus' reading agreed with the Vulgate, charging that Erasmus' reading was impious – a charge that irritated Erasmus so thoroughly that in 1519 he published a brief apologia that bluntly revealed Lefèvre's incompetence by demonstrating that there was no support at all in the biblical text or in patristic tradition or anywhere else for the purely theoretical objection that Lefèvre had raised. Although Guillaume Budé smoothed over the conflict, a certain residual coolness always marked Erasmus' relations with Lefèvre and his French disciples.

Many more attacks came from certain scholastic theologians. The Louvain theologian Martin van Dorp, who had tried to forestall the edition by urging Erasmus to abandon the project because it undermined the authority of the church, came over to Erasmus' side; but the young English theological student Edward Lee became a stubborn and unrelenting critic. A far more formidable critic was the Louvain professor Latomus (Jacques Masson, c. 1475–1544), who attacked a treatise by the young German humanist Petrus Mosellanus but really was aiming at Erasmus when he flatly denied the humanists' claim that knowledge of Greek and Hebrew was necessary for a theologian. Even more troublesome were the repeated attacks by the Spanish theologian Stunica (Diego López Zúñiga, d. 1531), who was a competent biblical scholar involved in preparation of the great polyglot Bible at Alcalá. Stunica was so aggressive that after exchanging controversial tracts with him, Erasmus used his connections at Rome to secure direct orders from two successive popes imposing silence on him. Even so, he remained a persistent critic, all the more troublesome because he had a good command of the biblical languages and could challenge Erasmus' editorial decisions on specific points with considerable plausibility. In later years, other scholastic theologians, notably

Pierre Cousturier (Sutor) and Noël Béda of Paris, joined in the attack, which involved not only the exchange of controversial tracts but also inflammatory public sermons, so that Erasmus had the questionable pleasure of hearing a preacher in the Netherlands conclude a denunciatory sermon by urging the congregation to pray for the conversion of Erasmus to the Catholic faith. From an early date, many theologians associated Erasmus' theological scholarship and his 'philosophy of Christ' with the new heresy being spread in Germany by Martin Luther.

Although Erasmus found association with Froben and the Basle humanists intellectually rewarding, many obligations drew him back to the Netherlands. He eventually settled in Louvain, where he matriculated in the theological faculty and maintained a fixed residence until 1521. Despite open attacks by some aggressively conservative members of the faculty, he established civil relations with most of his new colleagues and repeatedly sought their advice on his preparation of a revised edition of the New Testament. As the Protestant Reformation unfolded in Germany, however, Louvain became increasingly uncomfortable for him on account of the growing number of accusations that he was the source of Luther's heresies and perhaps even the real author of Luther's books. He stoutly defended his orthodoxy and denied any connection with Luther. Privately, however, he sympathized with Luther on some issues and believed that Luther was essentially a good man who was being pushed into unfortunate and rash statements by unscrupulous and corrupt opponents. He repeatedly expressed his fear that if Luther were condemned, all 'good learning' – that is, the humanist programme of religious and educational reform – would be endangered. It became clear that if he remained in the Netherlands, he would be drawn into the campaign against Luther or else forced into the untenable position of openly opposing both the university faculty and the princely court of which he was an honorary councillor.

Basle, where Erasmus had to travel repeatedly to work on his publications, seemed far more comfortable. It was a self-governing German city that in 1501 had affiliated with the Swiss Confederation. It was still relatively remote from the growing agitation over Luther; and yet as a major publishing centre and a university town, it was an excellent place from which to keep in touch with scholarship and religious developments. Erasmus had made many close friends on his visits there in 1515 and 1518, including Froben and his talented team of young humanist editors, also Ludwig Baer, the leading professor in the local theological faculty, and even the bishop of the diocese, who sympathized both with Erasmus' scholarship and with his programme of moderate and gradual church reform. The contrast between the friendly surroundings and opportunity for scholarly discourse at Basle and the increasingly hostile relations with the Louvain theologians was obvious, and in October 1521 Erasmus moved to Basle. He did not announce this as more than a temporary visit, but he never returned to the Netherlands and left Basle only when that city's adherence to the Reformation in 1529 made him unwilling to remain in a city where at least some conformity to the Protestant church would be expected. He lived for several years in the near-by Catholic university town of Freiburg-im-Breisgau, but in June 1535 he returned to Basle to work at the Froben press; and he never left, dying there in July 1536.

On the eve of the Protestant Reformation, Erasmus had emerged as the leading representative of a reformist humanism that challenged much of the academic, intellectual, and even religious heritage of the Middle Ages and aspired to a programme of reforms that would be led from the top by the most enlightened figures of both the church and secular society. This reform, inspired by the best principles and the noblest authors of both pagan and Christian Antiquity, would produce a more peaceful and more just secular society and a church that would foster true, inward spirituality and a benevolent personal morality, while de-emphasizing (but not abolishing) the outward, material expressions of piety that had developed gradually during the Middle Ages. Erasmus and his disciples were fully aware that they faced hostility from traditionalists who feared social upheaval, as well as from many political and ecclesiastical officials who had a vested interest in the status quo. But the humanist reformers believed that the spread of enlightened attitudes through better education, and the inspiring effects of greater familiarity with the Bible and the Church Fathers, would inevitably produce success. Their goal was gradually to capture the positions of power, and in that way within a generation or two to bring about decisive improvement. A famous letter from Erasmus to his young friend Capito in 1517 expressed his happy anticipation that the outbreak of peace among the principal rulers, the mild and benevolent character of Pope Leo X, and the spread of humanistic scholarship were on the verge of producing a new golden age of peace, justice, learning, and piety.

Erasmus and the 'Luther question'

Like the peace treaty that inspired it, this optimistic mood was fleeting. The actual course of religious reform was very different. Although most humanists hailed Luther as yet another powerful voice for the incipient humanistic reform, both Erasmus and Luther early sensed an underlying discord. Privately, Erasmus believed that Luther's attack on indulgences was justified not only on the grounds that indulgences promoted a superficial, mechanical kind of religious observance and had financial rather than truly spiritual goals, but also because the theological foundation on which they rested was highly questionable. He excused Luther's regrettable appeal to public agitation as an inevitable result of the crude and unprincipled response to Luther's questions by clergymen who cared only for power and money. Yet Erasmus also felt uncomfortable about some of Luther's statements about the total corruption of human nature and the inherent sinfulness of all human acts. He described such elements in Luther's published works as 'paradoxes' and insisted that they were not meant to be literally true. But Luther's Evangelical doctrines worried him, as did Luther's stubbornness and fiery temper and his tendency to descend to scurrilous invective along with his critics. Erasmus feared that Luther's movement would discredit and overwhelm the different reform for which he had been fighting. Yet he also realized that most of Luther's most vociferous opponents were his own opponents; and he feared that if they triumphed over Luther, they would immediately turn on him and his followers as well.

Though he has often been accused of religious indifference or moral cowardice, Erasmus did what he could to head off the impending schism in Christendom. He wrote directly to Luther, praising his good intentions but begging him to avoid extreme positions and to bridle his tongue. He wrote directly to Pope Leo, carefully distinguishing Luther's reform from his own, but also complaining that the papal bull against Luther had condemned Luther without a fair hearing. At the end of 1520 and early in 1521, for the only time in his life, Erasmus mounted a concerted political effort, travelling to the conference of the new emperor Charles V with the German princes at Aachen and helping to draft a memorandum that urged peaceful arbitration. In a personal interview with the Elector Frederick of Saxony, Luther's patron, he deplored Luther's extreme language and arrogance but also advised against surrendering Luther to the custody of the papacy. Suppressing the movement by brute force would not remove the scandals that had given rise to it, he argued. After publication of Luther's three famous treatises of 1520, which flatly denied the lawful basis of papal authority and repudiated the whole sacramental system of the medieval church, Erasmus realized that compromise was impossible, and he gave up direct personal involvement. He now tried to remove himself from direct participation in what he could only regard as a catastrophe for Christendom. His move from Louvain to Basle was designed to facilitate that withdrawal.

But Erasmus was so famous, so thoroughly identified with religious reform, that he could not withdraw. When Albrecht Dürer, the great Nuremberg artist, heard a false report that Luther had been killed, he wrote in his diary a passionate entry expressing the hope that Erasmus would now step forward and take command of the Reformation. But Erasmus never intended to lead a breakaway from the traditional church, and despite his conviction that there was much good in Luther, he still conceived his own proper task to be the encouragement of gradual reform within Roman Catholicism. Uneasily, he feared that Luther was turning reform in the wrong direction and that the result of total defeat for Luther would be the ruin of his own reform as well. Erasmus was trapped in the common predicament of a moderate caught in the middle of a violent and polarized conflict.

By the 1520s, as he and others of the older generation of humanists felt growing concern about Luther's actions and the even more extreme actions of his followers, more and more young German humanists who had started as Erasmian humanist reformers were undergoing a religious conversion that transformed them into dynamic young leaders of the Reformation, followers no longer of Erasmus but of Luther and others even more radical. Many brilliant young humanists developed into Protestant leaders: Melanchthon at Wittenberg itself, Zwingli in Zürich, Oecolampadius and Pellikan in Basle, Vadian at St Gallen, Bucer at Strasbourg, Capito at both Basle and Strasbourg, and a host of lesser figures. All of these men had been enthusiastic young Erasmians. As Erasmus and the older generation of humanists drew back from Luther, they were simply passed by. In 1518 and 1519, Erasmus was the leader of a growing band of disciples, while Luther was an isolated figure. The humanists' own favourable comments about Luther gave him the instantaneous fame that won for the Wittenberg Reformer a serious consideration of his ideas and a huge market for his books. As the established, older humanists drew back, culminating in Erasmus' reluctant but powerful direct attack on Luther in his *On Free Will* in 1524, they found that now Luther had the followers and they were the ones feeling isolated. Many of their most brilliant disciples chose Luther over Erasmus when choice became unavoidable, even though many of these still admired Erasmus. The choosing of sides was often painful. Although Erasmus stoutly claimed that he never turned away a friend because of charges of heresy, religious differences embittered relations between him and some of his ablest young disciples, such as Capito, Oecolampadius, and Pellikan.

Pre-Reformation northern humanism in general, like Erasmus or Lefèvre d'Etaples in particular, emerged from the early Reformation years badly damaged. Even before 1517, Erasmus found that application of humanist ideals and methods to the task of religious reform aroused bitter attacks. As Luther's opinions spread and posed an even more extreme challenge to tradition, conservative critics accused the Christian humanists of being the source of Luther's heresies. When Erasmus drew back from Luther and finally engaged him in open debate on fundamental theological issues, these conservative attacks on him did not cease, not even when he secured direct orders from the popes imposing silence on some critics. His early statements, both public and private, urging that Luther should be given a fair hearing, were dredged up and repeated against him; and his continuing public criticism of the materialism and corruption of the old church, expressed brilliantly in his widely read *Colloquies,* which he continued to expand, seemed to outweigh his direct challenge to Luther on major Reformation issues like grace, free will, and predestination. In the mid-1520s, a concerted attack on both Erasmus and Lefèvre, driven relentlessly by the syndic of the Paris theological faculty, Noël Béda, led inexorably to the formal condemnation of articles excerpted from the works of both humanists by the Paris faculty, even though the French king blocked efforts by the faculty and the supreme judicial court, the Parlement of Paris, to take punitive action. During the final decade of their lives, both Erasmus and Lefèvre remained embattled, constantly under attack from both sides, even though they were personally sheltered by the intervention of kings, nobles, bishops, and even the popes themselves. Certainly Erasmus' momentary dream of 1517, that a golden age of peace, justice, and orderly religious reform was about to dawn, had been shattered.

Consequences of the Reformation

The consequences of the Protestant Reformation for the humanist movement are a classic issue for debate in the history of early modern Europe. The Reformation has been seen as the logical and inevitable consequence of the rise of humanism. But it has also been viewed as a conservative Christian reaction against a humanist philosophy that was eroding the hold of religion on Western humanity and laying the foundations for the subsequent triumph of secular rationalism. Neither of these interpretations, though they are still widely held, is defensible in the light of modern scholarship. The latter view is especially ill-founded, since Renaissance humanism, despite its penchant for criticism of tradition, was not an inherently anti-religious movement. The view that the Renaissance produced the Reformation does have better justification, for the methods and reformist spirit of the Erasmians did lead many people towards Protestant faith, and the network of humanists in schools, universities, chanceries, and publishing houses was absolutely essential to the rapid diffusion that made Luther's ideas impossible to suppress. Yet the true driving force of the Reformation did not come from Renaissance humanism but from

Luther's striking insight into what he and his followers regarded as the true inner spirit of Christianity. For Luther and his most perceptive followers, the real issue of the Reformation was not crooked priests or even superstitious ceremonies, but true doctrine. For those humanists who became converts to the Evangelical faith, humanistic studies changed from being ends in themselves to being useful means for the discovery and diffusion of this true doctrine. And for the many humanists who remained in the old church, humanism became a useful means for the reconstruction and re-establishment of the Catholic faith. Moderate Catholic reformers of the Erasmian stripe were gradually eclipsed by conservatives who mistrusted and even hated the Erasmian heritage. The renewed emphasis on hierarchical authority and on tradition that characterized the assertive, tough-minded Catholicism dominant at the Council of Trent (1545–63) had no sympathy with the hope of Erasmus and a number of humanistic churchmen inspired by him that mild treatment, rational discourse, and limited concessions on some secondary issues could end the religious divisions peacefully. Nor, in an age when censorship of the press became increasingly stringent, was the candid and satirical criticism of abuses found in Erasmus' popular reformist books such as the *Colloquies* or *The Praise of Folly* permissible. One by one, Erasmus' books were placed on the indexes of forbidden books. Surviving copies of his books owned by persons in strictly Catholic countries such as Spain and Italy still survive, showing the name of Erasmus painstakingly defaced in order to render the author unidentifiable.

Erasmian humanism as a unified and self-conscious movement for religious reform and the spread of 'good learning' did not survive the bitter divisions of the Reformation. But the conclusion that therefore humanism had been destroyed is untrue. The following chapter will explain why.

The bright hopes of a dawning golden age of peace, social justice, and religious renewal that Erasmus expressed in his famous letter of 1517 to the young humanist Capito (Ep. 541, in *Collected Works of Erasmus* 4: 261–68) evaporated in the fires of religious controversy. For Erasmus personally, the bitter divisions that separated Protestant from Catholic were both a social disaster and a personal tragedy, causing sharp alienation between him and many of his younger disciples. Christian humanism, Erasmian humanism, as a coherent programme of religious and cultural renewal ceased to be a unified movement. Some historians would therefore end the history of Renaissance humanism with the outbreak and rapid spread of the Reformation, taking the open break between Erasmus and Luther in 1524 as the symbolic final act. Though such a conclusion reflects the bleak despair with which Erasmus and his friends viewed the religious schism, it overlooks some deeper and more lasting consequences of the spread of humanistic learning. Despite the uncertainties and violence of the Reformation era, humanism was alive. Although divided by confessional hostilities, humanism remained a major force in religion, both Protestant and Catholic. Its penetration of schools and universities continued almost everywhere, so that even the most self-consciously conservative educational systems produced graduates equipped with humanistic knowledge and skills. The humanist penetration of the schools inevitably led also to a more shallow but unmistakable diffusion of the new Latin culture into the vernacular world, through popular and courtly literature, translations, imitations, and the fine arts. The conviction that humanistic education was an essential preparation for high public office not only persisted but grew, and humanism established an educational hegemony that was not broken until nearly the end of the nineteenth century.

The quest for religious unity

Within each of the divided religious camps of the 1520s and after, a moderate tradition stressing restraint, respect for diversity, and the value of an education based on classical languages and literature survived, often affirming its respect for Erasmus and defending its own orthodoxy from attacks by co-religionists who rejected moderation and denounced Erasmus and all Erasmians as unprincipled temporizers. Among the first generation of Lutheran reformers, Philip Melanchthon remained the outstanding moderate leader. Unlike Luther, who openly denounced Erasmus as a mocking unbeliever without genuine Christian convictions, Melanchthon upheld the value of Erasmus' work and continued to correspond with him as long as he lived. Though Melanchthon was active in church politics and defence of Lutheran doctrine, he was also by far the most important figure in promoting educational reform of a clearly humanistic character. A largely humanistic educational reform became an integral part of the Reformation, not only in Lutheran lands but also in regions dominated by the rival Reformed tradition, such as Geneva, where John Calvin regarded his humanistic school, the Geneva Academy, as the capstone of his reform, guaranteeing not only to Geneva but to the whole world of Reformed Protestantism a succession of educated ministers and lay leaders.

Erasmus and his closest followers never gave up their forlorn hope that the divisions growing out of the Reformation could be healed by rational discourse and compromise. He wrote repeatedly about the need for moderation and goodwill and never regarded the Protestants as truly lost to the Christian religion. Moderate Protestants like Melanchthon and Martin Bucer joined moderate Catholics like Johannes Gropper and Cardinal Gasparo Contarini in a series of religious colloquies (1540–1) that attempted but ultimately failed to heal the theological divisions. Even so, these negotiations did show that the two sides continued to hold many beliefs in common. After both Luther and the pope repudiated the doctrinal compromises formulated at Regensburg, the influence of moderate Catholic humanists within the Roman church waned. Erasmus appeared on many lists of forbidden books, and the first Roman Index of Forbidden Books (1559) listed him among authors whose books were prohibited without exception. In Protestant lands, open profession of respect for Erasmus and other reforming humanists was easier. Anticlerical satires like *The Praise of Folly* and many of the *Colloquies* were welcomed as proof of the corruption of the old church, and Melanchthon in a public oration in 1557 honoured Erasmus as a great precursor of the Reformation.

Humanism as a critical method

One area of continuing vitality for humanism after the Reformation was the study of classical language and literature. Italian humanism had begun with a craze for the discovery and diffusion of ancient Latin literary texts and in the Quattrocento had added Greek as well. But early humanist study of classical languages and literature was unsystematic and lacked clearly defined goals and methods. As noted earlier, Lorenzo Valla practised and to some extent defined the principles of textual criticism and linguistic study that became the basis of the science of philology. He saw more clearly than any predecessor how evaluation of contemporary beliefs, traditions, and institutions could be conducted through critical analysis of documents and literary texts. In the next generation, only a few humanists realized the significance of Valla's discoveries and applied his philological principles to the emendation of defective classical texts. The most talented critical scholar of the late Quattrocento was Angelo Poliziano. His *Miscellanies,* a collection of essays explicating difficult passages in ancient works, not only applied philological learning but virtually invented the procedure of gathering variant manuscript sources and classifying them into genetic groupings, the first step (though a small one) towards the principles of textual reconstruction enunciated by German philologists like Karl Lachmann in the early nineteenth century.

Although this method of textual criticism originated in Italy, it attained its fullest development among the humanists of northern Europe. Erasmus never met Poliziano, but the scholars whose editorial and exegetical principles most directly shaped his own textual criticism were Valla, Poliziano, and the Venetian Ermolao Barbaro. The only contemporary who could rival Erasmus in learning and reputation was the Frenchman Guillaume Budé, and while Erasmus is the more intellectually attractive of the two because he linked his scholarly work explicitly to goals of cultural and spiritual renewal, Budé was more typical of the narrow focus of humanistic scholarship on questions of textual criticism. This tendency is represented by Budé's *Notes on the Pandects* (1508), demonstrating the Greek sources of Roman law, and his *De asse* (1514), which set out to be a study of Roman coinage and weights and measures but proved most fascinating to contemporaries because it collected a rich miscellany of facts about the material aspects of Roman life (Pfeiffer 1976, p. 101). The work of Budé and his disciples Jacques Toussaint and Jean Dorat made France the chief centre of this sort of specialized classical study in the middle and later parts of the sixteenth century. This scholarship produced not only many excellent critical editions of individual classical authors but also valuable manuals and aids to scholarship such as Robert Estienne's *Thesaurus* (1543), which remained the standard authority for Latin lexicography until the eighteenth century. Estienne's son Henri continued not only his father's record as a great printer but also his reputation as a great classical scholar. His remarkable command of Greek yielded not only several pathbreaking first editions of Greek works and an edition of Plato that remained authoritative for centuries (its page numbers are still the standard for citing the Greek text of Plato), but also an early history of classical scholarship (1587) and a five-volume Greek dictionary (1572) that has never been entirely superseded.

Many other scholars enriched this French tradition of specialized scholarship, but the culminating figure was Josephus Justus Scaliger (1540–1609). His outstanding scholarly work was in the fields of archaic Latin and chronology. His *De emendatione temporum* combined knowledge of classical historical texts with mastery of astronomy to create an integrated chronology of the ancient world and so to bring the histories of the different ancient societies into a credible chronological relationship to each other. In his work and that of his contemporary Isaac Casaubon (1559–1614), the humanist tradition abandoned the soaring idealism of the Renaissance and descended to the prosaic detail of scholarship written purely for scholars.

Though this line of development may seem uninspiring, abandonment of Antiquity as an idealized abstraction allowed these French classicists to open their eyes and see many parts of the ancient literary heritage with a clarity that had been impossible for enthusiastic and credulous pioneers like Marsilio Ficino and Lefèvre d'Etaples. In 1614 Casaubon demolished forever the credibility of belief that the so-called Hermetic books were a holy source of ancient wisdom going back to the beginnings of human civilization. His irrefutable analysis proved from their contents and their Greek style and vocabulary that they were a product of late Antiquity, composed long after the rise of both Christianity and Neoplatonism. Even more striking as a product of mature critical scholarship was Scaliger's redating of the treatises attributed to Dionysius the Areopagite. Both Valla and Erasmus had questioned the common belief that this author was identical with the Athenian philosopher converted to Christianity by St Paul (Acts 17:34), but in the face of bitter denunciations, they did not pursue the issue. Scaliger's demotion of pseudo-Dionysius from a convert instructed by St Paul to an inconsequential patristic writer of the sixth century was irrefutable (though many tried) because it was firmly based on a philologist's analysis of the language and a historian's analysis of the contents and their sources.

This development of critical historical thinking had obvious implications for the study of Roman law, which was based on the *Corpus Juris Civilis,* a compilation made in the sixth century for the Byzantine emperor Justinian. Poliziano had insisted that legal scholarship must focus exclusively on clarifying its textual sources and their transmission. The French humanist Budé had endorsed this general approach to study of law. This implied rejection of the voluminous commentaries created by Italian law professors of the fourteenth and fifteenth centuries, who had interpreted the law in terms of modern conditions. Budé regarded this medieval legal scholarship, which became known as the 'Italian method' (*mos italicus*), as a corruption of the law rather than practical and necessary adaptation. His idea of treating the ancient text as normative and rejecting the authority of medieval interpreters inspired a rival 'French method' (*mos gallicus*) for the interpretation of Roman law. The central figure in the rise of this humanistic, text-oriented legal scholarship was a young Italian jurist, Andrea Alciati (1492–1550), who had come north in 1518 to teach law at Avignon and who later taught with great success at Bourges. Though he spent only a few years in France, his commitment to humanist textual standards made him repudiate the Italian tradition. He regarded Poliziano as the one who put legal studies on the right track. He was also strongly influenced by Erasmus, and in 1519 he met Budé. His new 'French method' was based on the application of philological criticism to expound the text and on rejection of the medieval glosses and commentaries. When he returned to Italy, his ideas met sharp resistance from his students; but they swept the field in France.

The birth of medieval history

As this legal humanism focused on the origins of law, its leaders realized that not all of French law had Roman origins. Much of it had grown out of medieval feudalism. Rather ironically, therefore, the humanistic techniques of textual criticism became the foundation not only for a new approach to Roman law but also for textual scholarship devoted to medieval documents. French legal scholars probed the medieval origins of their own national institutions. François Hotman (1524–90), though he spent his career teaching Roman law, denied its relevance for modern French society. Legal humanism developed into an approach to French history based on critical evaluation of documents in quest of the origins of French laws, customs, and institutions, all of which were products not of Antiquity but of the Middle Ages. The fundamental interests of these pioneers of an archive-based history of France's medieval past and modern institutions arose not from humanism but from their national self-awareness. Their goal was to dignify their national identity by tracing its origins, shedding the prevailing notions of Trojan or other pseudo-classical ancestry and reconstructing the history of ancient Gaul and medieval France on the basis of a close reading of ancient and medieval sources ranging from Caesar's *Commentaries* to the charters and laws of medieval French kings. But the fundamental methods used by the makers of this new history to criticize and interpret manuscript sources came directly from the legal humanists. Etienne Pasquier, whose *Recherches de la France* (1560) was one of the first of the new genre, denied that the law of ancient Rome represented an unalterable ideal of pure justice. Rather, he viewed it as the specific and mutable product of a particular society at a particular time in the past. Hence he regarded Roman laws and values as obsolete. He probed ancient and medieval sources only to discover what French law was and how it came into being. His principal sources were the official acts of fourteenth-century kings and the registers of the high judicial court, the Parlement; but he also cited papal bulls, coins, statues, poems, trial records, and chronicles. Out of their study of old documents, Hotman and Jean Bodin created important statements of political theory that were rooted in historical evidence; and Bodin also put forth a comprehensive theory of history conceived not just as a chronicle of events but as a series of explanations tracing those events to purely human, non-miraculous causes.

Another direction in the historical work of sixteenth-century French legists was the collection, editing, and publication of documents (principally medieval documents) and the discussion of narrowly defined historical problems. This sort of work, which shunned broad theoretical systems like that of Bodin, is exemplified by the *Adversaria* (1564) of Pierre Pithou, which focused on local history. During his travels as a royal official, Pithou taught himself palaeography, in order to decipher old manuscripts, and diplomatics (the critical evaluation of ancient documents on the basis of their language and formal structure), in order to determine the authenticity and date of official documents. He also compiled inventories of local collections and extracts from significant documents. He did not cease to be a humanist: he also published editions of classical authors. But he was a great compiler of the documentary sources for French history; and his inventories and extracts from documents (many of which have subsequently been lost) were deposited in the Royal Library in the seventeenth century and still constitute an important source for early French history.

The fashion for this kind of documentary history waned in seventeenth-century France. Many of the legist-historians had been Protestants, and even the Catholics among them had expressed a critical spirit, an anticlericalism, and a Gallican mistrust of the papacy that were no longer acceptable under the Bourbon kings. Close probing of the historical origins of French society and government was not regarded favourably by a regime that emphasized the absolute character of its power and did not welcome publications that revealed the shaky and humble origins of the medieval monarchy and the many challenges that almost destroyed it in the fourteenth and fifteenth centuries.

The refined critical skills of Renaissance humanists survived and remained the basis of an erudite but very isolated tradition of classical scholarship. During the seventeenth century, the application of those skills to early Christian texts passed from the hands of possibly anticlerical or heretical laymen into the safer hands of monastic orders, particularly the Benedictines. The Benedictine Congregation of St Maur produced a remarkable series of editions of the Greek and Latin Church Fathers that in a sense fulfilled Erasmus' programme of patristic scholarship. Two other durable products of post-Renaissance Benedictine scholarship were the first great manual of diplomatics, *De re diplomatica* (1681) by Jean Mabillon, and the *Palaeographia Graeca* (1708) of Bernard de Montfaucon. Not all such scholarship was the work of monks. Charles du Cange, a Jesuit-educated friend of Montfaucon but a layman, compiled a massive dictionary of post-classical Latin, *Glossarium mediae et infimae Latinitatis* (1678), that drew much of its vocabulary from unpublished medieval manuscripts and still remains the most comprehensive dictionary of medieval Latin. Valuable though these seventeenth-century works of textual erudition were, however, they were no longer humanism, but rather the solid early foundations of what nineteenth-century German 'scientific' history would define as the 'auxiliary sciences': diplomatics, palaeography, chronology, and other methodological specialities.

Continuing educational change

While this highly technical scholarship marks a significant but narrow outgrowth of Renaissance humanism, for the general history of European civilization the steady penetration of schools and universities by humanistic subjects and textbooks was more important. The growth of humanistic influences in university faculties of arts, already evident in Germany from the second decade of the sixteenth century, continued through the rest of that century not only there but in England and France as well. New textbooks of Latin grammar, rhetoric, and logic replaced the old medieval ones that earlier humanists had denounced. The study of Greek as a formal academic subject became more common. At Paris, where the university remained cool towards Greek, King Francis I in 1530 appointed the first Royal Readers to teach Greek outside the structure (and hence also beyond the control) of the university, despite protests from the faculty. By the second half of the sixteenth century, most men who claimed any significant learning had a thorough knowledge of Latin language and literature, and at least some knowledge of Greek. This was true in Catholic as well as Protestant regions, north of the Alps as well as in Italy.

Far more numerous than universities were the Latin grammar schools. These had often been quicker than universities to adopt humanistic subjects and books. In 1524 Martin Luther wrote a famous open letter to the city councils of Germany urging the need to found or improve town schools for both boys and girls; and many of these schools taught Latin and Greek as well as vernacular literacy to boys. At least as striking was the founding of municipal *collèges* (Latin grammar schools) by the councils of many French towns during the sixteenth century. These schools provided for the sons of the local elite the kind of humanistic education that could prepare them for entry into a university, leading to careers in law and royal administration. Such education permitted sons of a determined and talented family to begin by acquiring public office, next to acquire respectable country estates, and ultimately, after two or three generations, to achieve the noble status and consequent tax exemptions to which ambitious bourgeois families aspired. Most of the masters who taught in these schools were young men who had taken BA and MA degrees at Paris. To the dismay of religious traditionalists, nearly all of them were laymen; and most of them were admirers of Erasmus, Lefèvre d'Etaples, and even Martin Luther, so that the spread of these *collèges* facilitated the penetration of the educated classes by reformist and even clearly Protestant ideas. In the following century, as the tone of French society became more resolutely Catholic, these municipal schools fell out of favour, and both political and ecclesiastical authorities placed the town councils under pressure to turn control of their schools over to religious orders such as the Jesuits. Indeed, under Louis XIII and Louis XIV, the royal government exerted systematic pressure in favour of closing nearly all provincial *collèges*, even safely Catholic ones, on the ground that easy access to education only made the lower classes discontented with their proper station in life.

Although Spain in the sixteenth century was a much more tightly controlled society than France and never experienced a serious Protestant threat, in education it followed a parallel line of development. Ambitious townsmen had the same conviction as their French contemporaries that giving their sons a good humanistic education would open the way to high government office and social advancement. By the sixteenth century, many municipal governments established grammar schools and (again like French cities) contracted with a university graduate to teach Latin grammar and the humanities. But operating a school and finding a competent headmaster were difficult for many towns, which tried both lay teachers and priests with equal lack of success. Jesuit control of municipal schools was more readily accepted in Spanish cities than in France, since the country lacked not only the anticlerical spirit but also, obviously, the anti-Spanish prejudice that made French cities resist pressure to turn schools over to the new order. By the early seventeenth century the Spanish monarchy, like the French, deliberately moved to decrease the number of municipal schools, and for much the same reasons. The monarchy did not in principle favour social mobility and hence sought to restrict access to Latin grammar schools so that only the privileged classes – nobles and the upper bourgeoisie – would be able to prepare their sons for high office in church and state. Teaching Latin to people of a lower rank would only create a large number of discontented, unemployable people who would never be satisfied with the humble employments to which their social rank limited them.

An important force in preserving (but also modifying) humanistic education was the Society of Jesus, the most important new religious order to emerge out of the Catholic Reformation. Although the founder, Ignatius de Loyola, disliked Erasmus' critical spirit and his tendency to spiritualize religious experience and to discount the objective, material, and sacramental aspects of Catholic religion, he was still a man of his time, convinced that mastery of classical languages and literature was a necessary preparation for the study of theology and other advanced subjects. The first Jesuit college, founded at Messina in 1548, adopted the same type of humanistic education responsible for the success of the Paris-trained teachers who controlled the municipal *collèges* in France. Education became and remained one of the principal fields of Jesuit activity; and though Jesuit schools remained conservative on religious questions and carefully inculcated respect for tradition and authority in conscious opposition to the critical stance fostered by Erasmian humanism, they made Latin, Greek, and classical literature the foundation of their curriculum. Before the end of the century, the order had developed a standardized curriculum for its schools, emphasizing humanistic studies in the earlier years, with a final two years of philosophy capping the course. By the 1540s, Jesuit professors were teaching in several German universities that had remained under Catholic control; and eventually the Jesuits took over all or part of the faculty of liberal arts at Ingolstadt, Cologne, and Vienna, while Jesuit colleges not linked to a university developed at many other places, not only in Germany but throughout Catholic Europe. The spread of conservative Catholicism and the eclipse of the Erasmian Catholics after the Council of Trent did not, therefore, spell an end to the influence of humanism on education in Catholic countries. Despite the disruption of certain aspects of humanism by the Reformation, the educational curriculum of humanism spread throughout Europe during the sixteenth century and became the educational foundation for the schooling of European elites, the functionaries of political administration, the clergy of the various legally recognized churches, and the learned professions of law and medicine.

The classics and vernacular culture

As humanism penetrated schools and universities, classical themes inevitably influenced vernacular literature. Some classical themes and ideas, though often in quaintly medieval form, had appeared in the popular literature of the Middle Ages; but in the Renaissance, both classical themes and classical literary forms established a dominance over the major national literatures that endured for centuries. Each body of vernacular literature retained many characteristics of the native medieval tradition, combining them with themes and forms drawn from Antiquity. The first major figures of Italian humanism, Petrarch and Boccaccio, wrote in Italian as well as Latin, and their works became a treasured part of the Florentine cultural tradition. Literary production in Italian seems to have fallen off in the late fourteenth century, but by the middle of the fifteenth century, vernacular prose works applying humanist concepts of civic and social ethics to the realities of contemporary life had appeared, notably *Della vita civile* by Matteo Palmieri and *Della famiglia* by the versatile humanist and architect, Leon Battista Alberti. The Neoplatonic philosophy of Marsilio Ficino also found vernacular expression. Ficino translated his own commentary on Plato's *Symposium* into Italian as *Il libro dell'amore*, expounding the doctrine of Platonic love, love based on spiritual rather than physical attraction. This popular Platonic idea is also reflected in the work of another client of the Medici, Cristoforo Landino; and just a generation later, Book Four of Castiglione's widely read and widely translated *Book of the Courtier* dealt with Platonic love in a way that made the doctrine one of the standard literary conventions of later Renaissance poetry. In fact, the household of Lorenzo de'Medici was the centre of a striking revival of vernacular poetry, characterized by a conscious effort to import the spirit and verbal fluency of ancient poetry into Italian verse. Lorenzo himself was not only the patron of this circle of poets but also a poet of considerable talent. Even more successful as a vernacular poet was one of Lorenzo's protégés, Angelo Poliziano, who was also the greatest classical scholar of the age. His verse play *Orfeo* was based on classical myth and written in a favourite classical genre, the pastoral. His *Stanze per la giostra* combines the medieval theme of knightly prowess with a spirit and elegance of form derived from ancient poems. This type of elegant vernacular poetry, artfully mixing ancient, medieval, and contemporary themes, continued in Italy into the sixteenth century. The verses produced are often criticized as artificial and stilted. Yet lyric poets like the curial humanist Pietro Bembo (1470–1547) and the artist Michelangelo Buonarroti, who as a youth lived at the 'court' of Lorenzo, continued an Italian poetic tradition, strongly shaped by humanist ideals, that influenced European poetry for centuries.

Even at the height of enthusiasm for the new humanistic culture, themes drawn from medieval romances also flourished, demonstrating clearly how humanistic culture and survivals of medieval culture overlapped. Luigi Pulci's *Morgante Maggiore* drew on the medieval Arthurian cycle of romances but was first presented in the household of Lorenzo de'Medici. At the elegant Renaissance court of Ferrara, a principal centre for humanistic influences, medieval chivalric themes combined with the classical epic form in long poems by two of the principal Italian Renaissance poets, Matteo Boiardo, author of *Orlando Innamorato* (1486), and Ludovico Ariosto, whose *Orlando Furioso* (1515) combined a Vergilian conception of epic with the medieval story of the Frankish warrior Roland. Two generations later, inspired by the spirit of Catholic reform, Torquato Tasso again glorified medieval chivalry and the crusades in his epic *Jerusalem Delivered* (1581), which, although written in Italian, followed the linguistic usage and metric form of the greatest Latin epic, Vergil's *Aeneid*. A similar blend of the medieval tradition with the humanist ideal of a life shaped by classical influences appears in Castiglione's *Book of the Courtier,* which is an idealized reflection of the Quattrocento court of the duke of Urbino. This book explicitly contrasted the Italian ideal of the learned gentleman with the traditional scorn for learning felt by the French aristocracy. Its many translations and editions attest to its value for social climbers and *parvenus* as a guide to the culture of ambitious courtiers. The importance of humanistic learning (lightly worn, but not absent) as one of the main qualities of the perfect courtier is a good example of the degree to which humanism had penetrated the vernacular culture of the aristocracy by the middle of the sixteenth century. From the time of Lorenzo de'Medici onward, Italian humanists repudiated the earlier humanist prejudice that serious literature should be written only in Latin. They adopted the Tuscan dialect of Dante and Petrarch as the proper medium for Italian authors to use. The talented and learned humanist and poet Pietro Bembo, though himself a Venetian, wrote a treatise, *Della volgar lingua* (1525), justifying his choice of Tuscan for his literary works.

French Renaissance literature

As interest in Italian humanism spread across the Alps, it inevitably coloured vernacular as well as Latin literature – all the more because the

Italian writings included vernacular works by Petrarch, Boccaccio, and others as well as their Latin writings. In France, a figure of particular importance was Marguerite d'Angoulême, sister of King Francis I and patron of Lefèvre d'Etaples and many vaguely 'evangelical' humanists. Marguerite was herself a poet and prose writer of considerable talent. In her *Heptameron,* a collection of tales, the Florentine idea of Platonic love is blended with medieval chivalric ideals and with a longing for Christian renewal based on faith in the redemptive power of Christ. She surrounded herself not only with mildly reformist priests and humanists but also with poets who shared her interests. The poems of Clément Marot (1496–1544), one of her clients, show strong connections in structure and style with medieval French poetry, but also clear influence both by ancient poets like Vergil, Ovid, and Catullus and by modern Italian poets like Petrarch.

Far more popular and talented than either Marguerite or Marot was the unpolished but broadly learned François Rabelais (1483–1553), whose tales *Pantagruel* (1532) and *Gargantua* (1534) and several sequels constitute the first great achievement of French Renaissance prose. Rabelais' tales continue a bawdy tradition deeply rooted in the French Middle Ages. Yet in their quest for an idealized pattern of life, their respect for ancient examples, and their irreverent contempt for scholastic learning and clerical worldliness, these books also reflect humanistic influence. While Rabelais had no sympathy for the dogmatic correctness of his contemporary John Calvin, his works do reflect the vaguely evangelical and reformist aspirations of many French humanists, especially those who inhabited the circle of Marguerite. As a former Franciscan friar, Rabelais had received a scholastic education, but his popular tales abound in contemptuous satires on scholasticism, and they also express his disdain for monastic life. Despite the hostility of his Franciscan superiors, Rabelais mastered Greek and made Latin translations of the Greek authors Herodotus and Lucian. Influential patrons such as Marguerite d'Angoulême helped to shield him from efforts by the Paris theologians and the Parlement of Paris to suppress his humorous tales. Although his books were formally censured for their irreverence, the numerous editions of *Pantagruel* and *Gargantua* and the publication of two sequels show that he had attained popularity among both the intellectual elite and ordinary French readers.

In Rabelais, humanism merged with and shaped a type of popular literature that appealed to many of the educated classes and yet propagated its ideals through a kind of broad, coarse humour that gave his books an enduring appeal. But humanist influence also shaped a very different sort of French literature, the elegant, refined poetry of a group of court poets whose seven principal figures were collectively referred to as *la Pléiade*, a constellation not of stars but of seven outstanding poetic talents. The programmatic statement of their ideal was a manifesto, *La défense et illustration de la langue française,* published in 1549 by Joachim du Bellay with the assistance of Pierre de Ronsard. The treatise defended the use of French (rather than Latin) as a literary medium for French authors, but it repudiated traditional French verse forms and stated the goal of founding a new poetic tradition that would combine the inherent beauty of the native language with the spirit, forms, and structures of classical poetry. These Renaissance precursors of later French neoclassicism remade the style and tone of French poetry. The most talented poets in *la Pléiade,* du Bellay and Ronsard, have maintained a high reputation through many shifts in literary taste.

The new culture in English literature

The penetration of French vernacular literature by ideas, values, and techniques derived from humanist study of classical literature had a parallel in the literature of England, where influences derived directly from study of the classics and modern Italian writers like Petrarch were reinforced by influences from France. As in France, humanistic literary influences never eradicated native themes and traditions but combined with them. Certain medieval English practices – for example, the old alliterative, unrhymed verse-forms – had already lost popularity in the late fifteenth century. But themes from the tradition of courtly love survived in English lyric poetry, modified by influences from classical, Italian, and French authors. Much writing, almost all of it now unread except by historians of literature, continued to deal with medieval topics and to use medieval verse-forms. But educated Englishmen looked abroad for models. In poetry, a landmark in the emergence of new themes and styles is a collection commonly known as *Tottel's Miscellany* (1557). The most important part of this poetic anthology is the work of two young aristocrats, Sir Thomas Wyatt (1503–42) and Henry Howard, Earl of Surrey (1517–47). Wyatt had travelled on diplomatic missions to both France and Italy and had been captured aesthetically by the Italians, especially Petrarch. He was the first English poet to use the sonnet as a metrical form. The Earl of Surrey is also important for the first significant and sustained use of blank (unrhymed) verse in his translations from Vergil's *Aeneid* (*c.* 1554). These reflect a humanist desire to purge serious poetry of rhyme, which various later English poets (Marlowe, Shakespeare, and especially Milton) avoided wholly or in part because it was a product of medieval barbarism. The new style of verse produced a major poet in

Edmund Spenser (1552–99), who adopted an archaic form of English language but also was strongly influenced by Platonism. In *The Shepherdes Calendar* (1579) and *The Faerie Queene* (1590, 1596) he artfully blended a pastoral form derived from Antiquity with national and chivalric themes derived from the Middle Ages. The most elegant and most admired of England's Renaissance authors was Sir Philip Sidney (1554–86). His humanistic learning, aristocratic birth, military heroism, and literary talent made him the exemplar of an ideal of human nature that had its roots in the Italian courts of the Quattrocento. These poets were realistic enough to use English, not Latin or Italian, as the proper language for literary work. Sidney's treatise on poetic theory, *An Apologie for Poetrie* (1595), had great influence; and his prose romance *Arcadia* (1590) drew inspiration from modern masters of the pastoral genre, Jacopo Sannazaro of Naples and the Portuguese Jorge de Montemayor.

Far outstripping any of these talented authors is William Shakespeare (1564–1616), not only because his many successful plays make him one of the greatest figures in world literature but also because the literary achievement of this socially obscure man, expressed not only in his plays but also in his poems, shows how thoroughly humanistic culture had penetrated English society. Shakespeare was no son of a peer or a gentleman, but the son of an undistinguished citizen of a small provincial town. He was no university-trained scholar but the product of some unidentified grammar school where he obviously acquired a command of Latin and perhaps a smattering of Greek, the 'small Latin and less Greek' of Ben Jonson's famous quip. His rise from obscurity to a solid financial success, his ability to attract great gentlemen as patrons of his theatrical company (and as the true authors of his poems and plays, if one believes a lunatic fringe of self-styled experts): these are testimony to a remarkable human talent. But despite his lack of much formal education, Shakespeare mastered the essentials of the humanistic heritage to the extent required by his literary work. His poems show a remarkable mastery of the sonnet form and of ancient mythological and historical lore; and his plays show him to be an author who could draw freely on ancient Roman as well as medieval English history, who could depict imaginary pastoral scenes and realistic urban scenes with equal skill, and who could express himself not only in the intricate rhymed verses of the medieval poetic tradition but also in the unrhymed blank verse that had been created by modern humanists who disdained rhyme as unclassical. The mysterious qualities that made Shakespeare a literary genius are no result of his exposure to second-hand (or even first-hand) humanistic and classical influences. But the ease with which he could reach into the armoury of humanistic literature and draw forth the stories, the names, the myths, the history, the verbal arts and tricks needed for his work are convincing evidence that humanistic learning had become an integral part of English culture.

The Spanish Golden Age

Spain was the other European nation that achieved a peak of literary greatness in the later Renaissance, an age conventionally known to Spanish literary historians as the Golden Age. Despite a strait-laced Catholic orthodoxy, humanism penetrated deeply into the educated classes of Spain, coming directly from Italy and also from northern Europe. The enthusiasm for Erasmus and his reformist kind of humanism began to wane in the later 1530s; and by mid-century, it became imprudent to cite Erasmus or his books by name. In the meantime, however, the scholarly classical and patristic aspects of humanism had inspired native scholars of real significance; and biblical humanism, though cautiously avoiding the sharply critical stance typical of Erasmus, had already produced the great Complutensian polyglot text of the Bible. Spain's rigorous orthodoxy and the harsh proceedings of the Inquisition may have channelled Spanish humanism, but they did not prevent it from flourishing.

Precisely the same was true of vernacular literature. No author could have been unaware of the dangers of running afoul of the Inquisition, but this consciousness did not prevent an outpouring of literature. As in other countries, vernacular writing was powerfully shaped by traditional native themes, forms, and attitudes; but humanism strongly affected it – more in some genres (lyric poetry, for example), less in others. Prose narratives such as the masterpiece known as the *Celestina* (1499) and the first and greatest of Spanish picaresque novels, *Lazarillo de Tormes* (1554), seem almost wholly native products with no humanistic admixture other than frequent allusions to classical mythology, even though the author of the *Celestina*, Fernando de Rojas, was a lawyer and a humanist fully conversant with Latin and Greek classics. *Lazarillo* remains anonymous. Poetry, on the other hand, felt the influence of the classics and of Italian humanism strongly. Good examples are the court poets Juan Boscán and Garsilaso de la Vega. Garsilaso moved from the Petrarchan style of poetry to a more up-to-date Renaissance style inspired by Horace and Vergil among the ancients and by Poliziano and Jacopo Sannazaro among recent Italians. Their poems were published in 1543, after both men were dead; but the frequency of new editions demonstrates their popularity. The school of poetry centred at Seville and dominated by Fernando de Herrera (1534–97) carried the adoption of Italian elegance and sophistication even further. Less ornately Italianate but far more successful poetically was the work of Luís de León (1527–91), an Augustinian friar, also a brilliant though controversial professor of theology at Salamanca, and an outstanding classical and biblical scholar, who mastered both Greek and Hebrew. Plato and the Bible influenced his verses as well as his theology, and the Roman poet Horace influenced his poetry. The contrived, artificial, but immensely influential poems of Góngora (Luís de Góngora y Argote, 1561–1627) represent a later stage in the penetration of Spanish poetry by the classics and the Italian poetry of the later Renaissance.

Spanish humanists, like their French counterparts, faced the problem of defining the proper role of their own language as a medium for serious literature. One of the principal humanistic scholars of the early sixteenth century, Antonio de Nebrija (1444–1533), contributed not only classical studies and bilingual dictionaries, but especially his *Gramática castellana* (1492), the first grammar of any modern European language. One of the most highly regarded examples of Erasmian influence in Spain, Juan de Valdés (1509–41), upheld the fitness of Castilian for serious literature in his *Diálogo de la lengua*. The fashionable Italian genre of the pastoral novel, associated with the Neapolitan poet Jacopo Sannazaro (1458–1530), was introduced into Spain in 1558 by a Portuguese author, Jorge de Montemayor, whose work inspired a number of imitations, including *La Galatea*, the first novel of the greatest Spanish author of the age, Miguel de Cervantes Saavedra (1547–1616). The prose works of Fray Luís de León are a major achievement in the emergence of serious literature in Spain, but except for the artful mastery of language, they are less clearly influenced by humanism than his poems. Cervantes, whose *Don Quixote* (1605 and 1615) was and remains the greatest masterpiece of Spanish literature, was exposed to humanistic education and dealt with classical materials in works like *La Galatea;* but his great novel is essentially a product of native Spanish culture, not strongly influenced by humanism.

The other major figure of Golden Age Spanish literature, Lope de Vega (1562–1635), received an excellent education in a Jesuit college and at the University of Alcalá. Though he began his career by writing pastoral verse and other poems influenced by the Italian poet Torquato Tasso and by classical poets, he is a major figure only on account of his dramatic works, which are dominated not by humanistic influence but by the combination of vernacular stage tradition with his own native genius.

Northern Renaissance art

Since even the new artistic styles of Renaissance Italy developed autonomously and intersected with humanistic learning only at certain times and in certain individuals, any relationship between humanism and the art of the northern Renaissance is open to question. Up to at least the

1490s, the Gothic styles of painting, sculpture, and architecture remained dominant north of the Alps; and artists (especially painters) looked to the tradition of Flanders more than to Italy for inspiration. Even a great painter like Matthias Grünewald (d. 1528) shows only faint traces of Italian influence. A few classical architectural details and his remarkably sophisticated mastery of perspective are the only tangible evidence of Italian influence. His paintings far surpass the work of most of his northern contemporaries, but they remain anchored in a native Gothic tradition that is linked to the work of the Flemish masters of the early fifteenth century, not to the painters of the Italian Quattrocento. The same is true of his contemporaries Lucas Cranach the Elder (1472–1553) and Albrecht Altdorfer (1480–1538).

The one great exception is Albrecht Dürer (1471–1528), the outstanding figure of northern Renaissance art. Though he was trained in the flourishing northern tradition and preserved many native elements in his works, three study-trips to Italy (1494–5, 1505, and 1506–7) made him a self-proclaimed disciple of the Italian Renaissance, both in his adoption of the scientific principles of perspective and in his conception of the artist as an intellectual, a person grounded in the liberal arts, and not just a skilled craftsman. Particularly noteworthy are his several self-portraits. Although the most striking of these, painted in 1500, shows the influence of Jan van Eyck and other northern portrait-painters, the self-conscious, Christ-like image reflects Dürer's exalted conception of the painter's importance. He is an especially significant figure in cultural history because he became his generation's greatest producer of woodcut illustrations, which were widely diffused through printing. Though some of his famous prints, such as the early *Four Horsemen of the Apocalypse* (1497–8), seem close to the native German tradition represented by the engraver Martin Schongauer (1430–91), his *Adam and Eve* (1504) presents two classically conceived nude figures against a northern background; and his *Knight, Death, and Devil* (1513) may have been inspired by the Christianized humanist ideal set forth in Erasmus' *Enchiridion*. It presents idealized forms inspired by both ancient and Italian Renaissance art. Dürer's own treatise on geometry reflects his interest in the scientific basis of painting. His religious ideals, shaped by the Christian humanism of Erasmus and later by Martin Luther, found striking expression in the panel painting, *The Four Apostles,* which he presented to his home town of Nuremberg just a year after it became officially Lutheran in 1525. The striking figures of saints Paul, John, Peter, and Mark reflect Dürer's close study of the works of Masaccio, Mantegna, and Piero della Francesca; and his treatise on geometry was based on Piero's treatise on perspective.

11 Albrecht Dürer, *Self-portrait at the Age of Twenty-Eight* (1500).
Alte Pinakothek, Munich (Bridgeman Art Library Ltd)

12 Albrecht Dürer, *St Jerome in his Study* (engraving, 1514).
© The Trustees of the British Museum, London

Renaissance influences, but not specifically humanistic ones, combine with established northern portraiture in the works of Hans Holbein the Younger (1497–1543), who admired Erasmus and painted a striking portrait of him but made most of his fortune and reputation painting portraits at the court of Henry VIII of England. The greatest 'Renaissance' painter of the sixteenth-century Netherlands, Pieter Bruegel the Elder (d. 1569), travelled extensively in Italy in 1552–3 but seems to have been more impressed by the Italian countryside than by the works of Italian painters or humanists.

Sixteenth-century architects in northern Europe generally maintained their Gothic traditions and only gradually incorporated Renaissance influence, beginning with classicizing decorative elements on buildings that remained Gothic in conception (for example, the choir of the church of St Pierre at Caen, 1528–45, by Hector Sohier). The royal chateau at Chambord, on the other hand, retained many traditional Gothic elements (turrets, high-pitched roofs, tall chimneys) but was built around a central section of Italianate style and possibly designed by an Italian architect. Its arches, window-forms, and layout of interior space are Italianate. Even more clearly Italian in spirit is the portion of the rebuilt Louvre at Paris designed by Pierre Lescot (1515–78) and constructed under Francis I and Henry II. Classical influences mediated through the Italian Renaissance abound in the Baroque style of building (and painting and sculpture) that spread from Italy to northern Europe in the later sixteenth and early seventeenth centuries; but it is doubtful whether any of this art can be conceived as a product of humanism except for the borrowing of neoclassical details.

Social utility of humanistic learning

If the influence of humanism on northern art was rather limited, the same is not true of the relationship between humanism and the ruling classes of the sixteenth and early seventeenth centuries. Humanism had made its first appearance as the distinctive culture of a ruling elite in the republic of Florence in the early fifteenth century and had adopted a distinctively republican, anti-monarchical coloration that looked back to the Roman republic for inspiration. But Italians soon discovered that it was easy to divorce the idea that humanistic education conferred skills and attitudes suitable for a ruling class from the republican political ideology. Humanism became the predominant cultural style at the courts of Renaissance princes and popes.

This courtly adaptation of humanistic culture was the form in which humanism established itself in Spain and north of the Alps. The popularity of Castiglione's *Book of the Courtier,* not only in its Italian original but also in translations into Spanish, French, English, German, and Polish, documents the courtly bias of most humanistic culture in the later Renaissance. Other popular books of manners, such as *The Boke Named the Gouvernour* (1531) by Sir John Elyot, *The Arte of Rhetorique* (1553) by Thomas Wilson, and *The Scholemaster* (1570) by Roger Ascham, are English examples of the victory of humanism as an essential part of the education of all who aspired to hold influential positions in the royal courts of northern Europe. Mastery of at least some classical language and literary culture became almost mandatory for the royal official and the court gentleman. This does not mean that all – or even many – courtiers and royal officials became deeply learned, but it certainly meant that any young man who wished to rise from low to high status in the service of the ruler would need to have a respectable familiarity with humanistic culture.

Such ideas about the utility of humanistic learning did not remain confined to the books of social and educational theorists. European governments in practice did begin to prefer men with humanistic education and humanistic skills for public employment. Ambitious families soon learned that sending a son to a humanist schoolmaster significantly enhanced his chances for a successful career in royal service. The clearest example of this development is in Tudor England, where the peculiar national system of maintaining the native common law and providing legal training at a separate set of non-university trade-schools prevented the near-monopoly of public office by graduates of university law faculties that developed in France, Spain, and Germany. The Tudor dynasty from the time of Henry VII had shown favour to humanists and humanistic education. The value of humanists for royal service was recognized early and is well illustrated in the career of Erasmus' English friend Richard Pace, who served as Henry VIII's ambassador to Venice and produced a short treatise on the utility of humanistic education. The founding of new colleges favourable to humanistic studies at Oxford and Cambridge by members of the royal family and by courtiers reflects the same tendency, as does the firm and durable support for Erasmus and Erasmian humanism shown by a number of English bishops sympathetic to humanism.

Humanism and the Henrician Reformation

Henry VIII's divorce and the eventual separation of the Church of England from the jurisdiction of the popes cost two of England's outstanding humanists, Thomas More and Bishop John Fisher, their lives. But this has obscured the absolutely central role played by humanists in planning and carrying out Henry's religious and dynastic policies. The executions of More and Fisher, tragic though they were, did not mean the end of English humanism. On the contrary, the emergence of Thomas Cromwell as the principal government minister placed England on a path that meant not only separation from Rome but also the adoption of a religious policy guided far more by Erasmian humanism than by Lutheran Protestantism, at least until the death of Henry VIII in 1547. Many of those who surrounded and advised the king sought a gradualist reform that was inspired chiefly by the writings of Erasmus. This was even true of some, such as the Archbishop of Canterbury, Thomas Cranmer, who were privately attracted to Protestant doctrines. Ultimately the Henrician reformers divided into a conservative group that abandoned Rome but struggled to maintain traditional liturgy and doctrines and a more radical group that favoured Protestant doctrines and practices. Yet in the crucial early years when England was cutting loose from Rome, an explicitly Erasmian programme held the reformers together. In the background was Thomas Cromwell, a shrewd political manipulator who was no humanist but who recognized the attractiveness of an explicitly humanistic reform programme and also the value of humanists as propagandists for royal policy.

Particularly striking was the large number of English translations of Erasmus' works published in this period. Erasmus' ideas of religious reform were already widely shared by English humanists, and these ideas were sufficiently vague and general to suit the needs of the government for propaganda that would favour reform without committing the regime to a specific and detailed programme. One of the first of these translations was an anonymous version of the *Paraclesis*, Erasmus' programmatic statement of his approach to Scripture. The most productive source of Erasmian translations was Richard Taverner. Already in 1531 he had published a version of Erasmus' *Encomium matrimonii*, a book often attacked by conservative theologians. Probably about the same time, an anonymous translator published an English version of another short Erasmian work that had incensed some conservative churchmen, *An Epystell . . . concernyng the forbedynge of eatynge of flesshe*. This work certainly preached no heresy, but it did point out that the complex rules for fasting enforced in the contemporary church rested only on human law and could, without endangering Catholic orthodoxy, be changed by lawful authority to meet the changing needs of society. By 1531–2, many humanists were turning to Cromwell for access to royal favour; and by the time he formally took office in 1534, he had surrounded himself with a group of able young humanists, eager to write and translate in defence of royal religious policy. Richard Wakefield, a leading Hebrew scholar who had taught at Louvain and Tübingen before becoming professor of Hebrew at Cambridge in 1523, published in 1532 a work that applied his mastery of the Hebrew Bible to prove that the king's marriage to Catherine of Aragon was unlawful. In 1533 Thomas Starkey and Richard Moryson, two humanists who had enjoyed the patronage of Henry VIII's humanist cousin Reginald Pole at Padua, courted royal favour and soon became active in the production of books defending Henry's policies. In that same year the humanist William Marshall translated Valla's famous work *On the Donation of Constantine* as well as books by Ulrich von Hutten and Nicholas of Cusa critical of that infamous historical forgery. Such translations at this juncture had the force of anti-papal propaganda. Also in 1533 Marshall translated Erasmus' tract on the Apostles' Creed, which presented a very broad definition of Catholic orthodoxy that was highly acceptable to the bishops of the English church. This flood of Erasmian translations continued throughout the 1530s and was accompanied by a second flood of apologetic tracts defending royal religious policy, the most important of which were Starkey's *An Exhortation to the People* (1536) and a defence of royal control over the church, *De vera obedientia* (1535) by Bishop Stephen Gardiner.

Cromwell's stable of authors was not limited to humanists. Gardiner, for instance, was a noted specialist in canon law and was valuable as a propagandist precisely because of his reputation in that field. But the general line of defence for the repudiation of papal authority and the assertion of royal supremacy was based on such Erasmian principles as the authority of Scripture, historical criticism of medieval traditions (which were always denounced as innovations and departures from the purity of the early church), the doctrine of adiaphora (things indifferent, not forming part of the essence of the true faith and hence subject to change according to the needs of society), and emphasis on inner spirituality rather than external ceremonies. A number of the Erasmian translations consisted of individual colloquies such as *The Funeral* and *A Pilgrimage for Religion's Sake,* both of them critical of abuses involved in traditional religious observances that Cromwell was actively reforming right out of existence (such as monastic orders and pilgrimage shrines). Most of these humanists were eager to write in support of official policy. James McConica (1965, pp. 166–67) has summarized the situation well: 'The Government leads them where they are inclined to follow, and induces a large group of official writers to flood the countryside with Erasmian literature wholly complementary to the official settlement.'

The fall of Cromwell from power and his execution in 1540 marked a clear swing in favour of the more conservative reformers but did not end the importance of Erasmian translations. At the very end of Henry VIII's reign, the royal injunctions of 1547 required all parish clergy to provide in a place accessible to the public not only a copy of the officially sponsored Great Bible (1539) but also the Paraphrases of Erasmus, even though the latter were not yet available in English. These translations, however, were already in progress and appeared in two volumes early in the reign of Edward VI. The first (1548) contained the Paraphrases on the Gospel of Luke in a translation by Nicholas Udall, and the Paraphrase of Matthew has sometimes been attributed to Henry's last queen, Catherine Parr; Mark was done by a little-known Oxford scholar, Thomas Key; and John by none other than Princess Mary Tudor, the future queen. Udall's prefaces present Erasmus as an authority comparable to the great fathers of the early church.

The increasingly Protestant character of religious policy under Edward VI confirmed the existing division between conservative and radical humanists. Bishop Gardiner bitterly opposed the overtly Protestant doctrines now gaining favour and drastically revised his earlier support of the use of Erasmus' works. Most of the conservative humanists, however, went along with the new regime, some reluctantly and some readily. Yet even the Protestant humanists in England seem to have favoured the more moderate and ecumenically inclined continental Protestants, such as Melanchthon, Oecolampadius, Bucer, and John à Lasco, all of whom were admirers of Erasmus.

The closing years of Henry VIII's reign and the reign of Edward VI are also important because a new generation of younger humanists was being formed, still committed to Erasmian ideals but increasingly attracted to Protestant doctrines and practices. The nucleus of this group came together between 1535 and 1544 at Cambridge University, many of them members of St John's College, one of the new colleges founded by Bishop John Fisher and Lady Margaret Beaufort for the express purpose of reforming religious life through humanistic education. The origins of the group go back to 1542, when Bishop Stephen Gardiner, chancellor of the university and leader of the conservative Anglo-Catholic faction at court, ordered the university to prohibit a new way of pronouncing Greek that had been proposed by Erasmus in 1528 as a return to ancient pronunciation. Use of this Erasmian pronunciation had been promoted by two young humanist fellows, John Cheke of St John's College and Thomas Smith of Queens'. Their adoption of the new pronunciation was symbolic of their intense commitment to humanistic studies. They attracted an enthusiastic following that came to be known as 'the Athenians', while their opponents were derisively dubbed 'Trojans'. The issue, of course, was not how to pronounce Greek but the conservative Gardiner's concern over the fashion for innovation, the lack of respect for tradition, and the general spirit of insubordination he sensed among the young humanists. What he really was trying to establish was not the old pronunciation of Greek but control of the university. He was never fully successful in suppressing the 'Athenian tribe'. Thomas Smith became an influential professor of civil law and a writer on political theory, and Cheke remained a charismatic tutor and friend of the zealous young humanists who (exactly as Gardiner had feared) were drawn not only to Erasmian pronunciation of Greek but also to a more clearly Protestant theology, especially in the reign of Edward VI.

Many of the young men associated with Cheke, sharing his sympathy for religious reform as well as for Erasmian pronunciation of Greek, were destined to hold high office not only in the university but in the English church and state. They included Roger Ascham and William Grindal, the future Archbishop of Canterbury, both of whom served as tutors to the future Queen Elizabeth I; William Cecil, who soon became an adviser to Princess Elizabeth and eventually was the most important of her government ministers; and a number of other prominent Elizabethans. All of these were Cheke's pupils at St John's. What is noteworthy about the 'Athenians' is not that a group of outstanding university men should rise to prominence but that this large and closely-knit group became almost entirely Protestant under Edward VI, and that they constituted most of the group who under Cecil's leadership took control of the church and state in 1558 and led the Elizabethan regime. This is a striking example of how humanism became the shaping educational force in the creation of England's Protestant ruling class. It also demonstrates that far from being shattered by the executions of More and Fisher, humanism extended in a direct 'apostolic succession' from Erasmus' English friends through all the religious changes under Henry, Edward, and Mary, down to the men who carried through the Elizabethan settlement in 1558–9. Perhaps nowhere else in Europe, not even in Italy, did education in humanistic subjects (as distinct from education in civil law) become so clearly a part of the common culture of the ruling elite.

Education and social advancement

On the Continent, despite the dominance of education in civil or canon law as a formal qualification for high office, mastery of the humanistic curriculum became an important part of preparation for entry into the privileged classes. This was an innovation of the Renaissance. Except for the clergy, education in Latin language and literature had not been an important qualification for the holding of high governmental office by laymen during the Middle Ages. In both France and Spain, the emergence of humanistic education as the essential first step towards social advancement is documented by the scramble to create local grammar schools in virtually every municipality, as described earlier. Well before the end of the sixteenth century, education in humanistic studies had established itself as the most widely accepted qualification for entry into the privileged classes of Europe, the classes that had access to high administrative and judicial office, to all teaching positions except those that imparted only vernacular literacy or some particular commercial or technical skill, and to all positions in the clergy. In many continental countries, to gain those very highest offices which could in two or three generations marvellously transform a wealthy bourgeois family into a noble one, study of law had to follow study of the humanities. The screening function of humanistic education – above all, the requirement to attain fluency in Latin – acted as a barrier to keep virtually all lower-class persons out of the privileged classes. The eagerness of socially reactionary monarchies in seventeenth-century France and Spain to limit access to grammar schools demonstrates that the filtering task of humanistic education was well understood.

Recently, some historians have not only demonstrated but also deplored this characteristic of Latin grammar schools, apparently overlooking what every bourgeois family then knew, that humanistic education had produced social advancement and tangible opportunity for ambitious and intelligent families during periods when the growth of free or inexpensive schools made humanistic education widely available. Renaissance society was elitist by design. But qualifications based on ability and education were more rational, more useful to the general welfare of society, than qualifications based on the accident of birth into a family of the aristocracy. Furthermore, educational qualifications were functional: they worked. Humanistic education no doubt undervalued originality and overvalued intellectual and social conformity, but it did impart skills that enabled graduates to perform the duties for which they were employed, especially skills in writing and speaking. In any case, the historian's task, like the anthropologist's, is not to sit in judgement on the moral or social purity of human societies, but merely to understand them.

Diffusion of the new culture

Although humanistic studies provided the common culture and social qualification for a ruling elite, their effects were not limited to that elite. The great Swiss historian Jakob Burckhardt, in his (literally) epoch-making book *The Civilization of the Renaissance in Italy,* devoted one section to a study of Italian Renaissance festivals, which he interpreted as proof that the elite culture was reflected in the popular culture and that the elaborate classical allegories of the festivals were thoroughly understood and appreciated by a popular audience because many elements of the Latin culture had become integral parts of the general culture as well. In the sixteenth century, the spread of printing and the employment of humanists to produce handbooks, summaries, and the earliest encyclopaedias organized on modern principles reflect the same process by which parts of humanistic culture penetrated far beyond the privileged elite. Obviously, full appreciation of both modern humanism and its ancient model was open only to those who had a classical education. But for those who lacked Latin or who had studied it but could not read it with ease, sixteenth-century translators unlocked the treasures of ancient Greece and Rome with a flood of vernacular editions. Of course some vernacular translations of ancient literature were made in the Middle Ages – for example, at the French royal court in the early fourteenth century or even at the Anglo-Saxon court of Alfred the Great. But in the sixteenth century, the power of the printing press spread the desire as well as the ability to read the classics far beyond the Latin-reading public. The French led the way, with the Italians close behind; but readers of English and Spanish also had a rich selection of ancient authors available in print by the end of the sixteenth century, while for some reason the Germans lagged far behind. If one omits minor authors and focuses on the five principal vernaculars of Western culture at that period (Italian, French, Spanish, English, and German), this availability is striking: Appian was available in English, French, Italian, and Spanish; some of Aristophanes in Italian and Spanish; some of Aristotle in all five languages (but only Italian had many of his works); Dioscorides in French, German, Italian, and Spanish; Euclid in English, French, Italian, and Spanish; parts of Euripides and Galen in all five languages; parts of Herodotus in English, French, German, and Italian but not in Spanish; Hesiod only in French; Hippocrates in English, French, and Italian; one or both epics of Homer, plus Isocrates and Lucian, in all five languages; Plato in all but German (though only one title in English); Plutarch, both the *Parallel Lives* and the *Moralia,* in all five languages; Polybius and some of Ptolemy in English, French, and Italian; Sophocles in French and Italian; and Thucydides and Xenophon in all five languages. Among major Latin authors, even more translations were made into the five vernaculars: Apuleius, Boethius, Caesar, Cicero, Horace, Livy, Ovid, Plautus, the elder Pliny, Sallust, the younger Seneca, Tacitus, and Terence into all five; Juvenal into all but English; Martial into all but Spanish; the younger Pliny into English, German, and Italian. Professional textbooks used in university study had a mixed record of vernacular translations. Thus the *Institutes,* the legal textbook prepared as part of Justinian's codification of Roman law, was available in French, German, and Spanish; but a scientific work like Pomponius Mela was published only in English and Italian, and medical works like Celsus (German) and Vegetius (Italian) were not widely translated. The influential *De architectura* of Vitruvius, while it appeared frequently in Italian, had only one printing in German and one complete version and one set of extracts in French, but no English or Spanish translation.[1] For a thorough mastery of ancient literature, mastery of Latin was essential and good control of Greek virtually essential. Nevertheless, the main point remains true: knowledge of classical literature spread far beyond the ruling elite and became (and still remains) an integral part of the literature and general culture of all European nations. By the late Renaissance, except for the peasants and the very lowest classes of the urban population, humanist influence was everywhere.

---

[1] Based on table in R. R. Bolgar, *The Classical Heritage*, 2nd edn (New York, 1964), pp. 508–41.

7   The end of an age

By the closing decades of the sixteenth century, Renaissance humanism had become the prevalent culture among the educated elite that dominated the political establishment, the officially recognized churches, and the schools of western and central Europe, north as well as south of the Alps. Even across the bitterly contested divide of the Reformation, and despite the limitations imposed by censorship of the press, inquisitions, and consistories, a broadly uniform higher culture prevailed. Books and ideas passed back and forth from Protestant to Catholic regions. A famous classical scholar and neo-Stoic moralist like Justus Lipsius (1547–1606) could make his academic career at different periods of his life at both Protestant and Catholic universities provided he was willing to conform to the established local form of Christianity, even though there were some bitter remarks about the slippery religious convictions of an author whose most famous book of ethics was called *Of Constancy.* Furthermore, though the humanistic culture that prevailed in the late Renaissance was in one sense restricted to the privileged few who could obtain an education, the work of translators and popularizers allowed a much larger proportion of the population to share the new culture. A man of the people like Shakespeare had access to themes, ideas, and values found in classical texts, even though he could never penetrate the classical heritage with the profundity of a brilliant and privileged university graduate like John Milton. The humanistic tradition remained dominant in many respects, among plain folk as well as the educated classes, into the late nineteenth century.

Extent of humanism's triumph

The penetration of humanistic learning into the general society differed greatly from region to region, because it varied with the degree of economic development, urbanization, and literacy. Countries that were highly developed, such as the Netherlands and the urbanized parts of England, France, and Italy, show strong classical influence even in their vernacular literature, while in largely peasant districts, only a privileged few had much appreciation or knowledge of classical and humanistic writings.

The triumph of humanism was never total. After all, humanism never really claimed to embrace every aspect of learning. In education, its nucleus always remained that limited group of subjects which since Cicero's time had been known as humanistic studies (*studia humanitatis*), those subjects most essential to the intellectual and moral formation of a mature human being: grammar and rhetoric (the arts of effective communication and persuasive argument), history and poetry (both conceived as parts of ancient literature), and moral philosophy (which involved not primarily a body of knowledge to be understood but rather a set of values to be internalized and applied in making the moral choices that arise in every human's life). The humanists touted the central importance of grammar, rhetoric, and moral philosophy and criticized traditional educators for neglecting them and giving too much attention to formal logic, but they never demanded the abolition of other academic subjects. In practice, they nowhere destroyed the basic outlines of medieval scholastic learning. Academic philosophy remained almost totally based on Aristotle, and the ultimate collapse of Aristotle's role as the central authority, *the* Philosopher, in the middle of the seventeenth century resulted not from humanistic educational reforms but from the shocking revelation by the new natural scientists that his natural philosophy was fundamentally unsound both in specific conclusions and in intellectual method. Until that happened, university education remained largely scholastic despite the humanistic reforms.

Humanism also changed academic life beyond the liberal-arts curriculum. Humanists made good their claim that the ancient texts on which all non-humanistic studies were based were subject to critical evaluation by the philological method invented by humanists like Lorenzo Valla and Erasmus. Here, in cases where humanists expressed opinions on the authoritative texts used by other academic fields, is where the ugliest academic conflicts occurred, for humanists were perceived as intruders into non-humanistic fields when they insisted that any study of an ancient legal or medical or even biblical text was invalid unless based on a critical assessment of the ancient text in the original language. Such conflicts pitted individual humanists against representatives of the natural sciences, against traditional legal scholars, and against medical scholars. But most contentious of all were the humanists' challenges to scholastic theology. With more or less radicalism, various humanists rejected the scholastic use of Aristotelian logic to organize and interpret the Bible. Their conception of theology, especially after the work of Valla and Erasmus, questioned or even denied the value of rationalistic argumentation and endorsed the predominance of the biblical text. Thus they would make theological learning depend on exegesis of the sacred text rather than on logical demonstration. In all these fields, if the authority of the ancient text in its original form became paramount, the humanist as the expert on the interpretation of texts really did take control of natural science, or law, or medicine, or theology. University education and professional study remained largely scholastic through the Renaissance, both in form and in content; but scholasticism survived at the price of gradual and often grudging concessions to reform.

Transformation of humanism

Any attempt to trace humanism in European high culture of the later Renaissance is difficult because, in some form and to some degree, humanism was everywhere. The truth was in the text, and the expert humanist critic controlled the text. Yet if traditional education and both Latin and vernacular literature had been permeated by humanistic learning, humanism also had changed. In a sense, humanism at the end of the Renaissance survived by dissolving into a number of separate though interrelated strands.

One aspect of humanism, the linguistic, philological, and textual, grew into the highly sophisticated but narrowly specialized fields of philology and classical studies. Another aspect, the literary and aesthetic, grew into a literary movement, producing Latin and vernacular poetry, history, and prose fiction inspired by classical models. This line of development also led to a conscious effort to discover and apply the artistic principles on which classical literature was founded and so led, guided by the newly influential *Poetics* of Aristotle, to the neoclassical movement of the seventeenth century.

While the humanistic curriculum dominated the leading grammar schools and expanded its position in nearly all universities, the humanistic curriculum as actually taught focused on a small and cautiously chosen segment of classical literature, tacitly renouncing the dream of enriching students' minds with the whole broad and exciting spectrum of ancient texts. Latin and Greek literature contained much that could challenge prevailing social, political, and religious ideas; but such books were carefully excluded from the classroom. Humanistic education in actual practice imparted familiarity with only a time-worn and often shop-worn body of safe texts. Humanistic education could lead a Niccolò Machiavelli or a John Milton to look beyond conventional pieties and to challenge the established social, political, and religious order; but such was not the purpose of those who authorized, financed, and controlled the schools; and such was not the usual result of humanistic study. The heroic if rather vague dreams of renewal through rediscovery of the whole classical past found in pioneering figures like Petrarch or Erasmus gave way to the humbler goal of graduating boys who had a reasonable facility in reading and even speaking and writing something akin to classical Latin and who also possessed a general familiarity with ancient times through the rather plodding study of a handful of 'safe' Roman and Greek authors. Humanism may have set out to revitalize both secular life and the church, but after two or three centuries it had become the bulwark of an authoritarian and carefully orthodox social and ecclesiastical order. The potentially radical implications of humanists' textual and historical criticism were carefully confined to narrowly defined details of classical erudition. A Machiavelli or a Milton might find in the classics the foundation of the same republican political ideals that had animated some Florentine humanists in the early fifteenth century, but for the most part humanism had been tamed into conformity to the needs of absolute monarchies and established churches (Grafton and Jardine, pp. xii–xv, 9–28). This is not necessarily to say that humanism had failed (though some modern critics claim just that), for it never set out with a clearly defined and highly detailed plan of action. Perhaps its conformity to the requirements of ruling elites ought not to be seen as a betrayal but only as a striking success in integrating itself into the very fabric of its world. The humanists as a group had never been truly radical reformers, not even in education; and their ready accommodation to the authoritarian political structures of the late Renaissance and the seventeenth century, however regrettable it may seem to some modern critics, was in no sense a betrayal of the vague reformist dreams of the first humanists.

There were lasting successes. Education really had become more literary and classical and less dominated by dialectic than in the late Middle Ages. The ruling elite really had become less exclusively feudal and military and far more literate and literary in outlook; religion really had been reformed, though at the cost of losing religious unity. Each of the major religious reforms – Roman Catholic, Lutheran, Calvinist, and Anglican – had drawn heavily on the ideas and achievements of Renaissance humanism, even though after the Council of Trent, reformed Catholicism had rejected certain directions of humanistic thought and certain individual humanists (Erasmus in particular) and had also reaffirmed the value of much of its medieval heritage. As humanistic learning permeated all fields of high culture, it seemed to melt away since its very success made it no longer seem to be a distinct and challenging movement.

Rebellion against philosophy

Viewed as a distinct intellectual movement, humanism seems hesitant
and unclear. After all due respect is paid to intellectually attractive figures
like Petrarch, Lorenzo Valla, Nicholas of Cusa, and Marsilio Ficino, it
remains true that humanism – indeed, the whole Renaissance period, late
scholasticism included – did not produce a single major philosopher who
can rank with figures like Plato, Aristotle, or Aquinas in earlier centuries,
or with Galileo, Descartes, Hume, or Kant in the following period. This
philosophical mediocrity is no accident. The humanists did not set out to
develop a new philosophy. As professional rhetoricians, they challenged
the whole enterprise of philosophy, especially the attempt to elaborate a
comprehensive picture of reality. Most of the clearest-headed and most
influential humanists regarded human intellectual activity as instrumen-
tal and showed little interest in metaphysics. The human intellect, they
believed, is suited only to making response to specific problems – generally, problems of moral choice – that arise in the ongoing process of living;
it is not suited to the elaboration of broad, abstract philosophical systems.
The first major humanist thinker, Petrarch, shows this tendency very
clearly in his disdain for the intellectualist moral philosophy of Aristotle
and his preference for the eclectic blend of Academic scepticism and
Stoicism found in the philosophical works of Cicero. This same disdain
for abstract thought and system-building underlies the humanists' puzzling but unmistakable emphasis on rhetoric, which the best humanist
thinkers (Petrarch, Valla, Erasmus) did not conceive as just a technique of
embellishing human discourse but rather as a means of arguing for or
against a specific course of action in an effective, persuasive way (Gray
1963; Seigel 1968). Moral philosophy, the only branch of traditional philosophy to be numbered among the *studia humanitatis,* seemed the most
important kind of philosophy because it deals with the problems faced
daily by real people. Underlying this exaltation of moral philosophy and
rhetoric (the true core subjects of humanistic educational theory, even if
repetitive drilling on the details of grammar and Ciceronian style constituted the daily reality of the classroom) is a widely held view of human
nature: that human beings are primarily creatures of passion, not of intellect; that the goal of human life is to act in a real world of flesh and blood,
not to disdain the material world and seek fulfilment in contemplation of
a purely spiritual reality; that God must be approached through love and
grace and not primarily (or not at all) through rationalistic argumentation.

Conceivably, these ideas could have been developed into a comprehensive philosophical system that might have been labelled 'humanism'. But

the humanists' general hostility to all past philosophical systems, even
ancient ones, stood in the way. P. O. Kristeller was right on this issue:
there was no distinctive philosophy of humanism. Humanists generally
avoided metaphysical issues, preferring to dwell on the concrete. That is
precisely why figures like Ficino and Pico, though they possessed humanistic skills, should not be regarded as typical representatives of humanism,
but should be seen for what they were, leaders of one particular type of
fifteenth-century philosophy.

Humanism as an intellectual solvent

The true function of humanism in European history was not to shape
some new philosophy called 'humanism' but to act as an intellectual
solvent, striking down traditional beliefs of all kinds. Late medieval
thought and society were riven by disagreement, by conflict, by uncertainty. Though we can no longer dismiss late scholasticism as moribund or
incompetent, its principal accomplishment was the negative criticism of
the works of the great synthetic philosophers of high scholasticism such as
Aquinas. Late scholastic thinkers like Scotus and Ockham and their disciples were far more successful at picking apart the systems of thirteenth-
century scholasticism than in creating a broadly acceptable synthesis.
Their wrangling contentiousness and sectarian bickering were among the
accusations hurled at current scholastic philosophers by their humanist
critics, beginning with Petrarch and continuing down to and beyond
Erasmus and Rabelais. Humanists did not propose to provide better
answers to the questions debated by scholastic philosophers and theologians. Their tendency rather was to suggest that the old questions were not
worth debating or were beyond the reach of human abilities. As we have
seen, the humanists turned not to philosophy but to an idealized and
largely mythical Antiquity – Christian as well as classical – as the source of
knowledge and wisdom.

   In the long run, this idealized and vague 'Antiquity' to which humanist
authors referred their readers did not contain adequate solutions to the
problems that puzzled and worried their contemporaries. Humanists
made a strenuous effort to rediscover all of the treasures – literary, philosophical, religious, even artistic – of ancient civilization. In philosophy,
this included not only a systematic effort to replace the medieval Latin
text of Aristotle's works with new translations based on the original Greek
but also an effort to challenge Aristotle's overwhelming authority as *the*
Philosopher. In part they did this by discovering and publishing the works
of rival ancient philosophers. The desire for an alternative authority to
replace Aristotle was a major motive behind the hard work of finding and

translating other Greek philosophers. The outstanding example was the translation of the whole corpus of Plato's works from Greek into Latin by Marsilio Ficino.

Although Platonism became and remained the most widespread of the revived ancient philosophies, Lorenzo Valla had asserted the value of Epicurean philosophy. In the late sixteenth century, neo-Stoicism, a philosophy that emphasized the moral earnestness of Roman Stoics like Cicero, Seneca, and Marcus Aurelius, had a certain vogue, represented by writers such as Michel de Montaigne and Justus Lipsius. Yet none of these revived forms of ancient philosophy gained a profound hold on the conscience of more than a few scattered individuals. Not even Platonism managed to crack the monopoly of Aristotle in academic philosophy, largely because Aristotelianism was the only system that embraced the whole range of philosophical issues and in particular the only one that dealt in detail with natural philosophy (that is, natural science). In the long run, therefore, humanist attacks on the medieval traditions of interpreting Aristotle and on the sharp divisions among the various scholastic 'ways' merely increased the uncertainty and doubt already generated by wrangling among rival scholastic traditions. The movement produced better translations of Aristotle and promoted awareness of discordant ancient interpretations of his thought. Humanist exploration of alternative philosophical authorities demonstrated that even the revered ancients were unable to reach agreement on philosophical truth. Rediscovery of texts and more information about ancient thought were supposed to lead to harmony, concord, and unity in philosophy, a goal especially dear to the fifteenth-century Platonists. But deeper study of ancient philosophy merely revealed deeper levels of disagreement. Neither the ancients nor modern interpreters such as Ficino, nor the wrangling rival traditions of scholasticism, could end disagreement.

Rebirth of philosophical scepticism

One possible response to this failure to attain philosophical concord was the conclusion that all human knowledge is open to doubt and that all human learning, ancient as well as scholastic, is unreliable. The humanists' attack on the value of scholastic tradition and the Protestants' challenge to unscriptural practices and beliefs combined to create an attitude of doubt among many intellectuals. In addition, at the highest level of belief, in theology, the Protestants' rejection of the ultimate authority of the church hierarchy to determine religious truth raised in both theological and philosophical contexts the question of what constitutes the criterion (the intellectual yardstick, so to speak) by which truth is determined.

The Protestants offered as an alternative to the rulings of the church hierarchy the words of the Bible as the criterion of religious truth; but since
experience soon demonstrated that different people understood the Bible
in different ways, that criterion was inevitably less certain than the
authoritative determination of religious truth by one single human agent,
the pope – provided, of course, one accepted the belief that the pope
would always make the correct decision. Theological debates that
reached no resolution and the continuing emergence of new systems of
Christian truth (or heresy) were probably the most important source of
the re-emergence of a philosophical scepticism that questioned whether
anyone could gain metaphysical certitude – that is, knowledge that could
be shown to be true beyond any possible doubt.

Another source of scepticism, but probably a less decisive one, was
increased attention to sceptical philosophers of ancient times; and this, of
course, was made possible by humanistic textual studies. Ancient scepticism had not been of much interest to medieval thinkers, though in the
form of Academic scepticism, some sceptical opinions continued to be
known (and rejected) as presented in the readily available works of Cicero
and St Augustine. The more radical scepticism of the Pyrrhonist school
was much less known because only one author representing that school,
Sextus Empiricus, survived into modern times; and his works were virtually unknown until rediscovered and published by humanist editors and
translators in the mid-sixteenth century. In 1562, Henri Estienne, one of
the great scholar-printers of Parisian humanism, published a Latin
edition of Sextus' *Pyrrhonian Hypotyposes* (*c.* AD 200), followed in 1569
by a Latin edition of all of Sextus' works. The original Greek text did not
see print until 1621. The important part of Sextus' work was his presentation of tropes which put forth intellectual conundrums that could not be
resolved, either affirmatively or negatively, and which therefore ended in
the desired Pyrrhonian attitude, suspense of judgement. The ultimate
goal of both forms of ancient scepticism was to oppose philosophical dogmatism. Academic sceptics, while denying that human reason could
attain certitude on any question, did concede the possibility of showing
that one conclusion was more probable than another. Pyrrhonists,
however, insisted that all judgements were open to question and that the
only proper reaction to a debatable question was suspension of judgement. Ancient sceptics also vigorously attacked the very sources of all
knowledge by engaging in a vigorous critique of the reliability of sensory
experience, showing how often and how easily the senses are misled into
false conclusions. But mere availability of ancient sceptical texts was less
important than the raising of the whole issue of the criterion of truth by
Luther's attack on the infallibility of the church hierarchy.

Authors concerned about these problems of knowledge began citing Sextus Empiricus. Gianfrancesco Pico della Mirandola (1470–1533), nephew of the more famous Giovanni Pico, became convinced that arrogant rationalism was undermining faith and so published a book (*Examen vanitatis doctrinae gentium,* 1520) attacking human reason, especially the principal rationalist authority, Aristotle. His book draws on the works of Sextus Empiricus for much of its argument against the reliability of human reason. His intended conclusion was that since reason leads only to sin and error, divine revelation is the only reliable source of truth. A slightly earlier and somewhat similar use of scepticism to attack trust in reason and endorse reliance on revelation is the book *De vera philosophia* (1509) by Cardinal Adriano Castellesi da Corneto. He opposed Ficino's attempt to make Platonism into a philosophical foundation for Christian doctrines, drawing his underlying arguments against reason from Cicero's Academic scepticism. He organized his book as an anthology of anti-philosophical quotations from the four great doctors of the ancient Latin church, Saints Ambrose, Jerome, Augustine, and Gregory.

Distrust of rationalism as a potential threat to religion went back to the earliest age of the church and was an issue on which Christian intellectuals had always disagreed, so that the patristic authorities themselves were divided on the value of reason. Suspicion of reason was an important source of opposition to the growth of early scholasticism in the twelfth century. An example is the hostility of St Bernard of Clairvaux to the founder of the dialectical method in theology, Peter Abelard. Similar suspicion motivated much of the hostility to the rationalism of Thomas Aquinas, especially after the famous condemnation of rationalistic theses by the bishop of Paris in 1277. In the movements for spiritual renewal during the fourteenth and fifteenth centuries, such as the Dutch *Devotio Moderna,* the arrogance and unbelief of philosophically educated scholars was a common theme, expressed clearly in *The Imitation of Christ* by Thomas à Kempis, who was no rationalist but also no humanist. The fideistic attitude expressed by Gianfrancesco Pico and Cardinal Adriano, with its emphasis on blind faith rather than philosophical proof, was very similar to the *Imitation,* except that Pico and Cardinal Adriano drew on sceptical arguments to strengthen their case.

This religious suspicion of reason was independent of humanism in many respects, but the work of Gianfrancesco Pico and Cardinal Adriano shows that its supporters sometimes drew on ancient texts like Sextus Empiricus or Cicero's *Academica* for support. Erasmus of Rotterdam, the greatest humanist of the early sixteenth century, expressed the critical mentality of the major humanists and gave witty and persuasive expression to the widespread hostility to scholasticism. He particularly emphasized the sectarian divisions and petty factionalism of the rival scholastic traditions. Although Erasmus did not challenge the reverence shown by earlier humanists for classical (as distinct from scholastic) tradition, his famous dispute with Martin Luther over the freedom of the will led him to challenge directly Luther's confidence that the truth on issues raised by the Reformation, such as predestination and free will, could be determined with absolute certainty. Erasmus deliberately raised the sceptical issue, arguing that issues like free will and predestination are highly complex, that even the scriptural evidence is ambivalent, and that the very fact that such issues have been repeatedly debated by earnest and sincere Christians since the earliest times suggests that certainty is unattainable. Christians would be wise to admit that they can attain only probable truth on such issues and hence should prudently remain tolerant of those who judge the probabilities differently. While in addressing conservative Catholics Erasmus used such arguments to plead for moderation in dealing with Luther, his fundamental purpose was to support his own personal decision to remain in the old church. Absent convincing proofs showing beyond doubt that the old religion was wrong on major doctrines, it seemed more prudent to remain with the traditional institution.

Shortly after Erasmus' open break with Luther in 1524, the German occultist and humanist Heinrich Cornelius Agrippa von Nettesheim (1486–1535) wrote a work attacking all fields of human learning and worldly endeavour, *On the Vanity and Uncertainty of Arts and Sciences* (1530). To some extent, this book is just an example of a genre of satires, partly humorous and partly serious, aimed at various social classes and professions, including especially the clergy, and urging the targets of the satire to reform their evil ways. Such books included Sebastian Brant's *Ship of Fools* (1494), which was widely diffused in the original German and in Latin and French translations, and also Erasmus' *Praise of Folly,* which is by far the most penetrating and effective humanistic satire. But Agrippa's *Vanity* shows a savage bite and an unremitting determination to prove that all fields of learning, all social and occupational groups (especially the clergy), and all human institutions, both church and state, are corrupt, involve people in sin, and lack any secure intellectual foundation, being based purely on conjecture and false reasoning. The book ends with a fideistic insistence that the only true and certain knowledge is to be found in the Gospel, and that the humble Christian believer, symbolized by the simple fool or the patient ass, is closer to truth and to salvation than the learned scholar. This ideal is closely akin to the *idiota,* or humble believer, idealized by the fifteenth-century philosopher Nicholas of Cusa, whose masterpiece *On Learned Ignorance* is cited by Agrippa. The same idea, with less overtly fideistic overtones, appears in Erasmus' *Praise of*

Folly, where the perfect Christian is presented as a fool when judged by merely worldly standards.

Aside from its bitterness of tone and vehemence, Agrippa's *Vanity* is distinct from most social satires because of its explicit, though unsystematic, use of sceptical arguments. Agrippa cannot be called a sceptic in the same sense as Montaigne or Hume, but he did refer to both the Academics and the Pyrrhonists and like the ancient sceptics directly questioned human ability to know causes. Though his direct discussion of epistemological issues is brief indeed, he employs a major sceptical argument when he demonstrates the unreliability of sensory experience in order to prove that all human knowledge is open to question. He also points out that since human senses cannot produce anything but the perception of singular objects, there is no sure way to progress from knowledge of singular objects to knowledge of causes or to any sort of general principles. All higher generalizations in all sciences are nothing but arbitrary opinions, and any generalization can be disproved just as easily as it can be proved. Real truth is too elusive to be captured by syllogisms or any human proofs; it can be gained only by faith. Agrippa's book was often presented (by his French translator in 1582, for example) as a humorous, witty, but not wholly serious paradox, useful because of the extreme statements that could be used by courtiers and others who liked to uphold unconventional opinions in conversation. But under the humour and the rather superficial denunciation of all professions, doctrines, and social classes, there remains the unsettling generalization that no tradition, no field of knowledge, no philosophical demonstration was certain and reliable. While there is no way of knowing how seriously readers took Agrippa's pessimism, his book was frequently reprinted in Latin and received an English translation (by James Sandford, 1569) as well as the French translation by Louis de Mayerne-Turquet.

An even more widely known expression of cultural nihilism, also serious in purpose but humorous in expression, was the discussion of Pyrrhonism in the *Tiers Livre* of François Rabelais (1546). His 'Pyrrhonist' character, Trouillogan, does not employ the standard Pyrrhonist tropes available in the still-unpublished works of Sextus Empiricus. Instead he offers evasive and ambiguous answers in order to spread confusion and avoid giving a clear answer to Panurge's effort to get advice on whether he should marry. Scepticism is only a passing fancy in Rabelais, though like many humanists he poured contempt on traditional scholastic learning. He shows his opinion of the university education received by the young giant Gargantua by having Gargantua purged with a powerful laxative before beginning his re-education in a more natural and essentially humanistic manner.

Prior to the first edition of Sextus Empiricus in 1562, discussions of scepticism were frequent but generally superficial and jocular – more like Rabelais than like Gianfrancesco Pico and Agrippa. The obvious failure of theologians and philosophers to attain unity created a sense of uneasiness that was usually masked by humour. Pico's and Agrippa's books are more serious and strike not just at scholastic studies but also at grammar, rhetoric, moral philosophy, and the whole range of humanistic studies as well. What makes them unusual is that they challenge the humanist dream of cultural and social renewal through the recovery of ancient wisdom almost as savagely as they attack scholasticism. The only clear advantage they concede to humanistic learning is that its emphasis on languages and original texts leads directly to Scripture, which is the only real source of certain knowledge, based on faith rather than reason.

The war against Aristotle

These criticisms of reason, tradition, and learning went far beyond conventional humanist complaints about the established academic culture. Not all such criticisms took a sceptical direction. Many of them took the form of attacks on Aristotle, even though he remained the central authority for academic study of philosophy and natural science. One major line of attack is represented by a number of Italian philosophers who tried to reconstruct philosophy on the basis of Platonism but also to deal with questions of natural science, a subject that all known Platonic sources neglected. They are often labelled 'Italian philosophers of nature'. The most important individuals were Francesco Patrizi (1529–97), Bernardino Telesio (1509–88), and two Dominican friars, Giordano Bruno (1548–1600) and Tommaso Campanella (1568–1639). None of them achieved a viable and coherent philosophical synthesis, but each drew on humanistic discoveries of philosophical texts to suggest alternatives to Aristotelian natural science. Except for Telesio, each of them was a Platonist, a disciple not only of Plato and the Neoplatonists (Porphyry, Proclus, and Plotinus from ancient Alexandria and Ficino and Pico from the Florentine Renaissance) but also of pseudo-philosophical and occultist texts and authors who were historically associated with Platonism: the Cabala, Hermes Trismegistus, Zoroaster, Orpheus, the Sibylline oracles, Pythagoras, and pseudo-Dionysius. Patrizi, Bruno, and Campanella followed Ficino in believing that these occultist texts represented an ancient theological wisdom divinely revealed to Hebrew and gentile sages. Like Ficino, Patrizi and Campanella emphasized the harmony of these ancient or pseudo-ancient sources with Christianity. Patrizi even tried to persuade the pope to mandate the teaching of his new philosophy in all Catholic schools. Campanella, despite being imprisoned by the Dominican order for more than thirty years, still thought of himself as a Catholic and in his famous utopian political treatise, *The City of the Sun* (1623), aspired to a just society that would be ruled politically as well as spiritually by a high-priest (the pope) who could draw down magical and astrological powers from the heavens.

Bruno's devotion to the occult was even more extreme and heterodox. He regarded the Hermetic books as the true revelation of divine wisdom and discounted Aristotelian rationalism and orthodox Christianity as materialistic corruptions that would be removed when he purified Catholicism and restored the true magical–astrological religion of ancient Egypt. He also interpreted Platonic philosophy in an obviously pantheistic way, teaching that everything is God. Thus his execution by the Inquisition in 1600 was based on religious and philosophical doctrines that had nothing to do with his endorsement of Copernicus' heliocentric astronomy or his conclusion that the universe is infinite.

Unlike the three Platonist occultists, Telesio had relatively little problem with charges of heresy. This was because unlike the others he was not much drawn to the occultist sources and the speculative astral magic that marked their thought. The major ancient influence on his thought was the materialistic Epicurean philosophy of the Roman poet Lucretius, not the spirit-ridden Neoplatonism of Ficino and his disciples. Though his doctrine that the soul is a subtle material substance must have sounded dangerous, he guarded his orthodoxy by insisting that humans also have a non-material soul, which is the source of immortality and all moral and religious instincts. This soul is infused miraculously by God and so is not a part of nature or natural philosophy.

Despite their many individual differences, all four of these 'philosophers of nature' were aggressively hostile to the philosophy of Aristotle and his scholastic disciples. All four concentrated their attack on what had been the principal source of Aristotle's dominance over scholastic thought, his philosophy of nature. The specific object of attack was his doctrine of substantial forms: his teaching that all material things consist of two distinct principles, an underlying, undifferentiated, and unshaped matter (which Aristotle but not his orthodox Christian disciples regarded as eternal and uncreated) and a specific individuating form, the principle that shapes the matter and makes each existing object become what it is. (For example, in a human being, the vivifying rational soul is the form, the individuating principle that shapes indeterminate matter into a man or a woman.) None of these four philosophers was able to put forward a convincing alternative to the doctrine of substantial forms, but they did focus on the major doctrine that perished when Aristotelian natural philosophy finally lost credibility in the seventeenth century. Their rather muddled philosophies cannot be equated with humanism, but they depended on the humanists' work of making ancient non-Aristotelian texts available to help them in formulating their attacks on Aristotle.

The attack on Aristotelian natural philosophy was by no means limited to Italian philosophers of nature such as Patrizi, Telesio, Bruno, and Campanella. At the University of Wittenberg, Luther's hostility to Aristotle spilled over from attacks on scholastic theology to a determined effort to find alternative texts to displace Aristotle's books of natural philosophy from the liberal-arts curriculum. Pliny's *Natural History* was the text substituted, but such an unsystematic hotchpotch of information and misinformation was unsuited for teaching, and Aristotle's *Physics* and other scientific books gradually crept back into the curriculum. Whatever their defects might be, they were well ordered and teachable; and Philip Melanchthon and other Evangelical humanists who directed educational reform could not find adequate replacements for them.

A considerable number of physicians speculated about the foundations of natural science and raised objections to the Aristotelian principles on which medical teaching and practice were based. Many of them drew on the humanists' descriptions of other ancient philosophies, for humanism had both uncovered alternative texts and created a more historical way of thinking about the development of ancient philosophy, so that Aristotle no longer seemed *the* Philosopher but only one among many. One dissatisfied physician was Girolamo Fracastoro of Verona (1470–1553). His *De contagione* (1546) was a pioneering study in epidemiology. He argued for the superiority of empirically based medicine over that which confined itself to the study of Aristotle and Greek medical authors like Galen. Influenced by the pre-Socratic philosopher Democritus and the Roman Epicurean philosopher–poet Lucretius, Fracastoro upheld an atomic theory of the nature of matter, in direct opposition to Aristotle's theory of substantial forms. He explained contagion by the diffusion of seeds or tiny particles of the disease that penetrated the body and caused illness.

A far rougher, less sophisticated, but even more famous critic of Aristotelian science and Galenic medicine was the Swiss physician Theophrast Bombast von Hohenheim (1493–1541), who repudiated all classical medicine and took the name Paracelsus to symbolize his claim to be greater than the most famous ancient Roman physician, Celsus. He rejected the standard classical and medieval categories used for classifying and explaining material substance and tried to explain material objects as varying combinations of three first principles or elements, which he called mercury, salt, and sulphur but which he did not exactly identify with the chemical substances known by those names. He was widely but unsystematically learned, drawing ideas from ancient texts but scornfully repudiating the respect for ancient authorities typical of humanists and most physicians. His writings are a turgid mix of theology, philosophy, chemistry, learned medicine, folk-remedies, magic, and personal experience. But he attracted a considerable following among nonconformist medical practitioners. His fame and following are a clear sign that a whole section of the medical profession was beginning to turn against the ancient classical sources as well as medieval Arabic medicine.

Yet another rebellious physician and philosopher of the sixteenth century was Girolamo Cardano (1501–76), who is now known primarily for his writings on arithmetic and algebra, especially for his interest in probability, but was then also famous for two philosophical books. The earlier was *On Wisdom* (1544), where he drew a sharp contrast between 'human sciences', which are largely rhetorical and moral in content and are used chiefly by rulers to dominate and deceive people, and 'natural knowledge', which aims at 'rational discovery of the structure of reality'. 'Natural knowledge' did not exclude occult sciences, especially astrology, which had always had an important role in European medicine. His *On Subtlety* (1550) was a strongly anti-Aristotelian and comprehensive study of natural philosophy. It is rather obscure, but it did challenge the adequacy of Aristotelian natural philosophy and was frequently reprinted.

Natural science and medicine were closely linked to the general study of philosophy in medieval and Renaissance universities. Both the 'philosophers of nature' and an assortment of nonconformist medical writers focused their attack on the validity of Aristotelian philosophy. The authority of Aristotle was also challenged in the field of theology, not only by Luther and Calvin and other Protestant theologians but also by humanistic theologians like Erasmus, who may have disagreed with the Protestants' repudiation of papal authority but who to a large extent agreed with them that the whole effort of high scholasticism to apply Aristotelian dialectic to the elaboration of a speculative theology was a misbegotten undertaking. Both humanists and Protestants conceived of the proper role of theology as the explication (largely through linguistic and philological methods) of the sacred text. Neither the Erasmian humanists' cautious but vague concession that scholasticism still had some limited value to religion nor the later Protestants' return to many scholastic practices as they strove to systematize their doctrines really reversed the unsettling effects of their anti-dialectical criticisms. Although a scholastic revival (especially a revived commitment to the thought of Thomas Aquinas) can be discerned from the early sixteenth century, and though neo-Thomism became the semi-official philosophy of post-Tridentine Catholicism, neoscholasticism flourished only in overwhelmingly Catholic countries, where it was imposed by ecclesiastical control of the schools and the press. Later scholastic thinkers did have some influence even in Protestant lands, but their work was and remains largely irrelevant and even antithetical to the main lines of philosophical and scientific development in modern Western culture. Not a single major figure of post-Renaissance Western thought functioned as a conscious disciple of any of the medieval scholastic doctors, or even as a genuine philosophical disciple of Aristotle or Plato. This demolition of the authority of Aristotle and the scholastics was largely a consequence of the new scientific thought that began to develop in the sixteenth century but attained its maturity only in the middle of the seventeenth century. But the growing rebellion against Aristotle in the sixteenth century forms part of the background for these later developments.

The search for a new logic

Anti-Aristotelianism emerged not only in medicine, natural philosophy, and theology but even in logic, the methodological inner sanctum of scholastic thought. The syllogistic reasoning that formed the core of medieval teaching of dialectic had never been very effective at explaining how new propositions can be derived and proved true. Its strength was in demonstrating by deductive reasoning the consequences of propositions already accepted. Its treatment of the inductive procedure by which individual phenomena are studied in order to discover valid generalizations was quite offhand and feeble. This weakness was already obvious to late-scholastic thinkers, and late scholasticism, almost wholly independently of humanist influence, produced during the period 1300–1600 a number of studies of the logic of scientific investigation that probed the thought-processes by which sensory experiences could be analysed and then synthetically recombined into valid generalizations. In fact, the first really successful practitioner of the experimental method of modern science, Galileo Galilei, was a product of this tradition, though he carried it further and applied it more successfully than any of his predecessors.

Humanist scholars had already joined in the criticism of scholastic logic in the fifteenth century, though on grounds very different from those applied by scholastic philosophers (chiefly Italians) who sought to devise a new logic of scientific discovery. The humanists challenged the intellectualist conception of human nature that dominated scholasticism. Their goal was not the pursuit of absolutely certain proofs but rather guidance in making the kinds of decisions that arise in everyday life, where determination of eternally valid general truth is rarely an issue. Most of the decisions involved in real life, they argued, deal with weighing the favourable and unfavourable consequences of choosing one of two or more alternative courses of action. In such essentially moral decisions – such as whether to marry or not, whether to invest in a business venture or not, whether to enter the service of a prince or not – determination of absolute truth is not an issue. The process of decision deals with probabilities. Thus rhetorical argumentation, which in ancient authors like Quintilian dealt largely with judgement of probability, seemed more important to human need than formal syllogistic reasoning, which had little utility outside the artificial disputations of the universities. This position favouring rhetoric over dialectic found clear expression in the *Dialectical Disputations* of Lorenzo Valla. His insistence on probable decisions as the essential activity of human life was also reflected in Erasmus' attempt to refute Luther's dogmatism with sceptical arguments, as shown in Chapter 5. As humanists struggled to reform education, one of their major goals was to replace the rigid and essentially useless formal logic of the scholastic tradition with a more broadly conceived dialectic that regarded formal logic as a purely elementary subject and gave major attention to the determination of probability. Hence textbooks of logic written by humanists gave more attention to rhetorical and probable proofs. As noted earlier, the most influential such textbook was *On Dialectical Invention*, written in 1479 by Rudolf Agricola but not published till 1515. After its publication, Agricola's manual and a number of works derived from it rapidly won the upper hand in the universities; and from about 1530, the old medieval manual of logic, the *Summulae logicales* of Peter of Spain, dropped out of use and was rarely reprinted.

The new humanistically structured logic did not explicitly attack Aristotelian logic, but the step of making such a direct challenge to Aristotle was taken by an iconoclastic teacher at the traditional centre of scholasticism, the University of Paris. This was Peter Ramus (Pierre de la Ramée, 1515–72), whose works on dialectic were especially attractive to Calvinists, not only in France but also in the Netherlands and England, perhaps less because of any intrinsic merit than because Ramus was one of the Huguenot martyrs killed in the St Bartholomew's Day massacre at Paris in 1572. From early in his career, Ramus was openly critical of Aristotle and even questioned the authenticity of the works attributed to him. His attack on Aristotle grew out of his experience as a teacher in the faculty of arts. He concluded that Aristotle's logical treatises were unnecessarily complex and difficult to teach to undergraduates, also that they took up so much of the undergraduate curriculum that more useful and important subjects like rhetoric received too little attention. Two early publications in 1543, denouncing the traditional arts curriculum and demanding total abandonment of Aristotelian logic, aroused such fury that King Francis I suppressed the books and forbade Ramus to teach philosophy. His own writings on dialectic, derived in good part from Agricola's manual and culminating in his *Dialectic* (1555), were neither so free of Aristotelian influence nor so intellectually significant as he claimed. But his publications made reform of logic a topic of current debate among philosophers and educators. His impact was also due to his immense personal success as a teacher. After he regained royal favour under a new king and was appointed lecturer at the Collège Royal in 1551, students flocked to his classes; and a whole generation of young philosophers became avowed Ramists. In addition, though his books impress most modern readers as dull and complicated, he skilfully employed the graphic potential of the printed book to organize knowledge into tables that seem to have helped contemporaries to visualize relations between ideas and to become confident of their mastery of dialectic. While Ramus failed to deliver on his promise to present a new logic that would liberate human thought from its centuries of bondage to an unnatural, artificial Aristotelian system, his work expressed and stimulated discontent with traditional learning. Ramus did much to make intellectual method a hot issue and so to prepare the way for thinkers of the next century, notably Bacon and Descartes, to propose new methods for the pursuit of truth.

Danger of intellectual anarchy

All of these developments raised from many different directions the spectre of intellectual anarchy that would be incurable through any method other than the blind faith recommended by fideists like Gianfrancesco Pico. The humanist dream, always quite vague and general, that rediscovery of ancient texts would somehow lead to easy solutions of contemporary social, religious, and intellectual uncertainties, had not worked out. Indeed, the tendency of many later humanists to plunge into the occult, magical, and astrological pseudo-sciences contained in supposed sources of ancient wisdom like the Cabala and the Hermetic books demonstrates how helpless most humanists were as their favourite solutions for uncertainty and doubt failed. Magic, astrology, witchcraft, and other forms of occult lore were deeply imbedded in the ancient culture that they struggled to recover and had always had a place in the learned high culture of scholasticism as well as in medieval popular culture. Among the educated classes, at least, such cultural flotsam had been restricted to some extent by the predominantly rational principles of Aristotelian philosophy. The frantic embrace of ancient and pseudo-ancient occult sources by serious and generally competent thinkers like Ficino and Pico suggests that as the major works of ancient literature and philosophy failed to produce intellectual concord and only revealed deeper and deeper layers of conflict and uncertainty, people engaged in the humanistic enterprise of restoring ancient wisdom dug deeper and deeper into the literary remains of ancient civilization, credulously trusting that if the final wisdom was not to be found in Seneca and Cicero among the Latins and Plato and Aristotle among the Greeks, then it must be sought in the supposedly still more ancient texts of Egyptian Hermetism, Jewish Cabala, and Pythagorean mysticism. The craze for magic and astrology, and also the savage outbreaks of witch-hunting that characterized late Renaissance culture, had roots in the religious unrest associated with the Reformation and in the social conflicts of a culture that was abandoning traditional values and customs for the uncertainty of a market economy. But it also had intellectual sources that grew in influence as the scholastic rationalism that had accepted but also restrained occultist beliefs lost credibility.

Humanistic scholarship further deepened this incipient cultural anarchy by recovering the works of Sextus Empiricus and making them available in printed Latin translations in 1561 and 1569. Sextus Empiricus was not a major thinker, but his summary of the most radical form of ancient sceptical philosophy, Pyrrhonism, helped to shape the expression of all the accumulated doubts of late Renaissance thinkers. The emergence of a serious and comprehensive sceptical philosophy in France during the late sixteenth century is historically significant because, even more clearly than the emergence of the various (and abortive) 'philosophies of nature' among Italian thinkers of about the same period, it demonstrates that humanism, when conceived as an intellectual method and offered as an easy resolution of the intellectual uncertainties of the age, was just as thoroughly exhausted as scholasticism. Renaissance intellectuals had confidently trusted that rediscovered Antiquity would offer quick and ready-made solutions to all sorts of problems. The sceptics impolitely suggested that no one could be sure of any solutions and that truth and order appeared to lie wholly beyond the reach of the human mind.

There are a few hints of sceptical opinion in late scholasticism, especially in the challenge to philosophical realism by William of Ockham and some of his disciples, though these directions were not pursued. We have seen that Gianfrancesco Pico had used Sextus Empiricus to question the ability of human reason to reach certitude. Agrippa at least flirted with scepticism. Peter Ramus' friend Omer Talon interpreted the Academic scepticism of Cicero as justification for Ramus' attack on Aristotelian logic; and though Ramus was not a sceptic, his enemies accused him of being one. A dialogue by another friend of Ramus, Guy de Brués, although rejecting scepticism, suggests that sceptical viewpoints were well known and were being discussed among the influential group of poets known as *la Pléiade*. Both Protestant and Catholic religious controversialists (but mainly Catholic ones) frequently used sceptical arguments to suggest that the justifications presented for rejecting their own form of Christianity were invalid.

Sanches and Montaigne

The two central figures of sixteenth-century French philosophical scepticism were the Portuguese-born physician Francisco Sanches (*c.* 1550–1623), whose family moved to Bordeaux while he was a child and who practised and taught medicine at Toulouse, and the wealthy and aristocratic Michel de Montaigne (1533–92), who served as a counsellor in the Parlement of Bordeaux, was mayor of Bordeaux at a very violent period of the Wars of Religion, and played an important mediating role as a moderate Catholic adviser to the Protestant leader Henry of Navarre during those wars. Sanches' sceptical book, *That Nothing Can Be Known* (1581), is a penetrating analysis of the foundations of Aristotle's theory of knowledge. He attacked Aristotle's doctrine of definition but especially his doctrine of scientific proof, arguing that syllogistic conclusions are true (as distinct from formally valid) only if the propositions that form the major and minor premises are true, and that Aristotle fails to offer any valid and realistic way to prove the truth of propositions. Thus, Sanches argues, the logic of Aristotle is useless for scientific discovery. All that remains is intuitive apprehension of singular objects perceived by the senses, and even this knowledge is unreliable because the senses are easily deceived by appearances. Sanches' little treatise, unlike the works of Agrippa or Gianfrancesco Pico, was a thorough philosophical critique of the processes by which people gain knowledge, but it was rarely reprinted and seems not to have had much influence.

Very different is the case of Montaigne, whose *Essays*, written in French and published between 1580 and 1595, were explicitly influenced by the Pyrrhonism of Sextus Empiricus. These essays quickly attracted popular attention and established themselves as one of the masterpieces of French literature. The personal essay as a literary form is an invention of this author, who took himself as the main subject of his work. He was not a systematic philosopher; in fact, he did not regard himself as a philosopher at all. There are many elements in his thought besides Pyrrhonist scepticism, notably a tendency to favour moderate Stoic views on ethical questions. Though he was not a professional scholar, he was unusually skilled in Latin. His familiarity with classical Latin literature and with those Greek books available in French or Latin translation (many, by this period of the late Renaissance) was remarkable even for that age of humanist-dominated education. His *Essays* teem with classical quotations and allusions; yet the effect is not one of plodding erudition but of an active and playful rumination.

The general lesson Montaigne drew from his studies was that human beings had disagreed widely on all possible questions, and that nothing is certain. A radical cultural relativism runs through his discussion of ancient literature; and his thought is also striking because he drew further support for this cultural relativism from reports of the new European discoveries overseas, an early example of the long-term intellectual challenge posed to European traditions by increasing familiarity with non-European cultures unknown to Antiquity or the Middle Ages. He did not exempt even religion from this radical relativism and candidly confessed that 'we are Christians by the same title that we are Perigordians or Germans' – that is, by an accident of birth and geography. His cultural relativism is especially powerful in his famous essay 'Of Cannibals', describing his meeting of several American natives brought to France from Brazil. His classical references are a clear mark of his humanistic background, but his extreme relativism and his use of modern discoveries that contradict classical tradition show that he had left conventional humanism far behind.

Extending beyond this generally relativistic attitude was his explicitly Pyrrhonist philosophical position, most fully developed in his longest essay, 'An Apology for Raymond Sebond'. In form it is a defence of an obscure fifteenth-century theologian who tried to demonstrate that the truth of every single Christian doctrine can be proved by philosophical argument, an excessively zealous effort that had brought down ecclesiastical censure on the author because he left no room at all for faith. Montaigne's 'defence' of Sebond's failed proof is really a demonstration that every other philosophical proof is just as preposterous and unsound as those used by Sebond. Drawing sceptical arguments chiefly from Cicero and Sextus Empiricus, Montaigne claimed that the powers of the human mind are very few and that human beings not only are mere animals but in many respects must be judged inferior to other animals. He uses the example of primitive Americans to prove that the simple life of the savage is purer and nobler than that of the learned philosopher. He repeatedly cites the opinions of philosophers, both ancient and modern, to demonstrate that philosophy leads only to uncertainty and conflict. True religion can never be based on the quicksands of human reason but must rest securely on faith. Some interpreters of Montaigne regard this fideistic conclusion as an insincere screen for unbelief while others regard it as a serious justification of his own decision to remain Catholic despite

the corruption of the church and the inability of reason to prove its doctrines true. Montaigne explicitly commends Pyrrhonist scepticism,
endorsing its advice to suspend judgement on all philosophical questions.
He borrows from Sextus the standard tropes or paradoxes used to demonstrate that all positive assertions are open to question. He points out
the ambiguity of definitions and language, the mind's inability to control
or even pay heed to its own processes, and most crushing of all, the radical
unreliability of the sense perceptions that are the source – the unreliable
source – of all human knowledge. Montaigne's *Essays* were widely read.
But his ideas were also reinforced by the books of more systematic but less
sparkling disciples such as Pierre Charron (1541–1603), who consciously
applied Montaigne's Pyrrhonist philosophy to defend Catholicism
against Calvinist critics.

Death of the Renaissance dream

Renaissance humanism was not a philosophy. It most assuredly was not
identical with the scepticism of Montaigne and his disciples. But it was
closely linked to a dream, the dream of a sweeping and decisive solution to
the ills and inadequacies of European society through a rediscovery of the
texts – and more importantly, of the values, the inner secret – of Greek and
Roman civilization. In Montaigne's *Essays,* despite his remarkable familiarity with classical literature, the death of that dream is clearly proclaimed.
There is much exaggeration and not a little self-deception in the claim of
the architects of early modern science and philosophy, men like Francis
Bacon and René Descartes, that they had cast aside the stale burden of past
learning (not only medieval but also ancient) and had started the search for
truth anew. Modern studies have shown that Bacon was quite familiar with
the ideas of Telesio and Bruno and that his own system was influenced by
late Renaissance ideas of magic. Descartes admitted that as a youth, he had
been influenced by Campanella; and modern scholarship has traced in his
mature system many remains of the discarded Aristotelian natural philosophy he learned from his Jesuit schoolmasters. Yet it is true that in the seventeenth century, European science and philosophy made a new beginning,
even though both continued to be nourished – and impeded – by the heritage of the past. Both for rationalists like Descartes and for empiricists like
Bacon and Newton, the sceptics' assault on traditional learning provided a
starting-point beyond which they could advance only by carefully and consciously narrowing the scope of their inquiries to a limited and carefully
defined set of problems. Bacon's remark in *The Great Instauration* that the
Greeks and Romans represented not the wise conclusions of Antiquity but
the premature speculations of the callow youth of the human race, is

simply unthinkable in any generation before his own. It shows that the humanists' dream of a cultural rebirth through recovery of ancient wisdom was gone forever. In the two generations after Bacon's death in 1626, the whole definition as well as the practice of science was radically changed, so that by the end of the century, the term *science* was limited (at least in England, which led the way to the new culture) to questions that could be answered by quantitative responses derived from experience, while all other knowledge, including many subjects that had been at the heart of classical, medieval, and Renaissance civilization, had been relegated to the category of mere opinion. These developments, of course, lead far beyond the subject of this book.

The afterlife of humanism

Though humanistic learning was therefore in a sense outgrown, it continued to permeate Western culture for centuries and still survives today, though in altered and no longer exclusively classical form. Aspects of humanistic studies live on in classical philology, the study of ancient literature, and historians' distinctively modern, critical way of thinking about the past. More broadly, Renaissance humanism has permanently affected the way in which modern people conceive their own identity, for humanist historical thought first taught us that we, too, are the products of an ever-changing flow of events and that within the bounds set by human physiology, all human values, ideas, and customs are contingent products of time and place. This cultural relativism, one of the distinctive characteristics that differentiate modern from traditional culture, was powerfully reinforced by the European discovery of non-Western societies; but its earliest roots are in the ideas of humanists about history, an awareness of change and contingency not achieved by any other civilization, not even those of ancient Greece and Rome. Clearly linked to this historical consciousness is the reflective, critical mentality developed by those humanists who edited, translated, and interpreted ancient books. The application of critical analysis to one's own convictions is immensely difficult, as is illustrated by the resistance even of many competent humanist textual critics to surrendering their belief in the authenticity of beloved authorities like the pseudo-Dionysius and Hermes Trismegistus whose apocryphal nature should have been obvious. It took clear, steady, and courageous thinkers like Valla, Erasmus, Scaliger, and Casaubon to apply the critical knife to revered Antiquity and to winnow out the authentic from the fake, to cast aside forever Dionysius the Areopagite and the Egyptian sage Hermes. Such humanists were rare, but they were the great ones. Most humanists (like most scholastic thinkers or most academic persons at any time) were timorous, uncreative schoolmasters who avoided controversy, conformed carefully to the prevailing religious and political systems of their time and place, and reduced the potentially challenging intellectual treasures of the classical world to a small body of safe and approved authors, through whose texts teachers and pupils plodded page by page, word by word, not in search of electrifying intellectual challenges but rather in search of suitably classical Latin words, phrases, and usages, and assorted bits of information about ancient times, so that the pupils could write literate and safely dull compositions and orations that would demonstrate that they were becoming educated men.

Yet critical challenge to conventional wisdom always lurked within Renaissance humanism. The rank and file of humanists may have been conformist nonentities. Nevertheless, the critical potential was always there; and from Petrarch onward, the major humanists acted as critics of their own world. In modern Western civilization, often to the dismay of the authorities and even of the people, the intellectual functions as an outsider, as the critic who lays bare the prevailing evils and tries to effect remedial change. The intellectual is not necessarily a revolutionary, and sometimes he or she is a whining nag; but certainly he or she is a critic and would-be reformer of the world. This role was not typical of intellectuals in the ancient world, and certainly not in the medieval world, despite the activity of reformers like Gregory VII and Bernard of Clairvaux. Because of their unique new conception of history as a constantly changing succession of human cultures, humanists established themselves as critics, reformers, restorers of a better past. In differing ways and degrees, but always with the dream of creating a better future by capturing the essential qualities of Antiquity, humanists such as Petrarch, Valla, Machiavelli, and Erasmus pioneered in defining the role of the intellectual as conscience, gadfly, critic. Small wonder that the very best minds among them were attracted more to Socrates, who defined his own role as that of a gadfly to the Athenian people, and to Cicero, the patriotic statesman who struggled in vain to prevent the senatorial aristocracy of Rome from destroying their own republic, than to the fuzzy spirituality and political conformity typical of the Platonic and Neoplatonic parts of the classical heritage. By the time of Montaigne, and certainly by the seventeenth century, sublime trust in the curative powers of Antiquity had waned; but the critical spirit, the hope of improvement (no longer just by 'rediscovering' Antiquity), and even the habit of using the press to form and appeal to public opinion survived, all of them legacies from the culture of Renaissance humanism.

Bibliographical essay

Introduction (and general)

The classic study that shaped subsequent discussions of humanism and the Italian Renaissance is Jakob Burckhardt, *The Civilization of the Renaissance in Italy: An Essay*, trans. S. G. C. Middlemore, 3rd edn (many editions, including London: Phaidon, 1950); the first German edition came out in 1860. Though its interpretations have been challenged and some of its factual statements have been supplanted by modern research, it remains more than just an historiographical landmark; it is still well worth the attention of any serious student. The rise and fall of Burckhardt's interpretation, from the Renaissance to the end of the Second World War, is traced with great erudition in Wallace K. Ferguson, *The Renaissance in Historical Thought: Five Centuries of Interpretation* (Boston, 1948). A landmark in the challenge by medieval historians is Charles Homer Haskins, *The Renaissance of the Twelfth Century* (Cambridge, Mass., 1927), though it does not overtly attack Burckhardt. The extreme hostility of historians of medieval science to the Renaissance in general and to humanism in particular appears in Lynn Thorndike, 'Renaissance or Prenaissance?', *Journal of the History of Ideas* 4 (1943): 65–74, and more extensively in his massive *History of Magic and Experimental Science*, 8 vols. (New York, 1923–58), especially vols. 3–6. But he assumes tendentious definitions of 'Renaissance' and 'humanism' that no serious scholar would uphold today. Ferguson's book chronicled the near-collapse of Renaissance history as a field of study in the late 1940s; but the research on which subsequent reconstruction of the concepts 'Renaissance' and 'humanism' has been based had already begun to appear. Influential early efforts to integrate this new scholarship into a credible interpretation were Myron P. Gilmore, *The World of Humanism, 1453–1517* (New York, 1952), and Denys Hay, *The Italian Renaissance in Its Historical Background* (Cambridge, 1961; 2nd edn, 1977). A helpful guide to the specialized studies on which these early syntheses were based is the brief handbook by William J. Bouwsma, *The Interpretation of*

224

Renaissance Humanism (Washington, 1959; 2nd edn 1966), revised and reissued under a new title as *The Culture of Renaissance Humanism* (1973). A thoughtful re-evaluation of the 'Renaissance problem', giving considerable attention to the intellectual assumptions underlying the work of Kristeller, Garin, and Baron, is Christopher S. Celenza, *The Lost Italian Renaissance: Humanists, Historians, and Latin's Legacy* (Baltimore, 2004). See also Benjamin G. Kohl, *Renaissance Humanism, 1300–1550: A Bibliography of Materials in English* (New York, 1985).

On the general social and economic background in Italy, see Lauro Martines, *Power and Imagination: City-States in Renaissance Italy* (New York, 1979), and John Larner, *Culture and Society in Italy, 1290–1420* (New York, 1979). The classic presentation of the case for a depressed economy as the setting for the Renaissance is Robert S. Lopez, 'Hard Times and Investment in Culture', in *The Renaissance: A Symposium* (New York, 1953). This thesis has always been contested, and while it has been widely accepted, it seems now to be out of fashion among specialists in economic history. See Judith C. Brown, 'Prosperity or Hard Times in Renaissance Italy?', *Renaissance Quarterly* 42 (1989): 761–80. The real difficulty is the scantiness of evidence for any comprehensive picture of general economic conditions in the fourteenth and fifteenth centuries.

A pioneering study of Paduan pre-humanism and the importance of urban society in the rise of a new lay culture is Roberto Weiss, *The Dawn of Humanism in Italy* (London, 1947), but it has now been overwhelmed (in size as well as thoroughness) by Ronald G. Witt, *'In the Footsteps of the Ancients': The Origins of Humanism from Lovato to Bruni* (Leiden, 2000). Several standard college-level textbooks on the Renaissance–Reformation period (Ernst Breisach, De Lamar Jensen, Charles G. Nauert, Jr, F. H. New, Lewis W. Spitz) provide general political, social, religious, and cultural background; but these accounts are rather brief, with the notable exception of Wallace K. Ferguson, *Europe in Transition, 1300–1520* (Boston, 1962), which provides a rich, detailed, and learned account of those backgrounds but is disappointingly reticent when discussing the historical significance of humanism.

Any student of humanism ought to read the humanists themselves, an enterprise made difficult because most humanists wrote in Latin; except in the case of a handful of major figures, both critical editions of the Latin text and translations into English and other modern languages are few. This scarcity of modern critical editions and English translations is the central theme of Celenza, *The Lost Italian Renaissance*. Two exceptions, both involving major figures, are *Collected Works of Erasmus*, which aims eventually to make all of his works available in English, and *The Yale Edition of the Complete Works of St Thomas More*, giving both Latin and English, and partly paralleled by *The Selected Works of St Thomas More* (English texts only). There are also English editions of individual works of Erasmus and More, mainly *The Praise of Folly* and *Utopia*. There are several well-selected anthologies of Erasmian works: the most recent is by Erika Rummel. Machiavelli's *Prince* has appeared in many translations, the longer *Discourses* is also translated though not so often republished, and there are readable translations of his *History of Florence* and *The Art of War*. Despite his central importance to humanism, there are only a few English translations of Petrarch's Latin writings; most of the translations are of his vernacular poetry. The major literary figures associated with humanism and discussed in later chapters are widely accessible in English – for example, Boccaccio (but only his vernacular works), Castiglione, Rabelais, Marguerite d'Angoulême, and Montaigne. Pico della Mirandola's *Oration on the Dignity of Man* has received several editions. Works of Lorenzo Valla include a Latin–English edition of his *On the Donation of Constantine* (1922; reissued New York, 1971); selections from the same work and *The Profession of the Religious*, translated by Olga Zorzi Pugliese (2nd edn, Toronto, 1994); and *On Pleasure / De voluptate*, Latin–English, translation by A. Kent Hieatt and Maristella Lorch (New York, 1977). The gossipy but well-informed biographies of his contemporaries by the Florentine bookseller Vespasiano da Bisticci, *Lives of Illustrious Men*, was republished as *Renaissance Princes, Popes, and Prelates* (New York, 1963). For most humanists, students must rely on anthologies. *The Renaissance Philosophy of Man*, ed. Ernst Cassirer *et al.* (Chicago, 1948) has been widely used in teaching, as have a collection made by Benjamin G. Kohl and Ronald G. Witt, *The Earthly Republic: Italian Humanists on Government and Society* (Philadelphia, 1978), and Renée Neu Watkins, ed., *Humanism and Liberty: Writings on Freedom from Fifteenth-Century Florence* (Columbia, SC, 1978). Anthologies offering different choices of texts are Paul F. Grendler, ed., *An Italian Renaissance Reader* (Toronto, 1992); Kenneth R. Bartlett, ed., *The Civilization of the Italian Renaissance* (Lexington, Mass., 1992); Werner L. Gundersheimer, ed., *The Italian Renaissance* (Englewood Cliffs, NJ, 1965); and Arthur B. Fallico and Herman Shapiro, eds., *Renaissance Philosophy*, vol. 1: *The Italian Philosophers: Selected Readings from Petrarch to Bruno* (New York, 1967). Some northern humanists are anthologized in Fallico and Shapiro, eds., *Renaissance Philosophy*, vol. 2: *The Transalpine Thinkers* (New York, 1969), and Lewis W. Spitz, ed., *The Northern Renaissance* (Englewood Cliffs, NJ, 1972). Containing relatively brief selections but offering many authors are two anthologies compiled by James Bruce Ross and Mary Martin McLaughlin, *The Portable Medieval Reader* (New York, 1949), and *The Portable Renaissance Reader* (New York, 1960), whose contents show how permeable is the division between medieval and

Renaissance. The lack of accessible English-language texts of humanist authors is in the course of being remedied by the ongoing series 'I Tatti Renaissance Library', published by Harvard University Press. Volumes published so far offer both Latin and English texts of works by Petrarch, Boccaccio, Pope Pius II, Leonardo Bruni, Angelo Poliziano, Marsilio Ficino, and others, as well as a selection of *Humanist Educational Treatises* edited by Craig W. Kallendorf. For those who can read Latin, the older collection of educational treatises edited by Eugenio Garin, *L'educazione umanistica in Italia* (Bari, 1959), offers a valuable set of texts. Ironically, in view of the general misogyny of medieval and Renaissance society, the series 'The Other Voice in Early Modern Europe', directed by Albert Rabil, Jr, offers a rich collection of translations related to the role of women in Renaissance and post-Renaissance culture, published by the University of Chicago Press and including works about women by male authors such as Agrippa von Nettesheim and Juan Luis Vives but also by some of the exceptional female authors themselves, including Laura Cereta, Cassandra Fedele, Tullia d'Aragona, Olympia Morata, and Vittoria Colonna.

Chapters 1, 2, and 3 (Italy)

Modern discussion of Renaissance humanism begins with a rebellion against the vague attempts of writers of the late nineteenth and early twentieth centuries to define humanism as a comprehensive philosophical system counterpoised against medieval scholasticism and representing the emergence of forces which have dominated modern philosophy, such as materialism, secularism, and hostility to religion. The leader of the struggle to define Renaissance humanism in terms of its own expressions rather than the needs of this modern secular liberalism has been Paul Oskar Kristeller, whose numerous publications present the case for a strict and narrow definition of humanism, one that can be found in the works of the humanists themselves. His ideas are best expressed in a collection of lectures and essays, *Renaissance Thought: The Classic, Scholastic, and Humanist Strains* (New York, 1961), but also in *Renaissance Thought II: Papers on Humanism and the Arts* (New York, 1965), and *Renaissance Concepts of Man and Other Essays* (New York, 1972). On the other hand, a number of important studies explore the broader cultural implications of humanism; for example, Eugenio Garin, *Italian Humanism: Philosophy and Civic Life in the Renaissance*, trans. Peter Munz (New York, 1965); Charles Trinkaus, *In Our Image and Likeness: Humanity and Divinity in Italian Humanist Thought*, 2 vols. (Chicago, 1970); Jerrold E. Seigel, *Rhetoric and Philosophy in Renaissance Humanism: The Union of Eloquence and Wisdom, Petrarch to Valla* (Princeton, 1968); Nancy S. Struever, *The*

Language of History in the Renaissance: Rhetoric and Historical Consciousness in Florentine Humanism (Princeton, 1970); Hanna H. Gray, 'Renaissance Humanism: The Pursuit of Eloquence', *Journal of the History of Ideas* 24 (1963): 497–514. A broadly interpretive study of cross-currents in humanist thought is William J. Bouwsma, 'The Two Faces of Humanism: Stoicism and Augustinianism in Renaissance Thought', in *Itinerarium Italicum: The Profile of the Italian Renaissance in the Mirror of its European Transformations*, ed. Heiko A. Oberman with Thomas A. Brady, Jr (Leiden, 1975), pp. 3–60, reprinted in Bouwsma, *A Usable Past: Essays in European Cultural History* (Berkeley, 1990), pp. 19–73. A massive effort to present interpretive surveys of many sub-fields is Albert Rabil, Jr, ed., *Renaissance Humanism: Foundations, Forms, and Legacy*, 3 vols. (Philadelphia, 1988). Hay, *The Italian Renaissance*, deals succinctly with the meaning of humanism. An attempt at interpretive integration within a brief span is Sem Dresden, *Humanism in the Renaissance*, trans. Margaret L. King (London, 1968), which also gives attention to northern humanism. Eugene F. Rice, Jr, *The Renaissance Idea of Wisdom* (Cambridge, Mass., 1958), traces the fate of a single major concept from medieval times through the Renaissance.

On the emergence of a new historical consciousness in the thought of Petrarch, the crucial work is Theodor E. Mommsen, 'Petrarch's Conception of the "Dark Ages"', *Speculum* 17 (1942): 226–42, reprinted in his *Medieval and Renaissance Studies*, ed. Eugene F. Rice, Jr (Ithaca, NY, 1959), 106–29. On Petrarch, see also Garin, *Italian Humanism;* Trinkaus, *In Our Image;* J. H. Whitfield, *Petrarch and the Renascence* (Oxford, 1943); Ernest Hatch Wilkins, *Life of Petrarch* (Chicago, 1961); Charles Trinkaus, *The Poet as Philosopher: Petrarch and the Formation of Renaissance Consciousness* (New Haven, Conn., 1976); and Marjorie O'Rourke Boyle, *Petrarch's Genius: Pentimento and Philosophy* (Berkeley, 1991).

On the concept of 'civic humanism' and its origins in the republican ideology of Florence, the book that set up the debate is Hans Baron, *The Crisis of the Early Italian Renaissance: Civic Humanism and Republican Liberty in an Age of Classicism and Tyranny*, rev. edn (Princeton, 1966), sharply criticized by Jerrold E. Seigel, '"Civic Humanism" or Ciceronian Rhetoric? The Culture of Petrarch and Bruni', *Past and Present*, no. 34 (July 1966), 3–46, and resolutely defended by Baron, 'Leonardo Bruni: "Professional Rhetorician" or "Civic Humanist"?', *Past and Present*, no. 36 (April 1967), 21–7; cf. also Seigel, *Rhetoric and Philosophy.* Hay, *The Italian Renaissance*, inclines to Baron's view, while Gene A. Brucker, *Renaissance Florence* (New York, 1969), suggests a more gradual penetration of the Florentine ruling class by humanism, an opinion also evident in his *The Civic World of Early Renaissance Florence* (Princeton, 1977). A collection of essays on civic humanism that generally rejects Baron's thesis is *Renaissance Civic Humanism: Reappraisals and Reflections*, ed. James Hankins (Cambridge, 2000). On the real social status of Florentine humanists, Lauro Martines, *The Social World of the Florentine Humanists, 1390–1460* (Princeton, 1963), is especially valuable because the author set aside theories and looked at archival documents. Douglas Biow, *Doctors, Ambassadors, Secretaries: Humanism and Professions in Renaissance Italy* (Chicago, 2002), discusses the relation between humanist learning and the professional careers of several Italian humanists. Useful accounts of the establishment of humanism as the culture of the Florentine elite are George Holmes, *The Florentine Enlightenment* (London, 1969), and *Florence, Rome, and the Origins of the Renaissance* (Oxford, 1986), also Donald J. Wilcox, *In Search of God and Self: Renaissance and Reformation Thought* (Boston, 1975). On Salutati's role in establishing Florentine leadership of Italian humanism, see Trinkaus, *In Our Image;* Berthold L. Ullmann, *The Humanism of Coluccio Salutati* (Padua, 1963); and Ronald G. Witt, *Hercules at the Crossroads: The Life, Works, and Thought of Coluccio Salutati* (Durham, NC, 1983). On Machiavelli as a latter-day heir of Florentine republicanism, see Felix Gilbert, *Machiavelli and Guicciardini: Politics and History in Sixteenth-Century Florence* (Princeton, 1965); Roberto Ridolfi, *The Life of Niccolò Machiavelli*, trans. Cecil Grayson (London, 1963); Sebastian de Grazia, *Machiavelli in Hell* (Princeton, 1989); and, linking Machiavelli to the Florentine humanists of the Quattrocento but rejecting the concept of civic humanism, Peter Godman, *From Poliziano to Machiavelli: Florentine Humanism in the High Renaissance* (Princeton, 1998). The classic study of the links between Florentine republican thought and the later career of republican ideology is J. G. A. Pocock, *The Machiavellian Moment: Florentine Political Thought and the Atlantic Republican Tradition* (Princeton, 1975). Non-Florentine humanism is often overlooked, but not by all. On Venice, William J. Bouwsma, *Venice and the Defense of Republican Liberty: Renaissance Values in the Age of the Counter-Reformation* (Berkeley, 1968), links the development of Venetian humanism to external challenges to local independence, much as Baron did for Florence; see also Oliver Logan, *Culture and Society in Venice, 1470–1790* (London, 1972); and Margaret L. King, *Venetian Humanism in an Age of Patrician Dominance* (Princeton, 1986). On humanism at Rome, see John F. d'Amico, *Renaissance Humanism in Papal Rome: Humanists and Churchmen on the Eve of the Reformation* (Baltimore, 1983); Charles L. Stinger, *The Renaissance in Rome* (Bloomington, 1985); John W. O'Malley, *Praise and Blame in Renaissance Rome: Rhetoric, Doctrine, and Reform in the Sacred Orators of the Papal Court, c. 1450–1521* (Durham, NC, 1979), and Ingrid Rowland, *The*

Culture of the High Renaissance: Ancients and Moderns in Sixteenth-Century Rome (Cambridge, 1998). On Naples, see Jerry H. Bentley, *Politics and Culture in Renaissance Naples* (Princeton, 1987). The later phases of Italian humanism are often neglected, except in the case of Venice; but see Eric Cochrane, ed., *The Late Italian Renaissance, 1525–1630* (New York, 1970), and his own *Florence in the Forgotten Centuries, 1527–1800: A History of Florence and the Florentines in the Age of the Grand Dukes* (Chicago, 1973). The difficulties encountered by critical humanist scholars in the face of tightened censorship in the late Italian Renaissance emerge clearly in William McCuaig, *Carlo Sigonio: The Changing World of the Late Renaissance* (Princeton, 1989).

The recovery of classical literary texts, both Latin and Greek, is covered by Witt, *Hercules*, Holmes, *The Florentine Enlightenment*, and Wilcox, *In Search of God and Self*, but in more detail by R. R. Bolgar, *The Classical Heritage and Its Beneficiaries: From the Carolingian Age to the End of the Renaissance* (Cambridge, 1954; repr. New York, 1964); Rudolf Pfeiffer, *History of Classical Scholarship, 1300–1850* (Oxford, 1976); and L. D. Reynolds and N. G. Wilson, *Scribes and Scholars: A Guide to the Transmission of Greek and Latin Literature*, 2nd edn (Oxford, 1974). On the growth of Greek learning in the West, see N. G. Wilson, *From Byzantium to Italy: Greek Studies in the Italian Renaissance* (Baltimore, 1992). Paul Botley, *Latin Translation in the Renaissance* (Cambridge, 2004), studies Renaissance practices of translation as exemplified by three important translators of Greek texts into Latin (Bruni, Manetti, and Erasmus). Ann Moss, *Renaissance Truth and the Latin Language Turn* (Oxford, 2003), is a stimulating discussion of the intellectual changes related to the humanists' shift from medieval to humanistic Latin style. On Lorenzo Valla, see Trinkaus, '*In Our Image*', chapter 3 *et passim*, the best English-language assessment of Valla's thought. On special aspects of Valla's work, see Anthony Grafton, *Joseph Scaliger: A Study in the History of Classical Scholarship*, vol. 1 (Oxford, 1983), Chapter 1; Jerry H. Bentley, *Humanists and Holy Writ: New Testament Scholarship in the Renaissance* (Princeton, 1983); and, for his contributions to philosophy and logic, Peter Mack, *Renaissance Argument: Valla and Agricola in the Traditions of Rhetoric and Dialectic* (Leiden, 1993). For those who read Italian, there are important modern studies of Valla by Franco Gaeta (1955), Giovanni di Napoli (1971), and Salvatore Camporeale (1972); for readers of German, Hanna-Barbara Gerl, *Rhetorik als Philosophie: Lorenzo Valla* (Munich, 1974). On Poliziano's importance in classical philology, see Anthony Grafton, *Defenders of the Text: The Traditions of Scholarship in an Age of Science, 1450–1800* (Cambridge, Mass., 1991), Chapter 2, and his *Joseph Scaliger*, Chapter 1.

On Renaissance education, especially the humanist theorists and academies, the old studies of William Harrison Woodward, *Vittorino da Feltre and Other Humanist Educators* (Cambridge, 1897; repr. New York, 1963), and *Studies in Education During the Age of the Renaissance, 1400–1600* (Cambridge, 1906; repr. New York, 1967), still have value. The former also reprints important treatises on education; the latter also deals with some non-Italian educators. A fresh new departure, based on painstaking archival studies, is Paul F. Grendler, *Schooling in Renaissance Italy: Literacy and Learning, 1300–1600* (Baltimore, 1989), continued at the university level by his book *The Universities of the Italian Renaissance* (Baltimore, 2002). Some of his conclusions on pre-university schools are challenged by Robert Black, *Humanism and Education in Medieval and Renaissance Italy* (Cambridge, 2001). On the narrowness of the humanistic curriculum in actual practice, see Anthony Grafton and Lisa Jardine, *From Humanism to the Humanities: Education and the Liberal Arts in Fifteenth- and Sixteenth-Century Europe* (Cambridge, Mass., 1986); R. R. Bolgar, 'From Humanism to the Humanities', *Twentieth-Century Studies* 9 (1973): 8–21; and Lisa Jardine, 'Humanism and the Sixteenth Century Arts Course', *History of Education* 4 (1975): 16–31. Grafton and Jardine, *From Humanism to the Humanities*, Chapter 2, deals with the education of women, which is also treated in Grendler, *Schooling*, and in Margaret L. King, *Women of the Renaissance* (Chicago, 1991); see also King's 'Book-lined Cells: Women and Humanism in the Early Italian Renaissance', in Rabil, ed., *Renaissance Humanism*, 1: 434–53, and an anthology of texts, Margaret L. King and Albert Rabil, Jr, eds., *Her Immaculate Hand: Selected Works By and About the Women Humanists of Quattrocento Italy* (Binghamton, NY, 1983). Discussion of women's place in Renaissance culture entered its modern phase with the challenging essay by Joan Kelly, 'Did Women Have a Renaissance?', in her *Women, History, and Theory* (Chicago, 1984), 12–50, reprinted in Renate Bridenthal *et al.*, eds., *Becoming Visible: Women in European History*, 2nd edn (Boston, 1987), 175–202. In general, most recent scholarship on the role of women in the Renaissance has dealt with topics of social rather than intellectual history.

The rise of printing has been chronicled by many hands, among which the most readable are S. H. Steinberg, *Five Hundred Years of Printing*, 2nd edn (Harmondsworth, Middlesex, 1961), and Lucien Febvre and H. J. Martin, *L'Apparition du livre* (Paris, 1958). Stimulating assessments of the long-term effect of printing on civilization are Elizabeth L. Eisenstein, *The Printing Press as an Agent of Change*, 2 vols. (Cambridge, 1979), and *The Printing Revolution in Early Modern Europe* (Cambridge, 1983), and Marshall McLuhan, *The Gutenberg Galaxy: The Making of Typographic Man* (Toronto, 1962).

Renaissance discussions on the conflicting ideals of active and contemplative life and on the theme of human dignity are treated in several previously cited books, including Holmes, *The Florentine Enlightenment*, Garin, *Italian Humanism*, and Trinkaus, *In Our Image*. On Renaissance Platonism, the works of Kristeller cited above contain important essays, and Kristeller also wrote the definitive study of Ficino, *The Philosophy of Marsilio Ficino*, trans. Virginia Conant (New York, 1943; repr. Gloucester, Mass., 1964). See also his *Eight Philosophers of the Italian Renaissance* (Stanford, Calif., 1964), and the books of Garin and Trinkaus cited above. Michael J. B. Allen, *Plato's Third Eye: Studies in Marsilio Ficino's Metaphysics and Its Sources* (Aldershot, 1995), reprints many of his valuable articles on Ficino. Also important are his introductory essays to several bilingual editions of works by Ficino. Important references for Neoplatonism and all other philosophical subjects are Brian P. Copenhaver and Charles B. Schmitt, *Renaissance Philosophy* (Oxford, 1992), and, for chapters by specialists, *The Cambridge History of Renaissance Philosophy*, ed. Charles B. Schmitt and Quentin Skinner (Cambridge, 1988). Two important recent books on Platonism are Arthur Field, *The Origins of the Platonic Academy of Florence* (Princeton, 1988), and James Hankins, *Plato in the Italian Renaissance*, 2nd edn, 2 vols. (Leiden, 1991). Most of these books also deal with the erudite occultism, magic, and religious universalism associated with Ficino and his disciples. A helpful introduction is Wayne Shumaker, *The Occult Sciences in the Renaissance: A Study in Intellectual Patterns* (Berkeley, 1972), usefully supplemented by a recent collection of essays, *Hermeticism and the Renaissance: Intellectual History and the Occult in Early Modern Europe*, ed. Ingrid Merkel and Allen G. Debus (Washington, 1988). A student who intends to read only one book on the esoteric side of Renaissance Platonism might well choose D. P. Walker, *Spiritual and Demonic Magic from Ficino to Campanella* (London, 1958; repr. Nendeln, Liechtenstein, 1969), though his *The Ancient Theology: Studies in Christian Platonism from the Fifteenth to the Eighteenth Century* (Ithaca, NY, 1972), is also valuable. Frances Yates produced several books on the same general theme, of which the most important is her *Giordano Bruno and the Hermetic Tradition* (Chicago, 1964). Those Florentine intellectuals who were not attracted to Platonism are discussed in Holmes, *The Florentine Enlightenment*. Broadly Marxist interpretations of Florentine Neoplatonism in humanism and art include Alfred von Martin, *Sociology of the Renaissance*, trans. W. L. Luetkens (London, 1944; repr. New York, 1963; German original, 1932); Friedrich Antal, *Florentine Painting and its Social Background* (London, 1948); and Arnold Hauser, *The Social History of Art* (New York, 1952). For the general history of Italian Renaissance art, the standard older studies are Heinrich Wölfflin, *Classic*

Art: An Introduction to the Italian Renaissance, trans. Peter and Linda Murray, 2nd edn (London, 1953); Bernard Berenson, *Italian Painters of the Renaissance* (London, 1938; repr. New York, 1957); and two works by Erwin Panofsky, *Studies in Iconology: Humanistic Themes in the Art of the Renaissance* (New York, 1939; repr. 1972), and *Renaissance and Renascences in Western Art*, 2 vols. (Stockholm, 1960). Other influential studies are Michael Baxandall, *Giotto and the Orators: Humanist Observers of Painting in Italy and the Discovery of Pictorial Composition, 1350–1450* (Oxford, 1971), and *Painting and Experience in Fifteenth-Century Italy: A Primer in the Social History of Pictorial Style* (Oxford, 1972); J. B. Trapp, *Essays on the Renaissance and the Classical Tradition* (Aldershot, 1990); Anthony Blunt, *Artistic Theory in Italy, 1450–1600* (Oxford, 1956); and S. Y. Edgerton, Jr, *The Renaissance Rediscovery of Linear Perspective* (New York, 1975). On the classical influence, see the works of Panofsky and also Jean Seznec, *The Survival of the Pagan Gods*, trans. Barbara F. Sessions (New York, 1953). Studies of individual painters are too numerous to discuss here.

Chapters 4 and 5 (Northern Humanism)

On the transmission of Italian humanistic culture to other countries, Hay, *The Italian Renaissance*, Chapter 7, offers helpful suggestions but no detailed development. Roberto Weiss, *The Spread of Italian Humanism* (London, 1964), despite its title, devotes less than half of its slim volume to non-Italian developments. Several collections of essays offer chapters on humanism in various countries, including Anthony Goodman and Angus MacKay, eds., *The Impact of Humanism on Western Europe* (New York, 1990); Roy Porter and Mikulás Teich, eds., *The Renaissance in National Context* (Cambridge, 1992), Rabil, *Renaissance Humanism*, and Oberman and Brady, *Itinerarium Italicum*. The latter contains important essays on individual countries by Sem Dresden, Jozef IJsewijn, Denys Hay, and Lewis W. Spitz.

The work most closely associated with the claim that the Dutch *Devotio Moderna* was a major source (or *the* major source) of humanism in northwestern Europe is Albert Hyma, *The Christian Renaissance: A History of the 'Devotio Moderna'* (Grand Rapids, Mich., 1924; 2nd edn, with five additional chapters, Hamden, Conn., 1965). Antedating Hyma is the somewhat similar claim made by Paul Mestwerdt, *Die Anfänge des Erasmus: Humanismus und 'Devotio Moderna'* (Leipzig, 1917). This thesis of predominantly northern sources for northern humanism became the prevailing view and still has influence, but it is hard to maintain after the scathing attack mounted by R. R. Post, *The Modern Devotion: Confrontation with Reformation and Humanism* (Leiden, 1968), even though

Post's shrill tone and verbosity weaken his case. On late medieval precursors of humanism, see Beryl Smalley, *English Friars and Antiquity in the Early Fourteenth Century* (New York, 1960), and Franco Simone, *The French Renaissance: Medieval Tradition and Italian Influence in the Shaping of the Renaissance in France*, trans. H. Gaston Hall (London, 1969). On precursors of humanism in Germany, see the essays by Frank L. Borchardt and Antonin Hruby in Gerhart Hoffmeister, ed., *The Renaissance and Reformation in Germany: An Introduction* (New York, 1977), and for subsequent development of genuine humanism, see Eckhard Bernstein, *German Humanism* (Boston, 1983), and *Die Literatur des deutschen Frühhumanismus* (Stuttgart, 1978). On early humanism in Spain, see Jeremy N. H. Lawrance, 'Humanism in the Iberian Peninsula', in Goodman and MacKay, eds., *The Impact of Humanism;* and for all Spanish literary subjects, Otis H. Green, *Spain and the Western Tradition: The Castilian Mind in Literature from El Cid to Calderón*, 4 vols. (Madison, Wis., 1963–6). On England, Roberto Weiss, *Humanism in England During the Fifteenth Century*, 2nd edn (Oxford, 1957), explores a little-known period in considerable detail. For the early humanist Rudolf Agricola, see Walter J. Ong, *Ramus, Method, and the Decay of Dialogue* (Cambridge, Mass., 1958; repr. New York, 1974), Chapter 5; Theodor E. Mommsen, 'Rudolph Agricola's Life of Petrarch', in his *Medieval and Renaissance Studies*, pp. 236–61; John Monfasani, 'Lorenzo Valla and Rudolph Agricola', *Journal of the History of Philosophy* 28 (1990): 181–200; F. Akkerman and A. J. Vanderjagt, eds., *Rodolphus Agricola Phrisius, 1444–1485* (Leiden, 1988); and, more broadly, Mack, *Renaissance Argument*. On the new direction in teaching Latin grammar in the Netherlands, see Jozef IJsewijn, 'The Coming of Humanism to the Low Countries', in Oberman and Brady, eds., *Itinerarium Italicum*, and James K. Cameron, 'Humanism in the Low Countries', in Goodman and MacKay, eds., *The Impact of Humanism*.

The role of universities in spreading humanism to transalpine Europe has been neglected until fairly recently. The standard older history of medieval universities, Hastings Rashdall, *The Universities of Europe in the Middle Ages*, new edn, ed. F. M. Powicke and A. B. Emden, 3 vols. (Oxford, 1936), is still valuable but emphasizes the high medieval period and thins out noticeably as it approaches its declared terminus of 1500. More recent research is presented by several scholars in James M. Kittelson and Pamela J. Transue, eds., *Rebirth, Reform and Resilience: Universities in Transition, 1300–1700* (Columbus, Ohio, 1984). An important article showing why humanist proposals for reform of grammar-teaching endangered the entire scholastic curriculum is Terrence Heath, 'Logical Grammar, Grammatical Logic, and Humanism in Three

German Universities', *Studies in the Renaissance* 18 (1971): 9–64. A general study exploring humanist penetration of German universities is James H. Overfield, *Humanism and Scholasticism in Late Medieval Germany* (Princeton, 1984); some of Overfield's conclusions are challenged by Erika Rummel, *The Humanist–Scholastic Debate in the Renaissance and Reformation* (Cambridge, Mass., 1995). A series of studies by Charles G. Nauert deals with this subject from a somewhat different perspective: two closely related articles, 'The Clash of Humanists and Scholastics: An Approach to Pre-Reformation Controversies', *Sixteenth Century Journal* 4, no. 1 (April 1973): 1–18, and 'Humanism as Method: Roots of Conflict with the Scholastics', *Sixteenth Century Journal* 29 (1998): 427–38; also 'Peter of Ravenna and the "Obscure Men" of Cologne: A Case of Pre-Reformation Controversy', in Anthony Molho and John A. Tedeschi, eds., *Renaissance Studies in Honor of Hans Baron* (De Kalb, Ill., 1971), pp. 609–40; 'Humanists, Scholastics, and the Struggle to Reform the University of Cologne, 1523–25', in James V. Mehl, ed., *Humanismus in Köln / Humanism in Cologne* (Cologne, 1991), pp. 39–76; and two studies with a broader focus, 'Humanist Infiltration into the Academic World: Some Studies of Northern Universities', *Renaissance Quarterly* 43 (1990): 799–812; and 'The Humanist Challenge to Medieval German Culture', *Daphnis: Zeitschrift für mittlere deutsche Literatur* 15 (1986): 277–306. Most older histories of individual universities concentrate almost exclusively on institutional structures and so give little sense of any educational or intellectual life that may have inhabited those structures. Two exceptions are Erich Kleineidam, *Universitas Studii Erffordensis: Überblick über die Geschichte der Universität Erfurt*, 3 vols. (Leipzig, 1969–83), and Erich Meuthen, *Kölner Universitätsgeschichte*, vol. 1: *Die alte Universität* (Cologne, 1988). John M. Fletcher, 'Change and Resistance to Change: A Consideration of the Development of English and German Universities During the Sixteenth Century', *History of Universities* 1 (1981): 1–36, is an illuminating comparative study. On the English universities and humanism, see the comprehensive works of Allan B. Cobban, *The Medieval English Universities: Oxford and Cambridge to c. 1500* (Berkeley, 1988), and Hugh F. Kearney, *Scholars and Gentlemen: Universities and Society in Pre-Industrial Britain, 1500–1700* (Ithaca, NY, 1970). A landmark is Mark H. Curtis, *Oxford and Cambridge in Transition, 1558–1642* (Oxford, 1959), which pointed the direction fulfilled in two works of synthesis, James McConica, ed., *The Collegiate University*, vol. 3 of *The History of the University of Oxford*, ed. T. H. Aston (Oxford, 1986), and Damian Riehl Leader, *The University to 1546*, vol. 1 of *A History of the University of Cambridge*, ed. Christopher Brooke (Cambridge, 1988). Scholarship on humanism in French universities is scarce. The valuable studies by James K. Farge on the Paris faculty of theology deal only tangentially with humanism. For those who read French, Augustin Renaudet, *Préréforme et humanisme à Paris pendant les premières guerres d'Italie (1494–1517)*, 2nd edn (Paris, 1953), is venerable (first edition 1916) but still unsurpassed, though its subject is Paris intellectual life in general, not just the university. For Spanish universities, see Richard L. Kagan, *Students and Society in Early Modern Spain* (Baltimore, 1974).

On pre-university schools north of the Alps, the important school at Deventer and its great headmaster Alexander Hegius are covered by Post, *The Modern Devotion*, and by IJsewijn in Oberman and Brady, eds., *Itinerarium Italicum*. The scarcity of modern studies on German grammar schools is aptly summarized in the title of Susan Karant-Nunn, 'Alas, a Lack: Trends in the Historiography of Pre-University Education in Early Modern Germany', *Renaissance Quarterly* 43 (1990): 788–98. A valuable study of French municipal schools, mainly in the sixteenth century, is George Huppert, *Public Schools in Renaissance France* (Urbana, Ill., 1984). For England, see Joan Simon, *Education and Society in Tudor England* (Cambridge, 1969), and Rosemary O'Day, *Education and Society, 1500–1800: The Social Foundations of Education in Early Modern Britain* (London, 1982).

The principal comprehensive study on German humanism is by Lewis W. Spitz, *The Religious Renaissance of the German Humanists* (Cambridge, Mass., 1963), who also wrote a life of an important early humanist, *Conrad Celtis, the German Arch-Humanist* (Cambridge, Mass., 1957). There are many useful studies of other German humanists, some of which are listed in the bibliography of Lewis W. Spitz, *The Protestant Reformation, 1517–1559* (New York, 1985). Useful collections of essays are Reinhard P. Becker, ed., *German Humanism and Reformation* (New York, 1982); *XVIIIe Colloque International de Tours: L'Humanisme allemand (1480–1540)* (Paris, 1979); Hoffmeister, ed., *The Renaissance and Reformation in Germany*, and the essays by Paul Joachimsen and Hans Rupprich in Gerald Strauss, ed., *Pre-Reformation Germany* (London, 1972). Of capital importance is Bernd Moeller, 'The German Humanists and the Beginnings of the Reformation', in his *Imperial Cities and the Reformation: Three Essays*, trans. H. C. Erik Midelfort and Mark U. Edwards, Jr (Philadelphia, 1972). See also Maria Grossmann, *Humanism in Wittenberg* (Nieuwkoop, 1975); and Steven Ozment, *The Age of Reform, 1250–1550: An Intellectual and Religious History of Late Medieval and Reformation Europe* (New Haven, 1980), Chapter 8. On the concept of generational differentiation among German humanists, see Moeller's essay and also Lewis W. Spitz, 'The Third Generation of German

Renaissance Humanists', in Archibald R. Lewis, ed., *Aspects of the Renaissance* (Austin, Tex., 1967). On the troubles of Peter of Ravenna at Cologne, see the article by Nauert (above). On the much more prominent Reuchlin case, see Hajo Holborn, *Ulrich von Hutten and the German Reformation* (New Haven, 1937), and the reassessment by James H. Overfield, 'A New Look at the Reuchlin Affair', *Studies in Medieval and Renaissance History* 8 (1971): 167–207, and his *Humanism and Scholasticism*, Chapter 7. Francis Griffin Stokes edited and translated the *Letters of Obscure Men* (London, 1909); the English text has been reprinted under the title *On the Eve of the Reformation* (New York, 1964). Study of northern humanism, especially in Germany, is complicated by the involvement of many humanists in the Protestant Reformation, both for and against. An interpretation of this relationship is William J. Bouwsma, 'Renaissance and Reformation: An Essay on Their Affinities and Connections', in Heiko A. Oberman, ed., *Luther and the Dawn of the Modern Era* (Leiden, 1974), pp. 127–49, reprinted in Bouwsma, *A Usable Past*, pp. 225–46.

On French humanism, a good general introduction is Donald Stone, Jr, *France in the Sixteenth Century: A Medieval Society Transformed* (Englewood Cliffs, NJ, 1969). Already cited is Simone, *The French Renaissance*. Useful collections of essays are Werner L. Gundersheimer, ed., *French Humanism, 1470–1600* (London, 1969), especially the essay by Eugene F. Rice, Jr, on Lefèvre d'Etaples and his disciples; and A. H. T. Levi, ed., *Humanism in France and in the Early Renaissance* (Manchester, 1970). Also important are several books (all in French) by Augustin Renaudet, including his *Préréforme;* and Eugene F. Rice, Jr, ed., *The Prefatory Epistles of Jacques Lefèvre d'Etaples and Related Texts* (New York, 1971). On Budé, see David O. McNeil, *Guillaume Budé and Humanism in the Reign of Francis I* (Geneva, 1975). The origin and significance of biblical humanism is studied by Bentley, *Humanists and Holy Writ*. Erasmus has been the subject of many biographies. The standard older one is by Johan Huizinga (first English edition, 1924; repr. Princeton, 1984); two important newer ones are by Cornelis Augustijn (Toronto, 1991) and Lisa Jardine (Princeton, 1993). Also useful are biographies by Roland H. Bainton (New York, 1969); Margaret Mann Phillips (London, 1949); and two different studies by James D. Tracy, *Erasmus, the Growth of a Mind* (Geneva, 1972), and *Erasmus of the Low Countries* (Berkeley, 1996).

For English humanism under the Tudors, in addition to the university histories listed above, see the pathbreaking study by John B. Gleason, *John Colet* (Berkeley, 1989), and James McConica, *English Humanists and Reformation Politics* (Oxford, 1965), the latter supplemented now by Thomas F. Mayer, *Thomas Starkey and the Commonweal: Humanist Politics and Religion in the Reign of Henry VIII* (Cambridge, 1989), and by Winthrop S. Hudson, *The Cambridge Connection and the Elizabethan Settlement of 1559* (Durham, NC, 1980). On the most famous English humanist, Thomas More, see the older biography by R. W. Chambers (New York, 1935) and the more recent ones by Alistair Fox (New Haven, 1983), and Richard Marius (1984), and also J. H. Hexter, *More's Utopia: The Biography of an Idea* (Princeton, 1952), and R. S. Sylvester and G. H. Marc'hadour, eds., *Essential Articles for the Study of Sir Thomas More* (Hamden, Conn., 1977). An influential interpretative study is Douglas Bush, *The Renaissance and English Humanism* (Toronto, 1939). See also the essay by Denys Hay in Oberman and Brady, ed., *Itinerarium Italicum*.

On the development of humanism in Spain, the classic study is Marcel Bataillon, *Érasme et l'Espagne*, new edn, 3 vols. (Geneva, 1991). The original one-volume edition (Paris, 1937) was translated into Spanish as *Erasmo y España* (Mexico, 1950; repr. 1966), but no English version exists. Lu Ann Homza, *Religious Authority in the Spanish Renaissance* (Baltimore, 2000), challenges Bataillon on several points. Also helpful are Green, *Spain and the Western Tradition*, and Lawrance, 'Humanism in the Iberian Peninsula'.

Chapter 6

On the unsuccessful efforts of both Protestant and Catholic humanists to end religious conflict and restore unity, see Clyde L. Manschreck, *Melanchthon, the Quiet Reformer* (New York, 1958), and Elisabeth G. Gleason, *Gasparo Contarini* (Berkeley, 1993). Erika Rummel, *The Confessionalization of Humanism in Reformation Germany* (Oxford, 2000), studies the transformation of humanism caused by the conflicts of the German Reformation. The development of classical philology is treated in the works of Bolgar, Pfeiffer, and Reynolds and Wilson cited above, but especially in Grafton, *Joseph Scaliger* and *Defenders of the Text*. The latter provides a good account of the demise of Hermes Trismegistus and Dionysius the Areopagite as respectable authors and also demonstrates that early philological study dealt with many ancient texts beyond the scope of *belles lettres*. On the application of philology to legal texts and to the documentary sources of French medieval history, see Donald R. Kelley, *Foundations of Modern Historical Scholarship: Language, Law, and History in the French Renaissance* (New York, 1970), and George Huppert, *The Idea of Perfect History: Historical Erudition and Historical Philosophy in Renaissance France* (Urbana, Ill., 1970). Studies of humanism in schools and universities are listed above. For the late Renaissance, the Jesuit schools are of great importance but have received surprisingly little scholarly attention. In English there is little except A. Lynn Martin, *The Jesuit Mind: The Mentality of an Elite in Early Modern France* (Ithaca, NY, 1988), Chapter 3, which is useful but focuses on France. In other languages, see Karl Hengst, *Jesuiten an Universitäten und Jesuitenuniversitäten* (Munich, 1981), which deals only with German universities; Gabriel Codina Mir, *Aux sources de la pédagogie des Jésuites* (Rome, 1968); and François de Dainville, *Les Jésuites et l'éducation de la société française: La naissance de l'humanisme moderne* (Paris, 1940). On humanistic influences in French vernacular literature, there are useful studies of Rabelais by Marcel Tetel (New York, 1967) and M. A. Screech (Ithaca, NY, 1979), and a broader study that has become a classic of cultural history, Lucien Febvre, *The Problem of Unbelief in the Sixteenth Century: The Religion of Rabelais*, trans. Beatrice Gottlieb (Cambridge, Mass., 1982; original French edn, 1942). On classical and humanistic influences in Spanish literature, Green, *Spain and the Western Tradition*, and Gerald Brenan, *The Literature of the Spanish People* (Cambridge, 1965), are helpful guides. For English literature, a standard guide is C. S. Lewis, *English Literature in the Sixteenth Century, Exclusive of Drama* (Oxford, 1954). On the diffusion of classical influences through English schools, an older study of great value is T. W. Baldwin, *William Shakspere's 'Small latine and lesse Greeke'*, 2 vols. (Urbana, Ill., 1944). See also McConica, *English Humanists and Reformation Politics*.

On northern Renaissance art, Otto Benesch, *The Art of the Renaissance in Northern Europe*, rev. edn (London, 1965), is a standard older guide. A recent comprehensive treatment of the subject is Jeffrey Chipps Smith, *The Northern Renaissance* (London, 2004). On Dürer, incomparably the most important figure in the diffusion of Italian influences into northern art, see Erwin Panofsky, *The Life and Art of Albrecht Dürer*, 2 vols. (Princeton, 1953).

Chapter 7

On the survival of Aristotle as the dominant philosophical and scientific authority throughout the Renaissance period and well into the seventeenth century, the work of Charles B. Schmitt is essential, especially his *Aristotle and the Renaissance* (Cambridge, Mass., 1983). Studies of Renaissance Neoplatonism have been discussed above (Chapters 1–3), as have works on Valla as a critic of Aristotelianism and a defender of Epicurean philosophy; but on Platonism, see also the old (1926) but still influential work of Ernst Cassirer, *The Individual and the Cosmos in Renaissance Philosophy*, trans. Mario Domandi (Oxford, 1963). Jason L. Saunders, *Justus Lipsius: The Philosophy of Renaissance Stoicism* (New

York, 1955), studies the most prominent Renaissance neo-Stoic. A pioneering essay on the logic of scientific investigation, emphasizing scholastic rather than humanistic developments, is John Herman Randall, Jr, 'The Development of Scientific Method in the School of Padua', *Journal of the History of Ideas* 1 (1940): 177–206. More inclined to emphasize the contributions of humanistic scholarship to natural science are Marie Boas, *The Scientific Renaissance, 1450–1630* (New York, 1962), and Grafton, *Defenders of the Text*; but Thorndike, *History of Magic and Experimental Science*, scoffs at the idea of any humanistic contribution to science, and even at the notion that Renaissance humanism was historically significant in any way. A stimulating short synthesis is Robert Mandrou, *From Humanism to Science, 1480–1700*, trans. Brian Pearce (Harmondsworth, 1978). Most histories of philosophy give little attention to late medieval and Renaissance developments, but two notable exceptions are *The Cambridge History of Renaissance Philosophy*, and Copenhaver and Schmitt, *Renaissance Philosophy* (both cited above). The Italian 'philosophers of nature' are well covered in these two histories. On them, see also Kristeller, *Eight Philosophers*, Chapters 6–8, and Yates, *Giordano Bruno*. An important study of Peter Ramus is Ong, *Ramus, Method, and the Decay of Dialogue*, but also useful are Wilbur Samuel Howell, *Logic and Rhetoric in England, 1500–1700* (Princeton, 1956); Neal W. Gilbert, *Renaissance Concepts of Method* (New York, 1960); and Frances A. Yates, *The Art of Memory* (London, 1966).

On the growth and significance of scepticism, see Richard H. Popkin, *The History of Scepticism from Erasmus to Descartes* (Assen, 1960), later expanded as *The History of Scepticism from Erasmus to Spinoza* (Berkeley, 1979). Luciano Floridi, *Sextus Empiricus: The Transmission and Recovery of Pyrrhonism* (New York, 2002), studies the role of ancient Pyrrhonism in this development. Also helpful are the *Cambridge History*; Copenhaver and Schmitt, *Renaissance Philosophy*; Victoria Kahn, *Rhetoric, Prudence, and Scepticism in the Renaissance* (Ithaca, NY, 1985); and Zachary Sayre Schiffman, *On the Threshold of Modernity: Relativism in the French Renaissance* (Baltimore, 1991). Works on Rabelais have been cited in the preceding chapter, but see also Barbara C. Bowen, *The Age of Bluff: Paradox and Ambiguity in Rabelais and Montaigne* (Urbana, Ill., 1972). On sceptical elements in Agrippa von Nettesheim, see Charles G. Nauert, Jr, *Agrippa and the Crisis of Renaissance Thought* (Urbana, Ill., 1965), Chapters 8 and 11; Michael H. Keefer, 'Agrippa's Dilemma: Hermetic Rebirth and the Ambivalence of *De vanitate* and *De occulta philosophia*', *Renaissance Quarterly* 41 (1988): 614–53; and Christopher I. Lehrich, *The Language of Demons and Angels: Cornelius Agrippa's Occult Philosophy* (Leiden, 2003). On Montaigne, see the brief biography by Peter Burke

(New York, 1982), and the longer one by Donald M. Frame (New York, 1968). There are now two excellent modern English translations of Montaigne's *Essays*, by Donald M. Frame (Stanford, Calif., 1948; repr. New York, 1960) and by M. A. Screech (London, 1991). Paolo Rossi, *Francis Bacon: From Magic to Science*, trans. Sacha Rabinovitch (London, 1968), unlike most studies of Bacon, shows the importance of Platonic and occultist influences; see also Lisa Jardine, *Francis Bacon: Discovery and the Art of Discourse* (Cambridge, 1974).

Index

NEW APPROACHES TO EUROPEAN HISTORY